Kershaw Penfold

Penfold on rating

Practical remarks upon the principle of rating railway, gas, water, and other

companies. Sixth Edition

Kershaw Penfold

Penfold on rating
Practical remarks upon the principle of rating railway, gas, water, and other companies. Sixth Edition

ISBN/EAN: 9783337143237

Printed in Europe, USA, Canada, Australia, Japan

Cover: Foto ©Andreas Hilbeck / pixelio.de

More available books at **www.hansebooks.com**

PENFOLD ON RATING.

PRACTICAL REMARKS

UPON

THE PRINCIPLE OF RATING

RAILWAY, GAS, WATER,

AND OTHER COMPANIES;

LAND, TITHES, BUILDINGS, MANUFACTORIES,

AND OTHER PROPERTIES

Liable to be Assessed towards the Relief of the Poor.

SIXTH EDITION,

RE-WRITTEN AND EXTENDED

BY

JOHN THOMAS KERSHAW AND WILLIAM MARSHALL,

Of the firm of Armstrong, Kershaw, & Marshall,
Civil Engineers and Rating Surveyors, 27, Norfolk Street, Strand, W.C.

LONDON:
KNIGHT & CO., 90, FLEET STREET, E.C.,
Publishers by Authority to the Poor Law Board,
and to the Home Office for the purposes of the Local Government Act.

PREFACE TO THE SIXTH EDITION.

The last Edition (the 5th) of " Penfold on Rating" was published on the 1st February, 1869, and was, before the end of the same year, entirely exhausted.

The work of revision and extension of the present Edition was commenced by the late Mr. Kershaw the able Editor of the last, but owing to his violent and untimely death the labour of its completion has fallen upon me.

In the present volume the law as it now stands, both for the Metropolis and the Country, is shown in parallel columns, the various clauses being arranged in the order in which they should be chronologically applied.

I have considered it necessary also to make several alterations and additions in the present instance—first, in consequence of some recent decisions of the Court of Queen's Bench; and secondly, on account of certain obvious omissions in the last Edition.

Some independent remarks, having reference to the present unsatisfactory system of valuing railway property, together with some suggestions as to the best method of effecting a remedy,

A 2

which may be taken to represent real property in the simplest
form; thence, progressing by regular stages, to those which
determine the same values of general tenements, houses, and land;
and finally, of the property of gas, water, railway, and other
public companies. Mr. Penfold did not use this mode of treat-
ment, but dealt with the several subjects as each presented itself
to his mind.

With regard to the opinions herein stated, it should be remarked
that they are, with one or two exceptions, those held by Mr.
Penfold, some of which were not confirmed as law until after his
death. The principal one in which the Editor has taken up a
position contrary to that held by Mr. Penfold, refers to the mode
of apportionment in the case of gas and water companies, and in
this he has always differed from Mr. Penfold, with whom, for
many years, he was associated.

Technical questions in matters of law have been unnoticed, such
matters being entirely without the sphere of a work like the
present.

Should the Editor prove, through the medium of this edition, to
be of any assistance to those whose unthankful, and at times per-
plexing duty it is to equalise the present unsatisfactory distribution of the poor-rates, by transferring their burden from the
shoulders of those who now bear it in an unjust proportion, as he
cannot but think, to those of the shareholders of many public
companies, the rateable value of whose various properties is so
imperfectly understood, he will consider himself amply repaid for
the time and trouble he has necessarily expended in producing
this edition.

The diminished bulk of the present volume, as compared with

that of its predecessor, is due to the omission of the unimportant and cumbersome extracts from Acts of Parliament and Court judgments, which, in the last, tended more to confuse than to elucidate the subject.

The Editor cannot conclude this brief introduction without expressing his thanks to the representatives of the late Mr. Penfold for the confidence they have reposed in him by the transfer of all the valuable manuscripts and data which Mr. Penfold accumulated as the result of many years of professional labour and experience ; and also to his partners, Mr. Armstrong, M.A. (Cantab), C.E., and Mr. Marshall (Lecturer on Surveying, King's College), who have at all times readily given him the benefit of their experience and advice during the progress of the work through the press.

37, NORFOLK STREET, STRAND. W.C.
January 1, 1869.

CONTENTS.

———◆———

GAS AND WATER WORKS.

SCHEDULE OF CASES NOTICED.

PRINCIPLE OF RATING PROPERTIES

RELIEF OF THE POOR.

CHAPTER I.

THE PRINCIPLE OF RATING.

THE declaration of our Saviour that "the poor ye have always with you," has at all times and in all countries been abundantly demonstrated. The presence in our own country of the poor unable to help themselves, has produced a voluminous code of laws, the object of which is to make provision for their due relief. These laws may be divided into two great parts: the first of which treats of the manner in which the money necessary is to be obtained; the second, of the manner in which it is to be expended. The foundation of all legislation, of which the poor have been the object, is the following statute:—

43 ELIZABETHE, CAP. 2 (A.D. 1601).

(An Act for the Relief of the Poor.)

" Be it enacted by the authority of this present Parliament, That the churchwardens of every parish, and four, three, or two substantial householders there, as shall be thought meet, having respect to the proportion and greatness of the same parish and parishes, to be nominated yearly in Easter Week, or within one month after Easter, under the hand and seal of two or more justices of the peace in the same county, whereof one to be of the quorum,

Overseers for the poor, their office, &c.

B

dwelling in or near the same parish or division where the same parish doth lie, shall be called overseers of the poor of the same parish; and they, or the greater part of them, shall take order from time to time, by and with the consent of two or more such justices of peace as is aforesaid, for setting to work the children of all such whose parents shall not, by the said churchwardens and overseers, or the greater part of them, be thought able to keep and maintain their children; and also for setting to work all such persons, married or unmarried, having no means to maintain them, and use no ordinary and daily trade of life to get their living by;

Who shall be taxed towards the relief of the poor. and also to raise weekly or otherwise (by taxation of every inhabitant, parson, vicar, and other, and of every occupier of lands, houses, tithes impropriate, propriations of tithes, coal mines, or saleable underwoods in the said parish, in such competent sum and sums of money as they shall think fit), a convenient stock of flax, hemp, wool, thread, iron, and other ware and stuff,

A convenient stock shall be provided to set the poor on work. to set the poor on work; and also competent sums of money for and towards the necessary relief of the lame, impotent, old, blind, and such other among them being poor, and not able to work; and also for the putting out of such children to be apprentices, to be gathered out of the same parish, according to the ability of the same parish, and to do and execute all other things, as well for the disposing of the said stock, as otherwise concerning the premises, as to them shall seem convenient."

By this Act not only were the *occupiers* of the properties, specified therein, to be assessed, but also *every inhabitant*.

At the present time the occupiers of property alone are liable to be rated, except such be occupiers of houses let furnished, or of houses let unfurnished at rents under £20, payable weekly or monthly.

Neither does the property mentioned in the Act of Elizabeth include *all* real property, consequently such non-mentioned properties are **not** liable to be rated. As the incidence of rating is now the subject of legislation, it is unnecessary to dilate upon this.

Until last year the rating of all rateable property in England and Wales was effected under the authority of the 6 and 7 William IV. cap. 96, which is commonly called the Parochial Assessment Act. This Act, which was passed in 1836, enacted that:

"Whereas it is desirable to establish one uniform mode of rating for the relief of the poor throughout England and Wales, and to lessen the cost of appeal against an unfair rate: Be it enacted by the King's most excellent Majesty, by and with the advice and consent of the Lords spiritual and temporal, and Commons, in this present Parliament assembled, **All rates to be made on the net annual value of the property.** and by the authority of the same, that from and after such period, not being earlier than the twenty-first day of March next after the passing of this Act, as the Poor Law Commissioners shall by any order under their seal of office direct, no rate for the relief of the poor in England and Wales shall be allowed by any justices, or be of any force which shall not be made upon an estimate of the net annual value of the several hereditaments rated thereunto; that is to say, of the rent at which the same might reasonably be expected to let from year to year, free of all usual tenants' rates and taxes, and tithe commutation rent charge, if any, and deducting therefrom the probable average annual cost of the repairs, insurance, and other expenses, if any, necessary to maintain them in a state to command such rent: Provided always, **Proviso.** that nothing herein contained shall be construed to alter or affect the principles or different relative liabilities (if any) according to which different kinds of hereditaments are now by law rateable."

In addition to establishing one uniform principle of rating, it provided for a less expensive way of getting relief from an unfair rate. This it did by permitting an appeal to the Justices sitting in Petty Sessions, instead of those sitting in Quarter Sessions, to whom an appeal had up to this time been *obligatory*.

But this Act did not provide any machinery by which the adoption of one uniform mode of rating was secured.

When the question of the extension of the Franchise was being mooted, and inquiries were made as to the increase in the number of voters which the adoption of a £6 or an £8 qualification would effect, it was found that a most extraordinary inequality in the assessment of property prevailed throughout the country.

To remedy this inequality, the Union Assessment Committee Act of 1862 and the Union Assessment Committee Amendment Act of 1864 were passed, which, whilst making no alteration in the *principle* of rating, provided that machinery which was lacking for the purpose of securing uniformity of valuation.

Strangely enough, these Acts were so drawn as to be applicable to portions only of the Metropolitan area.

When the provisions of the Metropolitan Poor Act, 1867, came to be put in force, it was found that much inequality existed in the assessment of property in various parts of London, and that, moreover, there was no practical method of remedying this inequality.

To remedy this, the Valuation (Metropolis) Act, 1869, was passed. By this Act the operation of many of the sections of the Union Assessment Committee and the Union Assessment Committee Amendment Acts was extended to the Metropolis. Some of the sections of these Acts, as well as of the Parochial Assessment Act, were by it repealed; and by it a special tribunal for hearing appeals against rates was created.

The result of all the recent legislation is that the assessment of property in all parts of England and Wales, except the Metropolitan area, is under one law, whilst the assessment of property in the Metropolitan area is under another. But whether in the Metropolitan area or not, the *principle of rating* is practically the same.

The law as it now stands, both for the Metropolitan area and for the rest of England and Wales, is set forth below in the *exact words* of the various Acts of Parliament, but in an order which it is believed will make the subject clear to the reader.

THE LAW AS ENACTED FOR ENGLAND AND WALES.

UNION ASSESSMENT COMMITTEE ACT, 1862, 25 AND 26 VICTORIÆ, CAP. 103.

(*An Act to Amend the Law relating to Parochial Assessments in England.*)—*7th August, 1862.*

Whereas it is expedient that more effectual provision should be made for securing uniform and correct valuations of parishes in the unions of England: Be it enacted by the Queen's most excellent Majesty, by and with the advice and consent of the Lords spiritual and temporal, and Commons, in this present Parliament assembled, and by the authority of the same, as follows :—

Interpretation.

1. The words used in this Act shall be construed in like manner as the words contained in the Act fourth and fifth of King William the Fourth, chapter seventy-six, and the word "committee" shall signify the assessment committee provided for by

THE LAW AS ENACTED FOR THE METROPOLIS ONLY.

UNION ASSESSMENT COMMITTEE ACT, 1862, 25 AND 26 VICTORIÆ, CAP. 103.

(*An Act to Amend the Law relating to Parochial Assessments in England.*) — *7th August, 1862.*

Whereas it is expedient that more effectual provision should be made for securing uniform and correct valuations of *parishes in the unions* of England : Be it enacted by the Queen's most excellent Majesty, by and with the advice and consent of the Lords spiritual and temporal, and Commons, in this present Parliament assembled, and by the authority of the same, as follows :—

Interpretation.

1. The words used in this Act shall be construed in like manner as the words contained in the Act fourth and fifth of King William the Fourth, chapter seventy-six, and the word "committee" shall signify the assessment committee provided for by

The Law as Enacted for England and Wales.

this Act; and this Act shall be termed "The Union Assessment Committee Act, 1862."

Appointment of the assessment committee by board of guardians.

2. The board of guardians of every union, formed under the Act fourth and fifth years of King William the Fourth, chapter seventy-six, shall, as soon as convenient after the passing of this Act, and in every subsequent year, at their first meeting after the annual election of guardians, appoint from among themselves any number not less than six, nor more than twelve, to be a committee, consisting partly of *ex-officio*, and partly of elected guardians, to be called the assessment committee of the union, for the investigation and supervision of the valuations to be made, as hereinafter-mentioned within such union, and for the performance of such said acts and duties as hereinafter-mentioned: Provided always, that one-third at least of such committee shall consist of *ex-officio* guardians, in case there shall be an adequate number of such *ex-officio* guardians; but in

The Law as Enacted for the Metropolis only.

this Act; and this Act shall be termed "The Union Assessment Committee Act, 1862."

VALUATION OF PROPERTY (METROPOLIS) ACT, 32 AND 33 VICTORIÆ, CAP. 67.

(An Act to provide for Uniformity in the Assessment of Rateable Property in the Metropolis.)—9th August, 1869.

Whereas it is expedient to provide for a common basis of value for the purposes of government and local taxation, and to promote uniformity in the assessment of rateable property in the Metropolis:

Be it enacted by the Queen's most Excellent Majesty, by and with the advice and consent of the Lords spiritual and temporal, and Commons, in this present Parliament assembled, and by the authority of the same, as follows:

Act to be construed as one with 25 & 26 Vict. c. 103, and 27 & 28 Vict. c. 39.

1. The *Union* Assessment Committee Act, 1862, is in this Act referred to as "the prin-

case an adequate number of such *ex-officio* guardians shall not exist, then the number so deficient shall be made up of elected guardians.

Where union has the same bounds as borough, names of assessment committee to be transmitted to town council, who may appoint additional members.

3. Where any union shall have the same bounds as a municipal borough, the clerk to the guardians of such union shall, upon the appointment of the assessment committee, if directed by the said guardians to do so, transmit in writing the names of the persons so appointed to the town council of such borough, and such council may thereupon, if they think fit, appoint from themselves a certain number, not exceeding the number appointed by the board of guardians, who shall, until they respectively cease to be members of the town council, or decline to act, forthwith form part of the assessment committee for such union, and the said council may from time to time supply any vacancies in the number of persons appointed by them.

cipal Act;" and the principal Act, and the Union Assessment Committee Act, 1864 (amending the same), shall for the purposes of this Act, and so far as is consistent with the tenor thereof, be incorporated with this Act: and the expression "this Act" in the principal Act, and any expression referring to the principal Act which occurs in the said Act amending the same, or in any other Act or document, shall, as regards places to which this Act extends, be construed to mean the principal Act as incorporated with this Act.

Short title.

2. This Act (including the Acts incorporated herewith) may be cited as "The Valuation (Metropolis) Act, 1869."

Extent of Act.

3. This Act shall extend only to unions and parishes *not in union*, which are for the time being either wholly or for the greater part in value thereof respectively situate within the jurisdiction of the Metropolitan

8 THE PRINCIPLE OF RATING.

The Law as Enacted for England and Wales.

Provision for neglect to appoint.

4. If the guardians shall neglect or be prevented from making such appointment at the meeting above specified, the Poor Law Board shall by their order appoint some other day on which the guardians shall make such appointment.

Provision for vacancies.

5. If any *ex-officio* or elected guardian being a member of the committee cease to be guardian, or resign his seat at such committee, or die, or become incapable of acting as such member, the board of guardians shall with all convenient speed appoint an *ex-officio* or elected guardian, as the case may be, to supply the vacancy.

Continuing members may act during vacancies.

6. During any vacancy in any assessment committee, the other or continuing members of such committee may act, and shall have the same powers and jurisdiction as if no such vacancy had happened.

The Law as Enacted for the Metropolis only.

Board of Works appointed under the Metropolis Managements Act, 1855

Definitions.

4. In this Act, unless the context otherwise requires,—

" Metropolis."

The term "metropolis" means the unions and Parishes to which this Act extends:

" Parish."

The term "parish" means any place for which a separate poor rate is or can be made, or for which a separate overseer is or can be appointed:

" Union."

The term "union" means any union of parishes, and any parish for which there is a separate assessment committee under this Act and the Acts incorporated herewith:

"Ratepayer."

The term "ratepayer" means every person who is liable to any rate or tax in res-

Extent of committee's authority.

7. The authority of the committee appointed for any union under this Act shall extend over every parish comprised in such union.

First meeting, when to be holden.

8. The committee shall hold their first meeting at the board-room of the union on a day to be fixed by the board of guardians, and the subsequent meetings of the committee shall be holden at such time and at such place and upon such notice and requisition as they shall from time to time appoint; and any guardian of the union may be present at any meeting of the committee, but shall not be entitled to take part in the proceedings thereof.

Quorum of meetings.

9. All acts, orders, matters, and things by this Act authorised or directed to be made or done by the committee may be made or done by the major part of the members of such committee who shall be present at a

pect of property entered in any valuation list :

" Year."

The term " year " means the twelve months commencing with the sixth of April and ending with the succeeding fifth of April ; and words referring to a year refer to the same period :

" Surveyor of taxes."

The term "surveyor of taxes" means any surveyor of taxes, inspector of taxes, or other officer appointed or to be appointed by the Commissioners either of Inland Revenue or of Her Majesty's Treasury for the purposes of any tax in respect of which a valuation-list is by this Act made conclusive :

" Overseers."

The term " overseers " includes any person or body of persons performing the duties of overseers so far as regards the assessment, making, and collection of meeting, the whole number present together at such meeting not being less than three, and not less in any case than one-third of the whole number of which such committee consists; and when upon any question there shall be an equality of votes the presiding chairman shall have a second or casting vote.

Committee may employ and pay clerk.

10. The committee shall employ the clerk or assistant clerk of the board of guardians as their clerk, with such remuneration for his services as the Poor Law Board shall sanction.

Proceedings to be entered in books and signed.

11. The committee shall cause a minute of their proceedings, and of the names of the members who attend each meeting, to be duly made from time to time in books to be provided for that purpose, which shall be kept by their clerk, under their superintendence, and every such entry shall be signed by the presiding chairman of the assess-

rates for the relief of the poor :

" Vestry Clerk."

The term "vestry clerk" means the vestry clerk, if any, elected under the Act of the session of the thirteenth and fourteenth years of the reign of Her present Majesty, chapter fifty-seven, or under a local Act, or, if there is no such clerk, the vestry clerk appointed under the Metropolis Management Act, 1855:

" Hereditament."

The term "hereditament" means any lands, tenements, hereditaments, and property which are liable to any rate or tax in respect of which the valuation-list is by this Act made conclusive :

" Gross value."

The term "gross value" means the annual rent which a tenant might reasonably be expected, taking one year with another, to pay for

The Law as Enacted for England and Wales.

ment committee present at the meeting at which the proceed-

Such entries evidence.

ing took place; and such entry, purporting to be so signed, shall be received as evidence in all courts, and before all judges, justices, and others, without proof of such meeting having been duly convened or held, or of the persons attending such meeting having been or being members of the committee, or of the signatures of the members, all of which facts shall be presumed until the contrary be

Books to be open to inspection.

proved; and all such books shall at all seasonable times be open to the inspection of every person rated to the relief of the poor in any parish or place in the union, without any fee being demanded for such inspection; and all such persons shall be entitled at all seasonable times to take copies or extracts from the said books, without paying any fee for the same; and if, on request made for that purpose, the clerk of the committee refuse to permit any

The Law as Enacted for the Metropolis only.

an hereditament, if the tenant undertook to pay all usual tenant's rates and taxes, and tithe commutation rentcharge, if any, and if the landlord undertook to bear the cost of the repairs and insurance, and the other expenses, if any, necessary to maintain the hereditament in a state to command that rent:

"Rateable value."

The term "rateable value" means the gross value after deducting therefrom the probable annual average cost of the repairs, insurance, and other expenses as aforesaid :

The Acts specified in the first schedule to this Act are in this Act referred to by the short title placed opposite to them in that schedule.

SECTION 2 OF THE ACT OF 1862.

Appointment of the assessment committee by board of guardians.

The board of guardians of *every union, formed under the*

The Law as Enacted for England and Wales.   *The Law as Enacted for the Metropolis only.*

such person to inspect any such books, or to take copies or extracts therefrom, as aforesaid, such clerk shall for every such offence be liable to a penalty not exceeding five pounds, upon a summary conviction for the same before two justices of the peace.

Proceedings of committees to be reported.

12. The board of guardians shall in the month of April in every year report the proceedings of their assessment committee to the Poor Law Board.

Overseers to prepare valuation-lists.

14. Subject to any order as hereinafter referred to which may be made by the committee, the *overseers* of each parish in the union shall, within three calendar months after the appointment of such committee, make a list of all the rateable hereditaments in such parish, with the annual value thereof respectively, in so much of the form shown in the schedule annexed to the Act sixth and seventh William the Fourth, chapter ninety-six, as is set out in the schedule to this Act; and unless such overseers think that the valuation

Act fourth and fifth years of King William the fourth, chapter seventy-six, shall, as soon as convenient after the passing of this Act, and in every subsequent year, at their first meeting after the annual election of guardians, appoint from among themselves any number not less than six, nor more than twelve, to be a committee, consisting partly of *ex-officio,* and partly of elected guardians, to be called the assessment committee of the union, for the investigation and supervision of the valuations to be made, as hereinafter-mentioned within such union, and for the performance of such said acts and duties as hereinafter-mentioned; provided always, that one-third at least of such committee shall consist of *ex-officio* guardians, in case there shall be an adequate number of such *ex-officio* guardians; but in case an adequate number of such *ex-officio* guardians shall not exist, then the number so deficient shall be made up of elected guardians.

The Law as Enacted for England and Wales.

then last acted upon in assessing the rate for the relief of the poor correctly shows the full annual rateable value of all such hereditaments, they shall revise such valuation, and such overseers shall sign every list so made by them as aforesaid, and such list shall be styled "The Valuation-List."

SCHEDULE.

VALUATION LIST for (*the parish or place for which the list is made*) in the county of

Name of Occupier.	Name of Owner.	Description of Property.	Name or Situation of Property.	Estimated Extent.	Gross Estimated Rental.	Rateable Value.

Signed this   day of

A.B. } C.D. } Overseers of the poor of the Parish aforesaid.

The Law as Enacted for the Metropolis only.

SECTION 5 OF THE METROPOLIS ACT.

Election of assessment committee in single parish where there is a vestry.

Where, in any parish which *is not included in any union formed under the Poor Law Amendment Act, 1834*, and the Acts amending the same there is for the time being a vestry elected according to the provisions of the Metropolis Management Act, 1855, but no assessment committee under the principal Act, the following provisions shall have effect.

(1.) Where in any such parish there is a board of guardians having power under any Local Act to assess or to make the rates for the relief of the poor, that board of guardians shall appoint an assessment committee :

(2.) Where any two of such parishes are united under a Local Act for the purpose of assessing or making the rates for the relief of

The Law as Enacted for England and Wales.   *The Law as Enacted for the Metropolis only.*

Definition of gross estimated rental.

15. The *gross estimated rental* for the purpose of the schedule to this Act shall be the rent at which the hereditament might reasonably be expected to let from year to year, free of all usual tenants' rates, and taxes, and tithe commutation rent-charge, if any: Provided that nothing herein contained shall repeal or interfere with the provisions contained in the first section of the said Act (six and seven William the Fourth, chapter ninety-six), defining the *net annual value* of the hereditaments to be rated.

SECTION 1 OF 6 AND 7 WILLIAM IV., Cap. 96.

(*An Act to regulate Parochial Assessments.*) — *19th August, 1836.*

All rates to be made on the net annual value of the property.

Whereas it is desirable to establish one uniform mode of rating for the relief of the poor throughout England and Wales, and to lessen the cost of appeal

the poor, the guardians for such united parishes elected in pursuance of the Poor Law Amendment Act, 1834, and the Acts amending the same, shall appoint an assessment committee :

(3.) In cases other than those before mentioned the vestry of such parish shall appoint an assessment committee :

(4.) In the first year after the passing of this Act and every subsequent year, the body who appoint an assessment committee under this section shall on a day fixed by such body between the fifteenth and twenty-ninth of April in that year, or some other day fixed by the Poor Law Board, hold a meeting, and appoint from among themselves an assessment committee (consisting of not less than six nor more than against an unfair rate: Be it enacted by the King's most Excellent Majesty, by and with the advice and consent of the Lords spiritual and temporal, and Commons, in this present Parliament assembled, and by the authority of the same, that from and after such period, not being earlier than the twenty-first day of March next after the passing of this Act, as the Poor Law Commissioners shall by any order under their seal of office direct, no rate for the relief of the poor in England and Wales shall be allowed by any justices, or be of any force, which shall not be made upon an estimate of the *net annual value* of the several hereditaments rated thereunto; *that is to say, of the rent at which the same might reasonably be expected to let from year to year, free of all usual tenants' rates and taxes, and tithe commutation rent charge, if any, and deducting therefrom the probable average annual cost of the repairs, insurance, and other expenses, if any, necessary to maintain them in a state to command such rent :*

twelve in number) in the same manner, as near as may be, as if the parish or united parishes were an union and the appointing body a board of guardians within the meaning of the principal Act.

All the provisions of this Act and Acts incorporated herewith shall—

(a.) in cases where the assessment committee is appointed by guardians under this section be construed as if such guardians, and the monies applicable by such guardians for the relief of the poor were the guardians mentioned in the principal Act and the common fund; and—

(b.) in cases where the assessment committee is appointed by the vestry be construed, so far as is consistent with the tenor thereof, as if the terms vestry,

The Law as Enacted for England and Wales.   *The Law as Enacted for the Metropolis only.*

Proviso.

Provided always, that nothing herein contained shall be construed to alter or affect the principles or different relative liabilities (if any) according to which different kinds of hereditaments are now by law rateable.

Section 7 of the Act 1864.

Expenses of overseers incurred with consent of vestry, or allowed by assessment committee, may be charged on poor-rates.

When the *overseers* of any parish incur any expense in making out any valuation-list or supplemental list, or in revising or valuing any of the rateable hereditaments of such parish, under the provisions of the Union Assessment Committee Act, 1862, with the consent of the vestry given by express resolution, after due notice, they may charge such expense, so far as the same may be authorised by the vestry, upon the poor-rate; and if no vestry meeting be held, or no decision arrived at on the subject, then to the extent which the assessment

members of the vestry, vestry clerk, assistant vestry clerk, and monies applicable to the payment of the expenses of a vestry under the Metropolis Management Act, 1855, were respectively substituted for the terms board of guardians, guardians, clerk of the board of guardians, assistant clerk of the board of guardians, and common fund, but nothing in such Acts relating to *ex-officio* guardians shall have any application in the case of a vestry.

Provision for cases where no guardians and where no overseers.

59. With respect to any parish which is not included in any union of parishes, and in which there is no board of guardians, the following provisions shall have effect:

(1) The assessment committee of the adjoining union

committee shall allow: Provided that, as regards the valuation of the property, no expense shall be so charged upon the poor-rate unless the consent of such committee to the procuring of such valuation by the overseers shall have been given previously to the same being made.

SECTION 16, ACT 1862.

Committee may enlarge the time for making valuation-lists, and may give directions concerning valuations and valuation-lists, and may appoint persons to make the same.

The committee by their order may from time to time enlarge the time within which the first valuation-list under this Act shall be made by the overseers of all or any of the parishes in the union, and for ensuring a uniform and correct valuation of every parish in the union may direct that any existing valuation of the rateable hereditaments in any parish be revised, in whole or in part, or a new valuation of such hereditaments be made by the overseers, or *the committee* may, with the consent of the

shall act as the *assessment committee* of that parish, and where there is more than one such adjoining union the Poor Law Board shall determine the assessment committee which is to act for such parish :

(2.) Every such parish shall, for the purposes of this Act and the Acts incorporated herewith, but not for any other purpose, be deemed to be within the union of the assessment committee which acts for it :

(3.) The masters of the bench, treasurer, governors, or other body of persons in such parish, may, at the time appointed for the election of an assessment committee, appoint a person to be a member of such assessment committee in addition to the number elected

c

board of guardians of the union, after notice shall have been sent to every guardian thereof, in any case appoint some person for either purposes aforesaid, and may direct such person to make and sign the valuation-list instead of the overseers, and every valuation-list so made and signed shall be delivered by such person to the overseers of the parish to which the same relates.

Valuation-lists to be deposited for inspection, and afterwards transmitted to the committee.

17. The valuation-list of each parish, made and signed by the *overseers*, or delivered to them, as hereinbefore provided, shall be deposited *by the overseers* in the place in such parish in which rate books are deposited or kept, and a copy of such valuation-list shall be forthwith delivered to the board of guardians, and the *overseers* shall give public notice of the deposit of such list on the *Sunday next* following the deposit of such list, and such notice shall be given in the same manner, and all persons assessed, or liable to be assessed

under this Act and the Acts incorporated herewith:

(4.) Where there are no overseers the *assessment committee* shall appoint some person to perform the duties of the overseers under this Act and the Acts incorporated herewith, and may award him such remuneration as they think fit: and the person so appointed shall perform those duties, and shall, for that purpose, have all the powers of overseers:

(5.) A proportionate share of the expenses of the assessment committee under this Act and the Acts incorporated herewith, and any remuneration paid to or expenses incurred by the person appointed by them under this or any other section to make a valuation-list, shall be charged on such to the relief of the poor of such parish, shall have the like right of inspecting, and of demanding and taking copies of, and extracts from, such list, as in the case of a poor-rate allowed by the justices, and the overseers shall, at the expiration of *fourteen days* from the time of the notice given of the deposit of such list, transmit the same to the committee, and any overseer or other ratepayer within the union shall have the right of inspecting and taking copies of, and extracts from, any of the lists so transmitted.

parish, and the sums so charged shall be paid by the masters of the bench, treasurer, governor, or other body of persons; and sections sixty-six, sixty-seven, and sixty-eight of the Metropolitan Poor Act, 1867, shall apply to such sums in the same manner as if the assessment committee and their clerk were the Poor Law Board and the receiver mentioned in those sections.

SECTION 5 OF THE ACT OF 1864.

Notice of assessment to be given to certain companies.

Within *fourteen days* after the transmission to the assessment committee of any valuation or supplemental valuation-list, the *committee* shall give notice to every railway, telegraph, canal, gas, and water company named in such list as the occupier of any property included therein, and not having any office or

SECTION 4 OF ACT 1862.

Provision for neglect to appoint.

If the *guardians* shall neglect or be prevented from making such appointment at the meeting above specified, the Poor Law Board shall by their order appoint some other day on which the guardians shall make such appointment.

Provision for vacancies.

5. If any *ex-officio* or elected guardian being a member of

c 2

place of business in the parish to which such list relates, of the sum or sums set down as the rateable value of the property purporting to be occupied by such company or companies, and such notice may be served by being transmitted through the post to the principal office of the company, or one of their principal offices when there shall be more than one.

SECTION 18 OF THE ACT OF 1862.

Objections to valuation-list.

Any overseer or overseers of any parish in any union, who shall have reason to think that such parish is aggrieved by the valuation-list of any parish within such union, or any person who may feel himself aggrieved by any valuation-list on the ground of unfairness or incorrectness in the valuation of any hereditaments included therein, or on the ground of the omission of any rateable hereditament from such list, may at any time after the deposit as aforesaid of such list, and *before the expiration of*

the committee cease to be guardian, or resign his seat at such committee, **or** die, **or** become incapable of acting as such member, the board of guardians shall with all convenient speed appoint an *ex-officio* or elected guardian, as the case may be, to supply the vacancy

Continuing members may act during vacancies.

6. During any vacancy in any *assessment committee*, the other or continuing members of such committee may act, and shall have the same powers and jurisdiction as if no such vacancy had happened.

Extent of committee's authority.

7. The authority of the *committee* appointed for any union under this Act shall extend over every parish comprised in such union.

First meeting, when to be holden.

8. The *committee* shall hold their first meeting at the board room of the union on a day to be fixed by the board of guardians, and the subsequent meetings of the committee shall be

The Law as Enacted for England and Wales.

The Law as Enacted for the Metropolis only.

---

twenty-eight days after the notice of the deposit as aforesaid, give to the committee and to the overseers a notice in writing to his objection, specifying the grounds thereof, and where the ground of any objection shall be unfairness or incorrectness in the valuation of any hereditament in respect of which any person, other than the person objecting, is liable to be rated, or the omission of such hereditament, also give notice in writing of such objection, and of the ground thereof, to such other person.

Service of notices, &c., on the committee.

42. Any notice or statement required to be served *upon the committee* may be served by being left at the office of the clerk to the board of guardians, or sent through the post-office, addressed to the committee at such clerk's office, or by being delivered personally to their clerk, or at his usual place of abode.

Committee to hold meetings to hear objections.

19. *The committee* shall hold

holden at such times and at such place and upon such notice and requisition as they shall from time to time appoint; and any guardian of the union may be present at any meeting of the committee, but shall not be entitled to take part in the proceedings thereof.

Quorum of meetings.

9. All acts, orders, matters, and things by this Act authorised or directed to be made or done *by the committee* may be made or done by the major part of the members of such committee who shall be present at a meeting, the whole number present together at such meeting not being less than three, and not less in any case than one-third of the whole number of which such committe consists; and when upon any question there shall be an equality of votes, the presiding chairman shall have a second or casting vote.

Committee may employ and pay clerk.

10. *The committee* shall employ the clerk or assistant clerk

such meetings as they may think
necessary for hearing objections
to the valuation-lists, and shall,
twenty-eight days at least before
holding every meeting for hearing objections to valuation-lists,
other than meetings by adjournment, cause notice of such meeting to be given to the overseers
of the several parishes to which
such lists relate, and such overseers shall, on the Sunday next
following the receipt of such
notice, publish the same in the
manner in which notice of a rate
allowed by justices is by law required to be given, and the committee may at any such meeting
hear and determine such objections, or may from time to time
adjourn any such meeting, and
adjourn or postpone the hearing
or further hearing and determination of any such objections,
and may, where they think fit,
direct notice of any such objections to be given by the overseers or by the persons objecting
to third parties before the further hearing thereof; but the
committee shall not be required
to hold a meeting for hearing
objections to the valuation-list

of the board of guardians as
their clerk, with such remuneration for his services as the
Poor Law Board shall sanction.

Proceedings to be entered in books and signed.

11. *The committee* shall cause
a minute of their proceedings,
and of the names of the members who attend each meeting,
to be duly made from time to
time in books to be provided for
that purpose, which shall be
kept by their clerk, under their
superintendence, and every such
entry shall be signed by the
presiding chairman of the assessment committee present at the
meeting at which the proceeding took place; and such entry,
purporting to be so signed, shall

Such entries evidence.

be received as evidence in all
courts, and before all judges,
justices, and others, without
proof of such meeting having
been duly convened or held, or
of the persons attending such
meeting having been or being
members of the committee, or
of the signatures of the mem-

The Law as Enacted for England and Wales.	*The Law as Enacted for the Metropolis only.*

of any parish, unless such notice in writing as hereinbefore-mentioned of some objection or objections thereto have been given to the committee; and where a meeting is holden for hearing objections to the valuation-list of any parish, the committee shall not hear any objection to such valuation-list, unless such notice as aforesaid of such objection have been given to the committee and to the overseers; and where the ground of such objection is unfairness or incorrectness in the valuation of any hereditament of any other person than the person objecting, or the omission of such hereditament, also to such other person by the person objecting, except where the overseers, by themselves or any other person on their behalf, and in the case aforesaid such other person as aforesaid, by himself or any other person on his behalf, consent to the hearing of such objection, and in such case the committee may, if they see fit, hear the same; and where the committee see fit to hear the same, they shall act in relation thereto in

bers, all of which facts shall be presumed until the contrary be

Books to be open to inspection.

proved; and all such books shall at all seasonable times be open to the inspection of every person rated to the relief of the poor in any parish or place in the union, without any fee being demanded for such inspection; and all such persons shall be entitled at all seasonable times to take copies or extracts from the said books, without paying any fee for the same; and if, on request made for that purpose, the clerk of the committee refuse to permit any such person to inspect any such books, or to take copies or extracts therefrom, as aforesaid, such clerk shall for every such offence be liable to a penalty not exceeding five pounds, upon a summary conviction for the same before two justices of the peace.

Proceedings of committees to be reported.

12. The *board of guardians* shall in the month of April in every year report the proceed-

like manner as if notice of such objection had been duly given.

Committee may require returns from overseers, &c. ;

13. *The committee* by their order may from time to time require the overseers, assistant overseers, constables, assessors, collectors, and any other persons having the custody of any books of assessment of any taxes or rates, parliamentary or parochial, or of the valuations of any parish, or having the collection or management of any such rates or taxes, to make returns in writing to the committee, at such times and places as they may appoint, of all such particulars as they may direct in relation to such taxes, rates, or valuations, or any property included therein, so far as relates to the union for which they act, and may require the persons having the custody of any such books as aforesaid to make and transmit to the committee copies of or extracts from such books, or to permit such copies or extracts to be made by such persons as the committee may in that be-

ings of their assessment committee to the Poor Law Board.

SECTION 6 OF THE METROPOLIS ACT.

Making of valuation-list.

The overseers of every parish to which this Act extends, within the time in this Act mentioned shall make (*and deposit before 1st June, 1870, Sect. 42,* Metropolis Act) a valuation-list of their parish in duplicate, in accordance with this Act.

Occupier to make returns.

55. In the first year after the passing of this Act, and in every subsequent year in which a new valuation-list is made, or in the month of March preceding any such year, *every person who is liable* to be charged with any rate or tax in respect of which the valuation-list is made conclusive shall, when required, make to the overseers of his parish such statement or return as a person chargeable under the Income Tax Act and the Acts amending the same is bound to make.

and may require production of rates, &c., and examine persons attending before them.

half direct; and may from time to time require any persons having the custody of any such books, or the collection or management of any such taxes or rates as aforesaid, to attend before them at a time and place to be mentioned in the order in this behalf, and to produce all parochial and public books of assessment, rates, rate books, valuations, apportionments, tithe and other maps, plans, surveys, and other public documents in their custody or power, and may examine all persons who shall attend before them: Provided always, that nothing herein contained shall authorise the production of valuations or assessments which by any provision of law at present are not suffered to be made public.

Authentication and service of orders and notices of the committee.

41. Every order and notice made or given *by the committee* under this act may be in writing or print, or partly in writing

Surveyor of taxes to supply notices and forms for returns to overseers, who are to serve them.

56. For the purpose of securing the proper making of such returns, the *surveyor of taxes* shall in the month of February preceding send to the overseers of each parish in his district a sufficient number of printed forms and notices, and the overseers, within a month after the receipt thereof, shall serve a notice and form on every person in their parish required by this Act to make a return; and every person required by this Act to make a return shall make it within twenty-one days after the service of a notice and form on him.

The forms and notices shall be such as are prescribed by the Income Tax Act or the Acts amending the same, or as the Commissioners of Her Majesty's Treasury may from time to time prescribe, and any such form duly filled up and signed shall be deemed to be a sufficient return.

The return shall be delivered to the overseers of each parish,

The Law as Enacted for England and Wales.

The Law as Enacted for the Metropolis only.

and partly in print, and shall be sufficiently authenticated if signed by their clerk, and may be served by the same or a copy thereof being delivered personally or sent by post to the party on or to whom such order or notice purports to be made or given, or by being delivered at his usual place of abode.

Penalty for non-attendance, &c., in obedience to order of the committee.

40. *Every person who wilfully refuses* to attend in obedience to any lawful order of any such committee, or to give evidence, or refuses to produce any ratebook, assessment, or valuation which may be lawfully required to be produced before such committee, shall for every such offence be liable to a penalty not exceeding twenty pounds upon a summary conviction for the same before two justices of the peace; and every person who

Injuring, &c., rate-books a misdemeanor.

wilfully injures, defaces, conceals, or destroys such ratebook, or who upon any examination before any such commit-

and together with the valuation-list shall be sent by them to the surveyor of taxes, and by the surveyor of taxes to the assessment committee.

Form and contents of valuation-list.

51. The valuation-list shall be made out in the form given in the second schedule to this Act.

The *overseers* shall not include in such valuation-list any hereditaments (except tithes or payment in lieu of tithes) which are charged according to Rule two

5 & 6 Vict. c. 35.

in section sixty of the Income Tax Act, but shall include tithes and payments in lieu of tithes and every hereditament in their parish, and shall enter every hereditament in the valuation-list in accordance with the classes mentioned in the third schedule to this Act, so that the deductions to be made in ascertaining the rateable value may be calculated in accordance with that schedule.

The Law as Enacted for England and Wales.

tee wilfully gives false evidence, shall be deemed guilty of a misdemeanor.

Board may allow compensation for returns, &c., and expenses.

37. *The committee* may allow such compensation for any returns, copies, or extracts, or any valuation, or valuation-list, or other act, matter, or thing to be made or done in pursuance of their order, and such expenses connected therewith, as to the committee in each case seems just.

Remuneration to clerk and certain expenses of committee to be paid out of common fund.

38. The remuneration allowed by the *committee* to their clerk, and all expenses incurred by them for the common use and benefit of the several parishes within the union for which they are appointed, shall be paid by the guardians of the said union, and be charged upon the common fund thereof.

Board may direct further valuation, and correct valuation-lists, and when corrected to approve the same.

20. *The committee* may, whe-

The Law as Enacted for the Metropolis only.

SECOND SCHEDULE.

PART I.—VALUATION LIST for [*the parish or place for which the list is made*] in the the Metropolitan Union of .... in the County of ....

No	Name of Occupier.	Name of Owner.	Description of Property.	No. of Class.	Name or Situation of Property.	Extent	Gross Value as estimated by Overseers.	Gross Value (Gross Value as estimated by Surveyor per Cent. of Taxes.	Rate of deduction	Rateable Value.	Gross Value as finally determined by Assessment Committee.	Rateable Value as finally determined by Assessment Committee.

Signed this .... day of ....

A. B. } Overseers of the poor of the
C. D. } Parish aforesaid.

The Law as Enacted for England and Wales.

The Law as Enacted for the Metropolis only.

---

ther any objection be or be not made to any such valuation-list, and either before or after any meeting for hearing objections, make such alterations in the valuation of any hereditaments included in any valuation-list, and insert therein any rateable hereditament omitted therefrom, and make such corrections in names, descriptions, and particulars in any valuation-list, and upon such information as to them may seem sufficient, and may, with the consent of the guardians as aforesaid, appoint or employ a person to survey and value the rateable hereditaments comprised in any such valuation-list, or any of them, or omitted therefrom, or may take such other means as they may think necessary for ascertaining the correctness thereof, and when the committee have heard and determined all such objections as aforesaid, and have made such alterations, insertions, and corrections in any valuation-list as to them may seem proper, they shall approve the same under the hands of three members of the committee present at the

---

Saving of exemptions and exceptional principles of valuation.

54. Nothing contained in this Act or the Acts incorporated herewith shall affect any exemption or deduction from or allowance out of any rate or tax whatever, or any privilege of or provision for being rated or taxed on any exceptional principle of valuation.

Saving of powers to value property not included in a valuation-list.

75. Nothing in this Act shall in any way alter or affect the mode of valuing or taxing any hereditament which is not included in any valuation-list, or which is chargeable according to the profits and not according to the gross value, or the mode of charging the occupiers of land subject to a tithe rentcharge in respect of such tithe rentcharge.

Separate assessment of houses for purposes of house duty, income tax, and Licensing Acts.

76. Where for the purposes of the Acts relating to the duty on inhabited houses, or to the duties charged under schedule

meeting at which the same is approved, with the date of such approval.

Valuation-list when altered to be deposited, &c.

21. Where *the committee* make any alteration in the valuation of any hereditaments included in, or insert therein any rateable hereditament omitted from, any such valuation-list, they shall cause such valuation-list, with such alteration or insertion, to be deposited for inspection in manner hereinbefore provided concerning the valuation-list made by or delivered to the overseers, and shall cause the like notice to be given of such deposit as is required in the case of a valuation-list so made or delivered as aforesaid, and shall appoint a day, not *less than seven days* nor *more than fourteen days* from the re-deposit of such valuation-list, for the hearing of any objections to the valuation-list as so altered; and when the committee have heard and determined any such objections, or have made such further alterations, insertions, and corrections in such valuation-list, they shall

B. of the Income Tax Act, or to the sale of exciseable liquors, it is necessary to make a separate valuation of any hereditament by reason of its not being separately valued in any valuation-list, the value of such hereditament shall be ascertained in the same manner as if this Act had not passed.

Deductions for rateable value.

52. The per-centage or rate of deductions to be made from the gross value in calculating the rateable value for the purposes of this Act shall not exceed the amounts in the third schedule to this Act so far as the same are applicable.

THIRD SCHEDULE.

Showing the several classes into which the hereditaments inserted in a valuation-list under this Act are to be divided.

	Maximum Rate of Deductions.
	Per cent. r Proportion
Class 1. Houses and buildings, or either of them, without land other than gardens where the gross value is under £20	25 or ¼th.
„ 2. Houses and buildings without land other than gardens and pleasure grounds valued therewith for the purpose of inhabited house duty where the gross value is £20 and under £40	20 or ⅕th.

The Law as Enacted for England and Wales.   *The Law as Enacted for the Metropolis only.*

approve the same in manner hereinbefore provided.

SECTION 30 OF THE POOR LAW AMENDMENT ACT OF 1868.

Columns in the valuation-lists to be cast up by the committee, and fair copies of the approved valuation-lists to be given to the overseers instead of originals.

When the *assessment committee* in any union shall have finally approved of any valuation-list, whether original, substitutional, or supplemental, they shall cause the total of the entries in the columns for the gross estimated value and the rateable value to be ascertained and entered at the foot of the same, and shall retain such list for the use of the guardians, to be dealt with in the manner provided by the thirty-first section of the Union Assessment Committee Act, 1862, and shall deliver a fair copy of the same to the overseers, signed by the three members of the committee who approved of the same; and such copy shall be countersigned by the clerk of the committee, and

	Maximum Rate of Deductions. Per cent. or Proportion.
Class 3. Houses and buildings without land other than gardens and pleasure grounds valued therewith for the purpose of inhabited house duty where the gross value is £40 or upwards	16⅔ or ⅙th.
,, 4. Buildings without land which are not liable to inhabited house duty and are of a gross value of £20 and under £40	20 or ⅕th.
,, 5. Buildings without land which are not liable to inhabited house duty and are of a gross value of £40 or upwards	16⅔ or ⅙th.
,, 6. Land with buildings not houses	10 or ⅒th.
,, 7. Land without buildings	5 or 1/20th.
,, 8. Mills and manufactories	33⅓ or ⅓rd.
,, 9. Tithes, tithe commutation rentcharge, and other payments in lieu of tithe	To be determined in each case according to the circumstances and the general principles of law
,, 10. Railways, canals, docks, tolls, waterworks, and gasworks	
,, 11. Rateable hereditaments not included in any of the foregoing classes	

The Maximum rate of deductions prescribed in this schedule shall not apply to houses or buildings let out in separate tenements, but the rate of deductions in such cases shall be determined as in Classes 9, 10, and 11.

Provision where vestry are the overseers.

60. Where the *vestry* or the *guardians of any parish* perform the duties of overseers with respect to a valuation-list under this Act the list shall be signed by the *vestry clerk* or the *clerk of the guardians.*

|

shall be preserved by the overseers, and dealt with by them in all respects as the list made out by them would have been dealt with according to the law now in force, and it shall not be necessary for the said committee to cause any other copy to be made.

SECTION 31 OF THE ACT OF 1862.

Copy of valuation-lists to be deposited in board-room.

The committee shall cause a copy of the valuation-list for the time in force for every parish in the union to be made and deposited at the board-room or other convenient place to be appointed by the board of guardians in the custody of the clerk, which copy shall be open at seasonable times to the inspection of any of the guardians of the union, and of any overseer of any parish within the union, without charge, and of any rate-payer within the union on payment of one shilling, such fee to be carried to the account of the common fund.

SECTION 7 OF THE ACT OF 1864.

Expenses of overseers incurred with consent of vestry, or allowed by assessment committee, may be charged on poor-rates.

When *the overseers* of any parish incur any expense in making out any valuation-list or supplemental list, or in revising or valuing any of the rateable hereditaments of such parish, under the provisions of the Union Assessment Committee Act, 1862, with the consent of the vestry given by express resolution, after due notice, they may charge such expense, so far as the same may be authorised by the vestry, upon the poor-rate; and if no vestry meeting be held, or no decision arrived at on the subject, then to the extent which the assessment committee shall allow: Provided that, as regards the valuation of the property, no expense shall be so charged upon the poor-rate unless the consent of such committee to the procuring of such valuation by the overseers shall have

32　　　　　　THE PRINCIPLE OF RATING.

The Law as Enacted for England and Wales.　　*The Law as Enacted for the Metropolis only.*

In computing amount of contributions to common fund, the annual rateable value to be taken from approved valuation-lists.

30. When the assessment committee for any union shall have approved valuation-lists for all the parishes comprised within such union, the *guardians of such union*, in computing the amount of contribution to the common fund for the several parishes, shall thenceforward take the annual rateable value of the property in such parishes respectively from the valuation-lists for the time being lastly approved of for such parishes respectively, any statute to the contrary notwithstanding : Provided that in case any parish comprised in any union shall receive any sum of money as a contribution in aid of the poor-rate of such parish, for or in respect of government property within such parish and used for public purposes, the annual value of such property, according to the estimate (if any) of such value on which the amount of the sum of money so received is computed, or, if there be no such

been given previously to the same being made.

SECTION 16 OF THE ACT OF 1862.

Committee may enlarge the time for making valuation-lists, and may give directions concerning valuations and valuation-lists, and may appoint persons to make the same.

The committee by their order may from time to time enlarge the time within which the first valuation-list under this Act shall be made by the overseers of all or any of the parishes in the union, and for ensuring a uniform and correct valuation of every parish in the union may direct that any existing valuation of the rateable hereditaments in any parish be revised, in whole or in part, or a new valuation of such hereditaments be made by the overseers, or the committee may, with the consent of the board of guardians of the union, after notice shall have been sent to every guardian thereof, in any case appoint some person for

estimate, then the annual value
of such property, estimated in
the mode provided by the act
sixth and seventh William the
Fourth, chapter ninety-six, for
making an estimate of the annual rateable value of property
liable to be rated to rates for
the relief of the poor, shall be
included by the overseer or overseers in the valuation-list of such
parish, and shall be added to the
annual rateable value of the property in such parish in computing the amount of contribution
to the common fund for the several parishes in such union.

SECTION 9 OF THE ACT OF 1864.

Clerks of assessment committees to furnish
clerks of the peace with totals of valuation-lists.

The *clerk* of every assessment
committee shall send annually
in the month of December copies
of the totals of the gross estimated rental and rateable value
of the property included in the
valuation-lists of the several parishes within the union, and
where such totals have been
altered by any supplemental

either of the purposes aforesaid,
and may direct such person to
make and sign the valuation-
list instead of the overseers,
and every valuation-list so made
and signed shall be delivered by
such person to the overseers of
the parish to which the same
relates.

SECTION 7 OF THE METROPOLIS
ACT.

Valuation-lists to be dealt with under
25 & 26 Vict. c. 103. ss. 17 to 21.

After the valuation-list is
signed by the *overseers* the same
proceedings shall be had as are
directed by the seventeenth,
eighteenth, nineteenth, twen-
tieth, and twenty-first sections
of the principal Act subject to
the alterations made by this
Act.

SECTION 17 OF THE ACT OF 1862.

Valuation-lists to be deposited for inspection, and afterwards transmitted to
the Committee.

The valuation-list for each
parish, made and signed by the
overseers, or delivered to them,

D

valuation-list or lists then of such totals as altered, to the clerk or respective clerks of the peace of the county or counties within which such parishes respectively may be situate.

SECTION 32, ACT 1862.

Appeal against valuation-list.

If the *overseer* or *overseers* of any parish in any union shall have reason to think that such parish is aggrieved by the valuation-list of any parish within such union, whether it be on the ground that the rateable hereditaments comprised in the valuation-list of such parish are valued at sums beyond the annual rateable value thereof, or on the ground that the rateable hereditaments comprised in the valuation-list of some other parish in such union are valued at sums less than the annual rateable value thereof, it shall be lawful for such *overseer* or *overseers*, with the consent of a vestry summoned for the purpose of considering the expediency of giving such consent, to appeal to the quarter sessions

as herein-before provided, shall be deposited by *the overseers* in the place in such parish in which rate books are deposited or kept, * * * * * * and the overseers shall give public notice of the deposit of such list, on the *Sunday* next following the deposit of such list, and such notice shall be given in the same manner, and all persons assessed or liable to be assessed to the relief of the poor of such parish shall have the like right of inspecting, and of demanding and taking copies of and extracts from such list, as in the case of a poor rate allowed by the justices, and the overseers, shall, at the expiration of fourteen days (*and not later than seventeen days, Sect. 42, Metropolis Act*) from the time of the notice given of the deposit of such list, transmit the same to the committee, and any overseer or other ratepayer within the union shall have the right of inspecting and taking copies of and extracts from any of the lists so transmitted.

for the county or borough in
which the greatest number of
parishes belonging to the union
is situate, or, in case the number of parishes in any two or
more such jurisdictions is equal,
to the quarter sessions for the
county or borough having jurisdiction over the parish in
which the workhouse of the
union is situate, at the sessions
to be holden after the expiration
of a month after the allowance
of and deposit of such valuation-
list as aforesaid, against such
valuation-list of the parish which
shall appear to be over-valued
or under-valued; and if in any
case any such *overseer* or *overseers* appeal against the valuation-list of any other parish on
the ground that the rateable
hereditaments in such list are
valued at less than the annual
rateable value thereof, such overseer or overseers shall give fourteen clear days' notice in writing previous to the first day of
the said quarter session at which
the appeal is to be made of the
intention to appeal, and the
grounds thereof, to the overseers
of the poor of such parish, and

Section 10 of the Metropolis Act.

Notice to state time and mode of objection.

The notice of the deposit and
re-deposit of the valuation-list
published by *the overseers* shall
state the times at which and
the mode in which objections
are to be made.

Publication of notices by overseers.

66. Any notice required by
this Act to be published by *the
overseers* shall, on the Sunday
next following the receipt of
such notice, or the document to
which the notice refers, and
the two following Sundays, be
published by them in the manner in which notice of a rate
allowed by justices is required
to be published.

Notice to occupier of alteration of value, &c.

9 (PART OF). Where the *overseers* of the parish insert in the
valuation-list some hereditament
not previously assessed, or raise
the gross or rateable value of

36 THE PRINCIPLE OF RATING.

The Law as Enacted for England and Wales.

to the guardians of the union
comprising such parish; and if
any *overseer* or *overseers* of any
parish appeal against the valuation-list of such parish on the
ground that the rateable hereditaments in such list are valued
beyond the annual rateable value thereof, such *overseer* or *overseers* shall give *fourteen days'*
notice in writing previous to
the quarter sessions at which
the appeal is to be made of the
intention to appeal, and the
grounds thereof, to the *guardians of the union* in which such
parish is situate, the said court
shall be empowered to hear and
determine such appeal, and
either confirm such valuation-
list, or correct such irregulari-
ties or inaccuracies as shall be
proved to exist therein as to
them may appear fair and just;
but no such valuation-list shall
upon such appeal be quashed or
destroyed in regard to any other
parish unless the court deem it
necessary to proceed to the making of an entirely new valuation-
list as hereinafter provided.

Hearing and determining appeals.

33. It shall be lawful for the

The Law as Enacted for the Metropolis only.

some hereditament above the
value stated in the valuation-list
for the time being in force or
(where there is no valuation-
list) in the then last assessment
to the poor rate, *the overseers*
shall immediately after the deposit of the list serve on the
occupier of such hereditament, a
notice of the gross and rateable
value thereof inserted in the
valuation-list.

Duplicate sent to surveyor of taxes.

8. The *overseers* shall send one
duplicate of the valuation-list
to the surveyor of taxes of the
district at the same time that
the other duplicate is deposited
by them. The surveyor of taxes
shall insert in the duplicate so
sent to him the amount in his
opinion of the gross value of
the hereditaments comprised in
such list where such amount
differs from the amount inserted
by the overseers, and shall
transmit the duplicate to the
assessment committee within
twenty-eight days after he has
received the same.

If overseers do not transmit list, committee to appoint a person to do so.

13. If the *overseers* of any

court of quarter sessions upon any such appeal, instead of hearing the said appeal, to adjourn the same, and to order, upon the application of the appellant or respondent in such appeal, a survey or valuation of any of the parishes in respect of which such appeal shall be made, and to fix the next or some subsequent sessions for receiving such survey or valuation, and for hearing and determining such appeal; and such court shall also thereupon appoint a proper person to make such survey or valuation, and the person so appointed shall have power, with or without assistants, to enter upon and survey, measure, and value all the hereditaments liable to be assessed to the rates for the relief of the poor within the parish or parishes mentioned in such order, and such survey and valuation shall be reported to the quarter sessions on adjournment fixed as aforesaid for receiving the same, and the court then and there assembled shall hear and determine the said appeal in the manner hereinbefore set forth.

parish fail to transmit such a valuation-list as is required by this Act, the assessment committee shall appoint some person to make a valuation-list, and may allow such person such remuneration in addition to his expenses as they think fit; and all expenses incurred by the assessment committee in pursuance of this section shall be paid by the guardians, and charged by them to such parish.

The person so appointed shall have for the purposes of this section the same powers and duties as overseers, and the valuation-list so made shall be dealt with in the like manner as if it had been duly made and transmitted by the *overseers.*

SECTION 5 OF THE ACT OF 1864.

Notice of assessment to be given to certain companies.

Within *fourteen days* after the transmission to the assessment committee of any valuation or supplemental valuation-list, *the committee* shall give notice to, every railway, telegraph, canal, gas, and water company

Costs of valuation and appeal.

34. The charges and expenses of any such survey and valuation so ordered shall be deemed costs in such appeal, and abide the event thereof, and the court before which any such appeal is heard and determined may order the costs in and about the appeal to be paid by either the appellant or respondent party, as they in their discretion may think fit; but where any appeal is made on the ground that the rateable hereditaments of any parish comprised in the valuation-list of such parish are valued beyond the annual rateable value thereof, if the court on such appeal determine in favour of the appellants, such court shall ascertain the costs and charge incurred by such appellants in and about such appeal, and shall order the board of guardians of the union in which such parish is situate to pay the same to the appellants out of the money raised for the common fund for the several parishes in such union.

named in such list as the occupier of any property included therein, and not having any office or place of business in the parish to which such list relates, of the sum or sums set down as the rateable value of the property purporting to be occupied by such company or companies, and such notice may be served by being transmitted through the post to the principal office of the company, or one of their principal offices when there shall be more than one.

SECTION 18, ACT 1862.

Objections to valuation-list.

Any *overseer* or *overseers* of any parish in any union who shall have reason to think that such parish is aggrieved by the valuation-list of any parish within such union, or *any person who may feel himself aggrieved* by any valuation-list on the ground of unfairness or incorrectness in the valuation of any hereditaments included therein, or on the ground of the omission of any rateable hereditament

SECTION 23, ACT 1862.

Custody, &c., of valuation-list after approval.

Every valuation-list, when approved *by the committee*, shall be delivered to the overseers of the parish to which the same relates, and shall be preserved at the like place and in the like custody, and be subject to the like resort thereto, and be delivered over from time to time in like manner, as the books are wherein rates and assessments for the relief of the poor for the same parish are entered, and shall be produced by the overseers before the justices, upon application, for the allowance of rates, and at the special or general or quarter sessions when any appeal is to be heard, and also at such times and places as the committee may from time to time direct.

What shall be deemed valuation-lists in force.

24. Every valuation-list approved by the committee, and delivered to the overseers of the parish to which the same relates,

from such list, may at any time after the deposit as aforesaid of such list, and before the expiration of *twenty-eight days* after the notice of the deposit as aforesaid, give to the committee and the overseers a notice in writing of his objection, specifying the grounds thereof, and where the grounds of any objection shall be unfairness or incorrectness in the valuation of any hereditament in respect of which any person, other than the person objecting, is liable to be rated, or the omission of such hereditament, also give notice in writing of such objection, and of the ground thereof, to such other person.

SECTION 42 (3) OF THE METROPOLIS ACT.

Notice of any objection by *any person* other than the surveyor of taxes and the overseers shall be given before the expiration of *twenty-five days* after the list is deposited.

42. (6.) Notice of objection with respect to any list by the *surveyor of taxes* and by *the*

The Law as Enacted for England and Wales.

The Law as Enacted for the Metropolis only.

shall with and subject to the alterations and additions for the time being made therein or thereto by any supplemental valuation-list so approved and delivered, be the valuation-list in force in such parish, except in the case of any parish, as is hereinafter referred to, in which the poor-rate, or assessment for the poor-rate, is made under the authority of a local act, until a new valuation-list in substitution for the same be approved and delivered in like manner.

SECTION 31, POOR LAW AMEND-
MENT ACT, 1868.

Certified copies of valuation-lists rendered available, whose original is lost.

Where any valuation-list heretofore approved, or the copy hereafter to be made, shall be lost, injured, or destroyed, the overseers of the parish to which it relates may apply to the clerk of the guardians for a copy of the same; and the clerk, upon payment of a reasonable compensation, not exceeding three shillings for one hundred separ-

overseers shall be given not less than *seven days* before the meeting at which objections to such lists will be heard by the assessment committee.

Grounds on which persons may object before assessment committee.

11. Objections may be made before the assessment committee by *any person authorized by this Act* and the Acts incorporated herewith to object who feels himself aggrieved by reason of the unfairness or incorrectness of the valuation of any hereditament, or by reason of the insertion or incorrectness of any matter in the valuation-list, or by reason of the omission of any matter therefrom, or by reason of such valuation-list as is required by this Act not having been transmitted by the overseers to the assessment committee. The notice of objection shall specify the correction which the objector desires to be made.

Surveyor of taxes, &c., may inspect, copy, and object to valuation-list.

12. A *surveyor of taxes*, and *any ratepayer* in the parish, shall

ate rateable hereditaments, shall give such copy, and certify the same to be a true copy of the list deposited with the said guardians, and such certified copy shall be thenceforth available as the original.

SECTION 43, ACT 1862.

Provision as to form of poor rate.

In every parish, until a valuation-list has been approved, and delivered to the overseers under this Act, every rate made for the relief of the poor in such parish shall be made in the form and contain the particulars required by the said Act of the sixth and seventh years of King William the Fourth; and after such valuation-list has been so approved and delivered, every such rate, except in any parish where the poor rate or the assessment for the same is made under the provisions of a local act as aforesaid, shall show the annual rateable value of each hereditament comprised therein according to the valuation-list in force in such parish.

have the same right of inspecting, copying, taking extracts from, and objecting to any valuation-list which relates to his district or parish as is given to any person by this Act and Acts incorporated herewith.

42. (4.) The *assessment committee* shall revise the valuation-list before the first of October in the same year (*1870*), and before the same day, but not less than sixteen days after the transmission of the list to them by the overseers shall hold a meeting for hearing objections to such list.

42. (5.) The *assessment committee* shall give notice of a meeting for hearing objections to a list not less than sixteen days before such meeting.

SECTION 19, ACT 1862.

Committee to hold meetings to hear objections.

The *committee* shall hold such meetings as they may think necessary for hearing objections to the valuation-lists, and shall, *twenty-eight days* at least before

After a valuation-list is approved, no rate to be allowed unless made according to such list.

28. In every parish where a valuation-list under this Act has been approved and delivered to the overseers, *no rate* for the relief of the poor, or other rate which by law is required to be based upon the poor rate, shall be of any force, unless the hereditaments included in such rate, except as hereinafter provided, be rated according to the annual rateable value thereof appearing in the valuation-list in force in such parish; and *instead* of the declaration required by the second section of the said statute of the sixth and seventh years of William the Fourth, chapter ninety-six, the *overseers* shall, before the rate shall be allowed by the justices, sign a declaration according to the form set forth in the schedule hereunto annexed : Provided always, that where by reason of any alteration in the occupation of any property included in such list, such property has become liable to be rated in parts not mentioned in such list as rate-

holding every meeting for hearing objections to valuation-lists, other than meetings by adjournment, cause notice of such meeting to be given to the *overseers* of the several parishes to which such lists relate, and such overseers shall, on the Sunday next following the receipt of such notice, publish the same in the manner in which notice of a rate allowed by justices is by law required to be given, and the committee may at any such meeting hear and determine such objections, or may from time to time adjourn any such meeting, and adjourn or postpone the hearing or further hearing and determination of any such objections, and may, where they think fit, direct notice of any such objections to be given by the overseers or by the persons objecting to third parties before the further hearing thereof; but the committee shall not be required to hold a meeting for hearing objections to the valuation-list of any parish, unless such notice in writing as herein-before-mentioned of some objection or obable hereditaments, and separately rated therein, such parts may, where a supplemental valuation-list showing the annual rateable value of such parts has not been approved and delivered as hereinbefore required, and whether such list has or has not been made, be rated according to such amounts as shall be fair apportioned parts of the annual rateable value appearing in such valuation-list in force as aforesaid of the hereditaments out of which such parts have been constituted.

Section 2, Act 1836.

Rates to be made in a given form.

And be it further enacted, That *every such rate* made after the said period shall, in addition to any other particular which the form of making out such rate shall require to be set forth, contain an account of every particular set forth at the head of the respective columns in the form given in the schedule to this Act annexed, so far as the same can

jections thereto have been given to the committee; and where a meeting is holden for hearing objections to the valuation-list of any parish, the committee shall not hear any objection to such valuation-list, unless such notice as aforesaid of such objection have been given to the committee and to the overseers; and where the ground of such objection is unfairness or incorrectness in the valuation of any hereditament of any other person than the person objecting, or the omission of such hereditament, also to such other person by the person objecting, except where the overseers, by themselves or any other person on their behalf, and in the case aforesaid such other person as aforesaid, by himself or any other person on his behalf, consent to the hearing of such objection, and in such case the committee may, if they see fit, hear the same; and where the committee see fit to hear the same, they shall act in relation thereto in like manner as if notice of such objection had been duly given.

be ascertained; and the church-wardens and overseers or other officers whose duty it may be to make and levy the said rate, or such a number of the said churchwardens and overseers or other officers as are competent to the making and levying of the same, shall, before the rate is allowed by the justices, sign the declaration (given at the foot of the said form); and otherwise the said rate shall be of no force or validity: Provided

Nothing herein to prevent owners from compounding for rates.

always, that nothing herein contained shall be construed to prevent the owners of tenements from compounding for the rates to be assessed on the same, in such manner as they were by any statute or statutes enabled to do before the passing of this Act, so that the gross estimated rental of the hereditaments compounded for be entered on the rate in the proper column.

SECTION 35, METROPOLIS ACT.

Amount of gross value specified by the surveyor of taxes to be inserted, unless disproved.

When a *surveyor of taxes* gives notice of objection or of appeal, the amount specified in the notice as being in his judgment the gross value of any hereditament referred to in the notice shall be inserted in the valuation-list by the assessment committee, special sessions (*Section 18*) or assessment sessions (*Section 23*), unless it is proved to the satisfaction of the assessment committee, special sessions, or assessment sessions, that such amount ought not to be so inserted.

SECTION 13, ACT 1862.

Committee may require returns from overseers, &c. ;

The committee by their order may from time to time require the overseers, assistant overseers, constables, assessors, collectors, and any other persons having the custody of any

The Law as Enacted for England and Wales.

SCHEDULE TO WHICH THIS ACT REFERS.

Form of Rate.

An assessment for the relief of the poor of the parish of Merton, in the county of Surrey, and for other purposes chargeable thereon according to law, made this thirtieth day of March, in the year of our Lord one thousand eight hundred and thirty-seven, after the rate of sixpence in the pound.

No.	Arrears due, or if excused.	Name of Occupier.	Name of Owner.	Description of Property rated.	Name or situation of Property.	Estimated Extent.	Gross estimated Rental.	Rateable Value.	Rate at 6d. in the Pound.
	£ s. d.					A. R. P.	£ s. d.	£ s. d.	£ s. d.
1	· · ·	Jas. Smith	Jn. Green	Land and Buildings.	Whitemore Farm.	40 0 0	60 0 0	30 0 0	1 7 6
2	· · ·	Ditto	Ditto	House and Garden.	In West Street.	0 1 0	30 0 0	25 0 0	0 12 6
3	Excused	John Poor	Ditto	House ·	In Brick Lane.	· · ·	1 10 0	1 3 0	0 0 7
&c.	&c.	&c.	&c.	&c.	&c.	&c.	&c.	&c.	&c.

DECLARATION TO BE ADDED TO
THE RATE.

We, the undersigned, do hereby declare that one of us, or some person on our behalf, has

The Law as Enacted for the Metropolis only.

books of assessment of any taxes or rates, parliamentary or parochial, or of the valuations of any parish, or having the collection or management of any such taxes or rates, to make returns in writing to the committee, at such times and places as they may appoint, of all such particulars as they may direct in relation to such taxes, rates, or valuations, or any property included therein, so far as relates to the union for which they act, and may require the persons having the custody of any such books as aforesaid to make and transmit to the committee copies of or extracts from such books, or to permit such copies or extracts to be made by such persons as the committee may in that behalf direct;

and may require production of rates, &c., and examine persons attending before them.

and may from time to time require any persons having the custody of any such books, or the collection or management of any such taxes or rates as aforesaid, to attend before them

examined and compared the
several particulars in the respective columns of the above
rate with the valuation - list
made under the authority of
the Union Assessment Committee Act, of 1862, in force in
this parish (*or township*), and
the several hereditaments are, to
the best of our belief, rated according to the value appearing
in such valuation-list.

————————— } Churchwardens.

————————— } Overseers.

Section 11, Act 1864.

Penalty on overseers omitting to make declaration or making false declaration.

Any *overseer* who wilfully
omits to make the declaration
required to be made by the
Union Assessment Committee
Act, 1862, or makes the same
falsely, knowing the same to be
untrue, shall be liable for every
such offence to a penalty not
exceeding five pounds, upon a
summary conviction for the same
before two justices of the peace,

at a time and place to be mentioned in the order in this behalf, and to produce all parochial and public books of assessment, rates, rate-books, valuations, apportionments, tithe and
other maps, plans, surveys, and
other public documents in their
custody or power, and may
examine all persons who shall
attend before them : Provided
always, that nothing herein
contained shall authorise the
production of valuations or
assessments which by any provision of law at present are not
suffered to be made public.

Board may allow compensation for returns, &c., and expenses.

37. The *committee* may allow
such compensation for any returns, copies, or extracts, or any
other valuation, or valuation-
list, or other act, matter, or
thing to be made or done in
persuance of their order, and
such expenses connected therewith, as to the committee in each
case seems just.

Remuneration to clerk, and certain expenses of committee, to be paid out of common fund.

38. The remuneration allowed

The Law as Enacted for England and Wales.

SECTION 29, ACT 1862.

Provision for places under local acts.

The provisions of section twenty-eight shall not apply to any poor rate made by any vestry, trustees, guardians, commissioners, overseers, or other persons authorised by any local act to make the rate for the relief of the poor in any parish, or the assessment on which such rate is made.

Act not to prevent composition for rates.

35. Nothing herein contained shall be construed to prevent the owners of tenements from compounding for the rates to be assessed on the same, in such manner as they were by any statute or statutes enabled to do before the passing of this Act.

Saving of exemptions and special rules of rating.

36. Nothing herein contained shall extend or be taken to render liable to be rated any property, or any person in respect of any occupation not now by law rateable of any property, or to deprive any property, or the

The Law as Enacted for the Metropolis only.

by the *committee* to their clerk, and all expenses incurred by them for the common use and benefit of the several parishes within the union for which they are appointed, shall be paid by the guardians of the said union, and be charged upon the common fund thereof.

Penalty for non-attendance, &c., in obedience to order of the committee.

40. *Every person* who wilfully refuses to attend in obedience to any lawful order of any such committee, or to give evidence, or refuses to produce any rate-book, assessment, or valuation which may be lawfully required to be produced before such committee, shall for every such offence be liable to a penalty not exceeding twenty pounds upon a summary conviction for the same before two justices of the peace; and every person who

Injuring, &c., rate-books a misdemeanor.

wilfully injures, defaces, conceals, or destroys such rate-book, or who upon any examination before any such committee wilfully gives false evidence, shall

The Law as Enacted for England and Wales.

The Law as Enacted for the Metropolis only.

occupier of any property, of the benefit of any exemption, in whole or in part, to which such property or occupier is now by law entitled, from any poor rate or other rate which by law is required to be based upon the poor rate, or to render liable to be rated according to the annual rateable value thereof, any property which under any local act or otherwise is entitled to be rated upon a fixed amount, or according to any special or exceptional principle of valuation, whether such property shall or shall not be included in any valuation-list in force under this Act, or shall in anywise affect the provisions of "The Cambridge Award Act, 1856," or the Act of the seventeenth and eighteenth Victoria, relating to the relief of the poor in the city of Oxford.

Provisions concerning the assessment, &c., of poor rates to be applicable to rates made according to this Act.

44. All the powers, authorities, provisions, clauses, and regulations now in force relating to the assessment, collection, and levying of poor-rates (save so

be deemed guilty of a misdemeanor.

Section 57 of the Metropolis Act.

Assessment committee may require returns from owner and occupier.

An *assessment committee* may, by order, require any person who is the owner or occupier or reputed owner or occupier of any hereditament in their union to send them a return in writing of all or any of the following things—viz., of the rent receivable or payable by him (as the case may be) for such hereditament, and of the person entitled to any tithe rentcharge charged on such hereditament, and of the amount of the same, and of the several persons by whom any tithe rentcharge is paid to him, and of the amounts paid by each such person, and of any other particulars respecting such hereditament as are required for the due execution of this Act and the Acts incorporated herewith. And every such owner or occupier shall obey such order within fourteen far as the same are hereby repealed or altered) shall be good, valid, and effectual for the purposes of assessing, levying, collecting, and enforcing the payment of such rate and for carrying this Act into execution.

SECTION 5, ACT 1836.

Power to take copies or extracts of rates gratis.

And be it further enacted, That it shall be lawful for *any person or persons rated to the relief of the poor* of the parish in respect of which any rate shall be made, at all seasonable times, to take copies thereof or extracts therefrom without paying anything for the same, anything in any act of parliament to the contrary notwithstanding;

Penalty for refusing to permit.

and in case the person or persons having the custody of such rate shall refuse to permit or shall not permit such person or persons so rated as aforesaid to take copies thereof or extracts therefrom, the person or persons so

days after the service thereof on him.

Penalty for no or false returns.

58. If *any person* wilfully refuses or neglects to make any return lawfully required under this Act within the times respectively limited by this Act in that behalf, he shall be liable, on summary conviction, to a penalty not exceeding five pounds.

If *any person* wilfully makes or causes to be made a false return, he shall be liable, on summary conviction, to a penalty not exceeding ten pounds.

Service of notices, &c., by post, &c.

65. All orders and notices under this Act and the Acts incorporated herewith shall be in writing or print, or partly in writing and partly in print, and if made or given by an *assessment committee* shall be sufficiently authenticated if signed by their clerk; and all orders, notices, and documents required by the same Acts to be served on or sent to any person or body of persons corporate or unincorporate may be either delivered

The Law as Enacted for England and Wales.

The Law as Enacted for the Metropolis only.

refusing or not permitting such copy or extract to be made shall forfeit and pay any sum not exceeding five pounds, to be recovered in a summary way before any justice of the peace having jurisdiction in the parish or place.

SECTION 1, ACT 1864.

Notice of appeal against poor rate to be given to the assessment committee of the union.

Before any appeal shall be heard by any special or quarter sessions against a poor rate made for any parish contained in any union to which the Union Assessment Committee Act, 1862, applies, the *appellant shall give twenty-one days' notice* in writing previous to the special or quarter sessions to which such appeal is to be made, of the intention to appeal, and the grounds thereof, to the assessment committee of such union: Provided, that after the first day of August next no person shall be empowered to appeal to any sessions against a poor rate made in conformity with the valuation-list approved

to such person or the clerk of such body, or left at the usual place of abode of such person or clerk, or at the office of such clerk or body, or (if such abode or office cannot on reasonable inquiry be discovered) at the premises to which the order, notice, or document relates.

They may also be served and sent by post, by a prepaid letter, addressed to such person, or to the office of such body or to their clerk, and, if sent by post, shall be deemed to have been served and received respectively at the time when the letter containing the same would be delivered in the ordinary course of post, and in proving such service or sending it shall be sufficient to prove that the letter containing the notice was properly addressed and prepaid and put into the post.

Board may direct further valuation, and correct valuation-lists, and when corrected to approve the same.

20. The *committee* may, whether any objection be or be not made to any such valuation-list, and either before or after any

The Law as Enacted for England and Wales.

of by such committee, unless he shall have given to such committee notice of objection against the said list, and shall have failed to obtain such relief in the matter as he deems just; and which objection, after notice given at any time in the manner prescribed by the said Act with respect to objections, the committee shall hear, with full power to call for and amend such list, although the same has been approved of, and no subsequent list has been transmitted to them, and if they amend the same shall give notice of such amendment to the overseers, who shall thereupon alter their then current rate accordingly.

Committee may, with consent of guardians, be co-respondents.

2. The *assessment committee* of such union may, with the consent of the guardians of such union, after notice shall have been sent to every guardian, appear as respondents to such appeal, but in the name of the guardians of such union, in like manner, and with the same incidents, and subject to the same

The Law as Enacted for the Metropolis only.

meeting for hearing objections, make such alterations in the valuation of any hereditaments included in any valuation-list, and insert therein any rateable hereditament omitted therefrom, and make such corrections in names, descriptions, and particulars in any valuation-list, and upon such information, as to them may seem sufficient, and may, with the consent of the guardians as aforesaid, appoint or employ a person to survey and value the rateable hereditaments comprised in any such valuation-list or any of them, or omitted therefrom, or may take such other means as they may think necessary for ascertaining the correctness thereof, and when the committee have heard and determined all such objections as aforesaid, and have made such alterations, insertions, and corrections in any valuation-list as to them may seem proper, they shall approve the same under the hands of three members of the committee present at the meeting at which the same is approved, with the date of such approval.

E 2

liabilities, and entitled to the same remedies and rights, as in the case of persons other than the overseer to whom notice of appeal may be given.

SECTION 29, POOR LAW AMEND-
MENT ACT, 1868.

Power for guardians of unions mutually to bear the costs of several appeals involving the same common principle.

Where an appeal is brought against the poor rate of a parish in a union, and may appear to involve a principle in which some neighbouring parish has a common interest, it shall be lawful *for the guardians of the unions* comprising such parishes to enter into an agreement mutually to bear the costs which may be properly incurred in and about the trial of such appeals on the part of the several respondents, as well as the cost of the appellants, if any, which may be awarded against the respondents, in such proportions as shall be fixed and determined with reference to the amount of interest of the several unions in the

SECTION 8, ACT 1864.

Power to guardians, with the order of the Poor Law Board, to borrow money for valuation expenses.

If the *assessment committee* order a valuation, with the consent of the board of guardians, to be made of all the rateable hereditaments of any parish, *the guardians* of the union may, if they think fit, apply to the Poor Law Board for an order to enable them to borrow the requisite amount to pay the cost of such valuation; and if the said board shall issue their order, the said guardians may borrow the same and charge the poor rates of the several parishes in the union with the repayment of the same by not more than five equal annual instalments; and where the parish for which the valuation is made shall, by reason of any provision in the said union assessment committee Act or this Act, be liable to pay the cost of such valuation, the said guardians shall charge the annual instalments, and the interest payable therewith, to such parish, and question, or otherwise, as shall appear just; and the said agreement shall continue binding upon the several boards of guardians and their respective successors in succession until the several appeals shall have been finally determined.

SECTION 3, ACT 1864.

Provision as to costs of committee on appeals.

The costs which *the committee* may incur in consequence of becoming respondents to such appeal, or of having received notice thereof, shall, if not recovered from the appellants, as well as any costs the committee may be ordered to pay to the appellants, be paid by the guardians, and charged to the common fund of the union, unless the court before whom such appeal is heard shall direct that such costs, or any part thereof, shall be charged to the parish, the rate of which is appealed against.

may recover the same as and with the usual contributions.

Power to Poor Law Board to order map or plan to be made.

10. If there be no map or plan of any parish available for the use or sufficient for the purposes of the assessment committee, *the committee* may, with the consent of the guardians, after notice as aforesaid, and under the authority of an order of the Poor Law Board, appoint a competent person to make a map or plan of such parish, and the cost thereof shall be charged either to the common fund, or to the parish, as may be directed by the Poor Law Board.

SECTIONS 3 AND 4, ACT 1836.

Power to order new survey and valuation.

And be it enacted, That when it shall be made to appear to the Poor Law Commissioners by representation in writing from the *board of guardians* of any union or parish under their common seal, or *from the majority of the churchwardens and overseers or*

The Law as Enacted for England and Wales.   *The Law as Enacted for the Metropolis only*

SECTION 6, ACT 1836.

Justices acting in petty sessions to hold four special sessions in the year to hear appeals.

And be it enacted, that the *justices* acting in and for every petty sessions division shall four times at least in every year hold a special sessions for hearing appeals against the rates of the several parishes within their respective divisions, and shall cause public notice of the time and place when and where such special sessions will be holden to be affixed to or near to the door of the parish church of the said parishes twenty-eight days at the least before the holding of the same ; and such special sessions shall and may be adjourned from time to time by the justices there present, as they may think fit ; and at such special or adjourned sessions the justices there present shall hear and determine all objections to any such rate on the ground of inequality, unfairness, or incorrectness in the valuation of any hereditaments included therein, which decision shall be binding

other officers competent as aforesaid to the making and levying the rate, that a fair and correct estimate for the aforesaid purposes cannot be made without a new valuation, it shall be lawful for the Poor Law Commissioners, where they shall see fit, to order a survey, with or without a map or plan, on such scale as they shall think fit, to be made and taken of the messuages, lands, and other hereditaments liable to poor rates in such parish, or in all or any one or more parishes of such a union, and a valuation to be made of the said messuages, lands, and other hereditaments according to their annual value, and to direct such guardians to appoint a fit person or persons to make and take every such survey, map or plan, and valuation, and to make provision for paying the costs of every such survey, map or plan, and valuation, either by a separate rate or by a charge on the poor rates, as they may see fit ; but in case of such charge being made, then provisions shall be made for paying of not less than one-fifth

and conclusive on the parties,
unless the person or persons
impugning such decision shall
within *fourteen days* after the
same shall have been made cause
notice to be given in writing of
his, her, or their intention of
appealing against such decision,
and of the matter or cause of
such appeal, to the person or
persons in whose favour such
decision shall have been made,
and within *five days* after *giving
such notice* shall enter into a re-
cognizance before some justice
of the peace, with sufficient securities, conditioned to try such
appeal at the then next general
sessions or quarter sessions of
the peace which shall first happen, and to abide the order of
and pay such costs as shall be
awarded by the justices at such
quarter sessions, or any adjournment thereof; and such justices,
upon hearing and finally determining such matter of appeal,
shall and may, according to
their discretion, award such costs
to the party or parties appealing
or appealed against as they shall
think proper, and their determination in or concerning the

of the sum charged on the rates,
and such interest as may from
time to time be payable in
respect of such charge or any
part thereof, in each succeeding
year till the whole is repaid.

**Power for surveyors to enter and examine
lands, &c., for purposes of survey and
plans.**

4. And be it further enacted,
that for the purpose of making
every such survey, map or plan,
and valuation, it shall be lawful
for the person or persons so to
be appointed for making the
same respectively, together with
their and every of their assistants and servants, at all reasonable times, until the same
respectively shall be completed,
to enter, view, and examine,
survey and admeasure, all and
every part of the messuages,
lands, and other hereditaments
aforesaid, and to do or cause to
be done any act or thing necessary for making such survey,
map or plan, and valuation:
Provided always, that any map,
survey, plan, or valuation made
previously to the appointment
of such person or persons which

premises shall be conclusive and binding on all parties, to all intents and purposes whatsoever:

Seven days' notice to be given of objections.

Provided always, that no such objection shall be inquired into by the said justices in special session unless notice of such objection in writing under the hand of the complainant shall have been given, *seven days at least before the day appointed* for such special session, to the *collector, overseers,* or *other persons* by whom such rate was made:

Proviso.

Provided also, that the said justices in special session shall not be authorised to inquire into the liability of any hereditaments to be rated, but only into the true value thereof and into the fairness of the amount at which the same shall have been rated.

Justices may act with all the powers of justices at quarter sessions.

7. And be it enacted, that the *justices present* at any such special or adjourned session shall for the aforesaid purpose have

shall be tendered to him or them, and which shall be in his or their judgment and to his or their satisfaction a just and true map or survey, proper for the purposes aforesaid, may be used for such purposes.

SECTION 61 OF THE METROPOLIS ACT.

Guardians may appoint a paid valuer to assist the assessment committee.

The *guardians* may, upon the application of the *assessment committee*, after notice sent in the manner required by the principal Act, appoint some competent person to assist the committee in the valuation of the hereditaments in the union for such period as they see fit, at a salary or other settled remuneration, to be paid out of the common fund.

SECTION 4, ACT 1864.

Valuation to be made in writing.

Where a *valuer* is appointed by the assessment committee he all the powers of amending or quashing any such rate so objected to of any parish or other district within their division, and likewise of awarding costs to be paid by or to any of the parties, and of recovering such costs, which any court of quarter sessions of the peace has upon appeals from any such rate, except as herein excepted: Provided always, that no order of the said justices shall be removed by certiorari or otherwise into any of His Majesty's courts of record at Westminster: Provided also, that nothing in this Act contained shall be construed to deprive any person or persons of the right to appeal against any rate to any court of general or quarter sessions: Provided also, that no order of the said justices in special sessions shall be of any force pending any appeal touching the same subject-matter to the court of general or quarter sessions of the peace having jurisdiction to try such appeal, or in opposition to the order of any such court upon such appeal.

shall make his valuation in writing, showing the particulars of the several hereditaments comprised therein, and the amounts at which he has valued the same respectively, and shall sign such valuation, which shall be open to inspection in like manner and with the same incidents with respect to the taking of copies or extracts as the minute-books of the committee.

SECTION 21, ACT 1862.

Valuation-list when altered to be deposited, &c.

Where the *committee* make any alteration in the valuation of any hereditaments included in, or insert therein any rateable hereditament omitted from, any such valuation-list, they shall cause such valuation-list, with such alteration or insertion, to be deposited for inspection in manner hereinbefore provided concerning the valuation-list made by or delivered to the overseers, and shall cause the like notice to be given of such deposit as is required in the case

The Law as Enacted for England and Wales. *The Law as Enacted for the Metropolis only.*

SECTION 6, ACT 1864.

Justices in certain cases not disqualified for hearing appeals.

No *justice* of the peace shall be disqualified for acting in the determination of any appeal against a poor rate at any quarter or special sessions by reason of such justice being rated, or being liable to be rated, in some other parish in the union than that for which the rate appealed against is made.

SECTION 22, ACT 1862.

If on appeal a rate is amended, the valuation-list to be altered.

In case *any ratepayer* shall under the existing law appeal to the special sessions or quarter sessions against any rate made for the relief of the poor in any parish, and the result of such appeal shall be to amend the rate appealed against, the assessment committee shall alter the valuation-list of the said parish in conformity with the decision so made.

of a valuation-list so made or delivered as aforesaid, and shall appoint a day, not less than seven days nor more than fourteen days from the re-deposit of such valuation-list, for the hearing of any objections to the valuation-list as so altered; and when the committee have heard and determined any such objections, or have made such further alterations, insertions, and corrections in such valuation-list, they shall approve the same in manner hereinbefore provided.

SECTION 42 (7) OF THE METROPOLIS ACT.

The assessment committee shall send the valuation-list to be re-deposited within three days after it is approved by them, and shall appoint a day not less than fourteen nor more than twenty-eight days after such re-deposit for hearing objections to the alterations of which objections seven days' notice shall be given by the objector.

9 (PART OF). Where the as-

Overseers to prepare supplemental valuation-lists in case of additions to or alterations in the rateable property of the parish.

25. When and so often as any property not included in the valuation-list in force in any parish becomes rateable, or where, by reason of any alteration in the occupation of any property included in such list, such property becomes liable to be rated in parts not mentioned in such list as rateable hereditaments and separately valued therein, and when and so often as it shall appear to the overseers that any rateable property included in such list has been increased or reduced in value since the valuation thereof, whether by building, destruction of building, or other alteration in the condition thereof or otherwise, *the overseers* of the parish in each of the cases aforesaid shall, as soon as conveniently may be, make a supplemental valuation-list showing the annual rateable value according to the judgment of the overseers of the property so become rateable, or of the parts so become able, or of the parts so become

sessment committee (otherwise than in determining an objection) alter a valuation-list by inserting therein some hereditament, or by raising the gross or rateable value of some hereditament comprised therein, *the overseers* shall immediately after the re-deposit of the list, serve on the occupier of such hereditament, a notice of the gross and rateable value thereof inserted in the valuation-list.

Valuation-list to be revised, certified, and sent to overseers, &c.

14 The assessment committee, within the time in this Act mentioned (*before 1st October, 1870, Section 42*), shall revise the valuation-list in accordance with this Act and the Acts incorporated herewith. When they have finally approved such valuation-list they shall cause the totals of the gross and rateable value in such list to be ascertained and inserted in the list, and three members of the committee present at the meeting at which the list is finally approved shall sign at the foot thereof such declaration of ap-

liable to be rated separately, or of the property so increased or reduced in value, as the case may be.

Committee may from time to time direct new valuation and new or supplemental valuation-lists.

26. *The committee* by their order may from time to time, where they see fit, upon the application of any person aggrieved by the valuation-list in force in any parish, or where they themselves think the same expedient, direct a new valuation of all or any of the rateable hereditaments in such parish, and a new valuation-list in substitution for such valuation-list as aforesaid, or a supplemental list in substitution for any part thereof or in addition thereto, to be made by the overseers, or the committee may, with such consent as aforesaid (*Sect. 16, Act. 1862*), appoint a person for such purposes; and the committee may, in directing such new valuation, and the making of such new or supplemental valuation-list, give and make all such or the like direc-

proval and certificate of compliance with this Act as is contained in Part one of the second schedule to this Act. One duplicate, so certified, shall be sent to the clerk of the managers of the metropolitan asylum district (*before 1st November, 1870, Section 42*) and the other duplicate to the overseers of the parish to which it relates.

We do hereby approve the above valuation-list, and certify that in determining the gross and rateable value of the above hereditaments the provisions of the Valuation (Metropolis) Act, 1869, have been duly complied with.

Signed this   day of

A. B. ⎫   Members of the
C. D. ⎬ Assessment Committee
E. F. ⎭   of the Union.

Note.—The two last of the above columns (for gross and rateable value as determined by Assessment Committee) must be filled up, and the totals of those columns must be added up after the objections to the alterations have (if any) been heard,

The Law as Enacted for England and Wales.

The Law as Enacted for the Metropolis only.

tions and provisions in relation thereto, as they are authorised under this act to give and make in relation to the valuations and valuation-list first directed and authorised to be made under the act.

Expenses of valuation, &c., to be paid out of poor rates.

39. The expenses of making any valuation and valuation-list of any parish, or any of such expenses, whether such valuation and valuation-list respectively be made by the overseers, or by any person appointed by the committee, shall be charged upon the *poor rates* of such parish if the valuation made by direction of the committee *shall exceed by one-sixth* the amount of the valuation delivered to them by the overseers, and upon the *common fund* of the said union if the valuation so made as last-mentioned *shall not exceed by one-sixth* the valuation so delivered as aforesaid.

and before the list is *finally* approved.

(8.) The assessment committee shall finally approve and send the valuation-list to the overseers, and the clerk of the managers of the metropolitan asylum district, before the first of November in the same year (1870).

Deposit of duplicate of list in each parish.

15. The overseers of the parish, on receiving the duplicate of the valuation-list so sent to them by the assessment committee, shall immediately deposit it in the place in which the rate books of the parish are kept, and shall publish notice of such deposit, and of the time and mode of making appeals, and of the grounds on which an appeal is allowed by this Act to be made.

Valuation-lists to be equivalent to rate-books of parish.

68 (PART OF). The duplicate of the valuation-list, approved by the assessment committee,

SECTION 8 OF THE ACT OF 1864.

Power to guardians, with the order of the Poor Law Board, to borrow money for valuation expenses.

If the *assessment committee* order a valuation, with the consent of the board of guardians, to be made of all the rateable hereditaments of any parish, the guardians of the union may, if they think fit, apply to the Poor Law Board for an order to enable them to borrow the requisite amount to pay the cost of such valuation; and if the said board shall issue their order, the said guardians may borrow the same and charge the poor-rates of the several parishes in the union with the repayment of the same by not more then five equal annual instalments; and where the parish for which the valuation is made shall, by reason of any provision in the said Union Assessment Committee Act or this act, be liable to pay the cost of such valuation, the said guardians shall charge the annual instalments, and the interest payable therewith, to such parish, and may recover the

and sent to the overseers, as directed by this Act, the notices of alterations made on any appeal under this Act, and any provisional list, shall for all purposes be deemed to be part of the rate books of the parish, and shall be produced by the overseers before the justices upon any application for allowance of rates, and on any appeal under this or any other Act, and on any other occasion if so required, on which they are bound to produce such rate books, and any overseer who fails to produce such list in accordance with the provisions of this section shall be liable on summary conviction to a penalty not exceeding five pounds.

Inspection, &c., of documents deposited with rate books.

67. Where any documents are required by this Act to be deposited in the same place in a parish in which rate-books are kept, every ratepayer shall be at liberty to inspect and take copies of or extracts from such documents at any reasonable time, without fee or charge.

The Law as Enacted for England and Wales.

The Law as Enacted for the Metropolis only.

same as and with the usual contributions.

Power to Poor Law Board to order map or plan to be made.

10. If there be no map or plan of any parish available for the use or sufficient for the purposes of the assessment committee, *the committee* may, with the consent of the guardians, after notice as aforesaid, and under the authority of an order of the Poor Law Board, appoint a competent person to make a map or plan of such parish, and the cost thereof shall be charged either to the common fund, or to the parish, as may be directed by the Poor Law Board.

SECTION 3 OF THE ACT OF 1836.

Power to order new survey and valuation.

And be it enacted, That when it shall be made to appear to the Poor Law Commissioners by representation in writing from the *board of guardians* of any union or parish under their common seal, or from the majority of the churchwardens and

Deposit of list at office of the managers of metropolitan asylum district.

16. The certified valuation-list so sent to the clerk of the managers of the metropolitan asylum district by the assessment committee shall be deposited at the office of such managers, and within the time in this Act mentioned (*see Sec.* 42 (11) shall be returned by such clerk to the same assessment committee.

Ratepayer, &c., may inspect documents, &c., in hands of clerk of managers or assessment committee.

69. Any ratepayer, overseer, clerk of an assessment committee, or surveyor of taxes in the metropolis may, at all seasonable times, without payment, inspect and take copies of and extracts from all valuation-lists and documents which in pursuance of this Act are under the control of the clerk of the managers of the metropolitan asylum district, or of the clerk of the assessment sessions.

Any surveyor of taxes and any guardian and any overseer in a union, without payment, overseers or other officers competent as aforesaid to the making and levying the rate, that a fair and correct estimate for the aforesaid purposes cannot be made without a new valuation, it shall be lawful for the Poor Law Commissioners, where they shall see fit to order a survey, with or without a map or plan, on such scale as they shall think fit, to be made and taken of the messuages, lands, and other hereditaments liable to poor-rates in such parish, or in all or any one or more parishes of such a union, and a valuation to be made of the said messuages, lands, and other hereditaments according to their annual value, and to direct such guardians to appoint a fit person or persons to make and take every such survey, map or plan, *and* valuation, and to make provision for paying the costs of every such survey, map or plan, and valuation, either by a separate rate or by a charge on the poor rates, as they may see fit; but in case of such charge being made, then provisions shall be made for paying of not less

and any ratepayer in a union on payment of a fee not exceeding one shilling (to be carried to the common fund), may at any reasonable time inspect and take copies of and extracts from any valuation-lists, notices of objection, returns, and other documents in the possession or under the control of the assessment committee of that union.

Any clerk of an assessment committee in the metropolis may inspect and take extracts from any valuation-lists in the possession or under the control of the assessment committee of any other union in the metropolis.

Any person who hinders a ratepayer, overseer, clerk of an assessment committee, or surveyor of taxes from so inspecting or taking copies of or extracts from any valuation-list or document, or demands where not authorized by this Act a fee for allowing him so to do, shall be liable on summary conviction to a penalty not exceeding five pounds for each offence.

Printing and distribution of totals of gross and rateable value in valuation-list.

17. The clerk of the managers

The Law as Enacted for England and Wales.

The Law as Enacted for the Metropolis only.

than one-fifth of the sum charged on the rates, and such interest as may from time to time be payable in respect of such charge or any part thereof, in each succeeding year, till the whole is repaid.

Power for surveyors to enter and examine lands, &c., for purposes of survey and plans.

4. And be it further enacted, That for the purpose of making every such survey, map or plan, and valuation, it shall be lawful for the person or persons so to be appointed for making the same respectively, together with their and every of their assistants and servants, at all reasonable times, until the same respectively shall be completed, to enter, view, and examine, survey and admeasure, all and every part of the messuages, lands, and other hereditaments aforesaid, and to do or cause to be done any act or thing necessary for making such survey, map or plan, and valuation : Provided always, that any map, survey, plan, or valuation made previously to the appointment of

of the metropolitan asylum district shall, within the time in this Act mentioned, cause the totals of the gross and rateable values of all the valuation-lists to be printed, and a printed copy of all such totals to be sent to every assessment committee, and the overseers of every parish in the metropolis and in every county in which any parish to which any such totals relate is situate, to the clerks of the peace for every such county, to the Commissioner of the Metropolitan Police, the Corporation of the City of London, the Metropolitan Board of Works, every district board in the metropolis, and the Poor Law Board. Every assessment committee, overseer, and ratepayer within the metropolis and every such county shall respectively be entitled to have printed copies of such totals on payment of one penny for each copy of all the said totals.

SECTION 42.

(11.) The clerk of the said managers shall send

F

The Law as Enacted for England and Wales.   *The Law as Enacted for the Metropolis only.*

such person or persons which shall be tendered to him or them, and which shall be in his or their judgment and to his or their satisfaction a just and true map or survey, proper for the purposes aforesaid, may be used for such purposes.

SECTION 32 OF THE POOR LAW AMENDMENT ACT, 1868.

Guardians may appoint a paid valuer to assist the assessment committee.

The guardians may, upon the application of the assessment committee, after notice sent in the manner required by the Union Assessment Committee Act, 1862, appoint some competent person to assist the committee in the valuation of the rateable hereditaments of the union for such period as they shall see fit, at a salary or other settled remuneration to be paid out of the common fund.

SECTION 4 OF THE ACT OF 1864.

Valuation to be made in writing.

Where *a valuer* is appointed by the assessment committee, he

out the printed totals before the first of December in the same year (1870), and shall return the valuation-list to the assessment committee not sooner than fourteen nor later than twenty-one days after the totals are sent out:

68 (PART OF). The duplicate of the valuation-list returned to the assessment committee by the clerk of the managers of the metropolitan asylum district, and other documents in the possession of the assessment committee in pursuance of this Act shall be kept at the board room or other convenient place from time to time appointed by the guardians of the same union, but shall be deemed to be in the possession of the assessment committee, and shall be produced by their clerk to the district auditor whenever required by him.

The Law as Enacted for England and Wales.

shall make his valuation in writing, showing the particulars of the several hereditaments comprised therein, and the amounts at which he has valued the same respectively, and shall sign such valuation, which shall be open to inspection in like manner, and with the same incidents with respect to the taking of copies or extracts, as the minute books of the committee.

SECTION 27 OF THE ACT OF 1862.

This Act as to valuation-list first directed to be made to apply to new and supplemental valuation-lists.

All the provisions of this Act in relation to signature, deposit, objections, approval, and otherwise concerning the valuation-list first directed and authorised to be made under this Act of the rateable hereditaments in any parish shall be applicable to every new or supplemental valuation-list to be made under this Act.

The Law as Enacted for the Metropolis only.

SECTION 30, ACT 1862.

In computing amount of contributions to common fund the annual rateable value to be taken from approved valuation-lists.

When the assessment committee for any union shall have approved valuation-lists for all the parishes comprised within such union, the guardians of such union, in computing the amount of contribution to the common fund for the several parishes, shall thenceforward take the annual rateable value of the property in such parishes respectively from the valuation-lists for the time being lastly approved of for such parishes respectively, any statute to the contrary notwithstanding: Provided that in case any parish comprised in any union shall receive any sum of money as a contribution in aid of the poor rate of such parish, for or in respect of government property within such parish and used for public purposes, the annual value of such property, according to the estimate (if any) of such value on which the amount of

F 2

The Law as Enacted for England and Wales.

The Law as Enacted for the Metropolis only.

SECTION 28 OF THE ACT OF 1868.

11 and 12 Vict., cap. 110, sect. 7, extended to a parish.

The provisions of the seventh section of the Poor Law Amendment Act, 1848, empowering guardians of unions to cause valuations to be made upon application as therein set forth, shall apply to the guardians of a parish not comprised in any union.

SECTION 45 OF THE ACT OF 1862.

Power for unions under Gilbert's or local Acts to be included in this Act.

And whereas there are divers unions or incorporations for the relief of the poor formed under local Acts, and under the Act of the twenty-second year of King George the Third, chapter eighty-three, which may desire to adopt the provisions of this Act: Be it enacted, that any such union or incorporation, on resolution to that effect of a majority, at two successive meetings of the body,

the sum of money so received is computed, or, if there be no such estimate, then the annual value of such property, estimated in the mode provided by the Act sixth and seventh *William* the Fourth, chapter ninety-six, for making an estimate of the annual rateable value of property liable to be rated to rates for the relief of the poor, shall be included by the overseer or overseers in the valuation-list of such parish, and shall be added to the annual rateable value of the property in such parish in computing the amount of contribution to the common fund for the several parishes in such union.

SECTION 43, METROPOLIS ACT.

EFFECT OF VALUATION-LIST.

Duration of valuation-list.

The valuation-list as approved by the assessment committee, and, if altered on any appeal under this Act to any sessions or a superior court, as so altered, shall come into force at the beginning of the year (commencing

The Law as Enacted for England and Wales.

The Law as Enacted for the Metropolis only.

having under the constitution of such union or incorporation the management of the relief of the poor within the same, may, by writing under the hand of the presiding chairman of the second of such meetings, apply to the Poor Law Board to be included in this Act; and such union or incorporation, upon the consent of the Poor Law Board being given to such application under its seal, shall be so included; and such consent so signified shall be evidence that such application was in all respects duly made according to the provisions above mentioned; and such regulations shall thereafter be made from time to time by the said board, with the consent of such body, as may be necessary to render the provisions of this Act conformable with the provisions of the Act under which the said union or incorporation shall have been formed.

Extent of Act.

46. This Act shall extend only to England.

on the sixth of April) succeeding that in which it is made, and shall last for five years, subject to any alterations that may be made by any supplemental or provisional list as hereinafter mentioned.

Rate to be levied notwithstanding appeal.

44. Notwithstanding any appeal under this Act which may be pending at the commencement of the year, the valuation-list shall come into force unaltered, and every assessment, contribution, rate, and tax in respect of which the valuation-list is conclusive shall be made, required, levied, and paid in accordance with such valuation-list; and where in consequence of the decision on any appeal under this Act to assesssment sessions or a superior court an alteration in such valuation-list is made which alters the amount of the assessment, contribution, rate, or tax levied thereunder, the difference, if too much has been paid, shall be repaid or allowed, and if too little, shall be deemed to be arrears of the assessment, contribution, rate, or tax (except so far as any

The Law as Enacted for England and Wales.

Section 12, Act 1864.

25 and 26 Vict., cap. 103, incorporated herewith.

The provisions of the Union Assessment Committee Act, 1862, shall, so far as the same are not contrary hereto, be incorporated herewith, and the terms used herein shall be construed in like manner as in that Act.

Short title.

13. This Act may be cited as "The Union Assessment Committee Amendment Act, 1864."

[End of the
Law as Enacted for England and Wales]

The Law as Enacted for the Metropolis only.

penalty is incurred on account of arrears), and shall be paid and recovered accordingly.

Valuation-list to be conclusive for purposes of certain rates, taxes, and qualifications.

45. The valuation-list for the time being in force shall be deemed to have been duly made in accordance with this Act and the Acts incorporated herewith, and shall for all or any of the purposes in this section mentioned be conclusive evidence of the gross value and of the rateable value of the several hereditaments included therein, and of the fact that all hereditaments required to be inserted therein have been so inserted; that is to say:—

(1.) For the purpose of any of the following rates which are made during the year that the list is in force, namely, the county rate, the metropolitan police rate, the church rate, the highway rate, the poor rate, the police, sewers, consolidated and other rates in the city of London, the

sewers, the lighting, general, and other rates levied by
order of district boards or vestries, the main drainage
improvement and other rates, and sums assessed on any
part of the metropolis by the Metropolitan Board of
Works, assessments for contributions under the Metropolitan Poor Act, 1867, and every other rate, assessment,
and contribution levied, made, and required in the metropolis on the basis of value:

(2.) For the purpose of any of the following taxes which become
chargeable during the year that the list is in force,
namely :—

  (*a.*) The tax on houses levied under the House Tax
    Act (14 & 15 Vict., c. 36, &c.) and the Acts
    therein incorporated or referred to:

  (*b.*) Any tax assessed in pursuance of the Income
    Tax Act (5 & 6 Vict., c. 35, &c.) and any Acts
    continuing or amending the same, on any lands,
    tenements, and hereditaments, in all cases
    where the tax is charged on the gross value,
    and not on profits :

(3.) For the purpose of determining, so far as it is applicable,
the value of any hereditament included therein for the
purposes of the Acts relating to the sale of excisable
liquors, to the qualification of a juror, to the qualification
of a vestryman, and an auditor of accounts under the
Metropolis Management Act, 1855, and to the qualification of a guardian and of a manager under the "Poor
Law Amendment Act, 1834," or of the "Metropolitan
Poor Act, 1867," at any time at which such value is
required to be ascertained :

And in construing the Metropolitan Police Act (10 Geo. 4, c.44)
and the Acts amending the same, the last valuation for the time

being acted upon in assessing the county rate shall be deemed to mean the valuation-list for the time being in force :

And in construing the County Rate Act (15 & 16 Vict., c. 81, &c.) and Acts referring to the valuation, estimate, basis, or standard shall be deemed to be the rateable value stated in such list :

And in construing the House Tax Act (14 & 15 Vict., c. 36, &c.) and the Acts therein incorporated or referred to, the full and just yearly rent shall be deemed to be the gross value stated in such list :

And in construing the Income Tax Act (5 & 6 Vict., c. 35, &c.) and any Acts continuing or amending that Act, with respect to schedules A. and B. thereof, annual value shall be deemed to mean the gross value stated in such list.

APPEALS.—SPECIAL SESSIONS.

18. In every petty sessional division in the metropolis the justices of the peace acting in and for such division

Holding of special session to hear appeals.

shall, in every year at the time mentioned in this Act, hold a special sessions for hearing appeals under this Act against the valuation-lists of the several parishes within such division.

42. (10.) The justices may hold the special sessions at any time after the thirtieth of November in the same year (*1870*), which will enable them to determine all appeals before the ensuing first of January.

19. Any ratepayer and any overseers of a parish, so far as respects the valuation-list of such parish, and any

Persons entitled to appeal to special sessions.

surveyor of taxes, so far as respects the valuation-list of any parish in the petty sessional division, may, if he or they feel aggrieved by any decision of the assessment committee on an objection made with respect to the unfairness or incorrectness of the valuation of any hereditament included in such list, but not otherwise, appeal against such decision to the special sessions. The right to appeal to special sessions shall not deprive a person of any other right of appeal conferred on him by this Act.

PROCEEDINGS ON APPEALS.

33. Notice in writing of every appeal, whether to special sessions or the assessment sessions (*see Sec. 25*), specifying the correction which the appellant desires to have made in the valuation-list, must be served, within the time in this Act mentioned.

Notice of appeal to special or assessment sessions.

42. (9.) Notices of appeal to special sessions shall be given on or before the twenty-first of November in the same year (*1870*) on the following persons, namely:—

> In all cases on the surveyor of taxes of the district to which the appeal relates, and on the clerk of the assessment committee which approved the list wholly or partly questioned by the appeal:
>
> When the appeal relates to the unfairness or incorrectness of the valuation of, or to the omission of an hereditament occupied by any person other than the appellant, or to the incorrectness of any matter stated in the list with respect to any such hereditament, then on such person:
>
> If an assessment committee or a surveyor of taxes is the appellant, then also on the overseers of the parish to which the appeal relates:

Provided that it shall not be necessary to serve any notice of appeal on the surveyor of taxes in any case in which the appeal relates only to the rateable value of any hereditament.

The clerk of the assessment committee, on receiving notice of an appeal, shall forthwith serve notice thereof on the clerk of the special sessions or of the assessment sessions, as the case may require.

SECTION 2, ACT 1864.

The assessment committee of such union may, with the consent of the guardians of such union, after notice shall

Committee may, with consent of guardians, be co-respondents. have been sent to every guardian, appear as respondents to such appeal, but in the name of the guardians of such union, in like manner, and with the same incidents, and subject to the same liabili-

ties, and entitled to the same remedies and rights, as in the case of persons other than the overseers to whom notice of appeal may be given.

3. The costs which the committee may incur in consequence of becoming respondents to such appeal, or of having

Provision as to costs of committee on appeals. received notice thereof, shall, if not recovered from the appellants, as well as any costs the committee may be ordered to pay to the appellants, be paid

by the guardians and charged to the common fund of the union, unless the Court before whom such appeal is heard shall direct that such costs, or any part thereof, shall be charged to the parish, the rate of which is appealed against.

SECTION 20, METROPOLIS ACT.

The justices in special sessions under this Act shall not hear any appeal touching any matter with respect to

Extent of jurisdiction of special sessions. which notice of appeal to the general assessment sessions has been served in manner prescribed by this Act, and shall not hear any appeal touching

any part or alter any part of the valuation-list except the part relating to the value of an hereditament ; and a decision of such justices and an alteration by them of the value of an hereditament in the valuation-list of any parish shall affect only the rights of the ratepayers of such parish among themselves, and shall not of itself in any way alter the totals of the gross or rateable value of such list as settled by the assessment committee, but may form a reason for an appeal against such totals to the assessment sessions and superior court as hereinafter mentioned.

21. The justices in special sessions under this Act may adjourn their court from time to time, as may be necessary for the performance of their duties under this Act. **Powers of special sessions.** They shall have, with respect to the attendance and examination of witnesses, the taking of evidence, the keeping order in court, the enforcing their orders, and all matters necessary for the execution of their duties under this Act, the same powers and jurisdiction as if they were assembled in petty sessions.

22. The justices in special sessions shall send a written notice of the time and place at which they will hold a special sessions for the purpose of hearing appeals **Notice by special sessions of time of sitting.** with respect to any parish to the overseers of such parish, who shall publish it as soon as it is received by them.

SECTION 6, ACT 1864.

No justice of the peace shall be disqualified for acting in the determination of any appeal against a poor rate at any quarter or special sessions by reason of such **Justices in certain cases not disqualified for hearing appeals.** justice being rated or being liable to be rated in some other parish in the union than that for which the rate appealed against is made.

The Law as Enacted for the Metropolis only.

SECTION 63 OF THE METROPOLIS ACT.

Any room maintained out of the proceeds of any rate levied
wholly or partly in the metropolis may (with the
consent of the person or body corporate having
the control of it) be used for hearing appeals, and
for other purposes of this Act.

Use of public room for appeals, &c.

34. The justices in special sessions and in assessment sessions
respectively shall, in open court, hear and determine all appeals brought before them in such order
as they may respectively from time to time appoint.
They may adjourn the hearing from time to time,
and to any day not later than the day before
which all appeals to them are required by this Act to be heard;
and in the case of assessment sessions for the purpose of obtaining
the decision of any superior court to any day necessary for that
purpose; and if from accident or mistake due notice of appeal
has not been given, or if an additional notice of appeal appears to
be required, they may, if they think it just, order notice of appeal
to be given. They may confirm or alter the valuation-list, so far
as it is questioned by the appeal, in such manner as they think
just, but shall not make any alteration in contravention of this
Act. The clerk of the assessment committee, or some deputy
allowed by the assessment committee, shall attend the court with
the valuation-list to which the appeal relates, and any alteration
shall be made by the justice acting as chairman of the sessions in
that list, and the said justice shall place his initials against such
alteration.

Sessions to hear and determine appeals, and alter list accordingly.

64. A valuation-list may be proved by the production of a
duplicate or copy of such list purporting to be
certified to be a duplicate or a true copy by the
clerk of the assessment committee that approved
it, and such certificate shall state that the alterations (if any) made

Evidence of valuation-list, &c.

---

in the list in consequence of the decision on any appeal under this Act have been correctly made in the duplicate or copy so produced, and the clerk on application shall furnish a copy to any overseers on payment of a sum not exceeding the rate of three shillings for every hundred entries numbered separately. A provisional list may be proved by the production of a duplicate or copy thereof purporting to be certified to be a true copy by the clerk of the committee who signed it.

APPEALS.—ASSESSMENT SESSIONS.

23. For the purpose of hearing appeals under this Act against any valuation-list in the metropolis, the justices of the peace appointed as hereinafter mentioned shall at the time mentioned in this Act assemble and hold a court of general assessment sessions (in this Act referred to as the assessment sessions).

Court of general assessment sessions.

24. The justices who are to form the court of general assessment sessions shall be appointed annually as follows:

1. Three justices of the peace of the county of Middlesex (of whom the assistant judge of the court of the sessions of the peace of the said county shall be one) shall be appointed by the court of general quarter sessions or general sessions of the peace for the county of Middlesex.

Appointment of members of general assessment sessions.

2. Two justices of the peace of the county of Surrey shall be appointed by the court of general or quarter sessions of the peace for the county of Surrey:

3. Two justices of the peace of the county of Kent shall be appointed by the court of general sessions for the county of Kent:

4. Two justices of the peace of the city of London shall be appointed by the court of the mayor and aldermen of the city of London in the inner chamber.

The Law as Enacted for the Metropolis only.

The said justices shall be appointed in the month of October in every year, or at such other time as may be from time to time fixed by the appointing body. They shall hold office for twelve months, beginning on the first of November, and any casual vacancy may be filled up by the appointing body.

25. The justices in assessment sessions may from time to time appoint, with the consent of the Poor Law Board, a clerk, and other persons to assist them in the performance of their duties under this Act, and may assign him or them such remuneration and such duties as the Poor Law Board may approve.

Officers of general assessment ses-sions.

26. The justices in assessment sessions may from time to time appoint one of their own number to act as their chairman, who shall have a second or casting vote, and they may from time to time determine on their quorum so that it be not less than three.

Chairman, quo-rum, and powers of general assess-ment sessions.

The court of general assessment sessions may adjourn from time to time, as may be necessary for the performance of their duties under this Act, and (for the purpose of giving judgment only) from place to place in the metropolis. They shall, with respect to the attendance and examination of witnesses, to the taking of evidence, to the keeping of order in court, to contempt of court, to the enforcement of their orders, and to all matters necessary for the execution of their duties under this Act, have the same juris-diction and powers, and be in the same position as a court of quarter sessions; and, subject to the express provisions of this Act, shall conduct their proceedings, be convened, and be in the same position, as near as may be, as if they were a court of quarter sessions.

27. The justices in assessment sessions may, with the approval of one of Her Majesty's Principal Secretaries of State, make orders from time to time for the purpose of regulating the proceedings on appeals

Orders as to pro-ceedings and reto them under this Act, and for determining the **cognizances on appeals.** recognizances (if any) to be entered into by appellants in the case of appeals either to special sessions or to the assessment sessions.

28. The justices in assessment sessions may make a table of the fees which in their opinion should be paid to the clerks of special sessions and to the clerk of assessment sessions in the case of appeals under this **Fees on appeals under this Act.** Act, and shall lay such table before one of Her Majesty's Principal Secretaries of State in the same manner as the justices at quarter sessions may make and lay before such Secretary of State a table of fees, and all the provisions of section thirty of the Act of the session of the eleventh and twelfth years of Her Majesty's reign, chapter forty-three (which section relates to a table of fees and to the prohibition of clerks taking other fees), shall apply in the case of a table of fees made, and the business done by the said clerks under this Act.

All fees paid in the case of appeals to the assessment sessions shall be paid to the account of the receiver of the Metropolitan Common Poor Fund, and shall be so paid and taken and accounted for in such a manner as the Poor Law Board may from time to time by order prescribe.

29. The justices in assessment sessions shall from time to time appoint a place in the metropolis where the appeals **Places for hearing** relating to each parish in the metropolis are to be **appeals.** heard, and may, if they think fit, divide the metropolis into districts for the purpose of appeals, and appoint one or more places for every such district.

30. The justices in assessment sessions shall cause public notice to be given of the several times at which they will sit at the several places appointed for the hearing **Public notice of times of holding courts to be given.** of appeals; such notice may be given under the hand of their clerk, and shall be given by adver-

tisement in some newspaper circulating generally in the metropolis, and by sending a copy of such notice to every surveyor of taxes in the metropolis, to every assessment committee which would have a right to appeal at such court, and to the overseers of every parish to which any appeal relates, and to all the parties to the appeal.

The overseers shall publish the notice as soon as it is received by them.

42. (13.) The justices may hold the assessment sessions at any time after the first of February in the same year, which will enable them to determine all appeals (except where a valuation-list or valuation is ordered) before the ensuing thirty-first of March :

(14.) Notice of the times at which the assessment sessions will be held at each place shall be given by the clerk ten days at least before the first court is held.

32. Any ratepayer, and any surveyor of taxes, and any overseer, with the consent of the vestry of his parish, who **Persons entitled to appeal against assessment sessions.** may feel aggrieved by any decision of the assessment committee, on an objection made before them to which he was a party, or by any decision of special sessions, whether he was a party or not, may appeal against such decision to the assessment sessions.

Any assessment committee in the metropolis, or in the county in which the parish to which the appeal relates is situate, any overseers in the metropolis or such county, with the consent of the vestry of their parish, any ratepayer in the metropolis or such county, and any body of persons authorized by law to levy rates or require contributions payable out of rates in the metropolis or such county, may appeal to the assessment sessions, if they or he feel aggrieved by reason—

(1) of the total of the gross value of any parish being too high or too low ;

(2.) of the total of the rateable value of any parish being too
high or too low; or

(3.) of there being no approved valuation-list for some parish.

42. (12.) Notices of appeals to assessment sessions shall be given
on or before the fourteenth of January in the same year:
(*See Section 33, Metropolis Act; Sections 2 and 3, Act
1864; Section 34, Metropolis Act; Section 64, Metropolis
Act.*)

31. The justices in assessment sessions may order any clerk to
the commissioners of taxes, any surveyor of taxes,
clerk of assessment committee, overseer, assistant
overseer, or like officer in the metropolis to produce
any documents relating to rates or taxes which such
Summons of certain officers as witnesses.
justices may consider necessary for determining an appeal, and do
not relate to profits of trade or of concerns in the nature of trade.

Any person who refuses, after tender of a reasonable sum for his
expenses, to obey any order under this section shall be liable (on
summary conviction before the justices in assessment sessions or
any other two justices) to a penalty not exceeding five pounds.

35. If it appears to the justices in assessment sessions on any
appeal that there is no approved valuation-list for
some parish, they may appoint some proper person (with such remuneration as they may appoint)
to make a valuation-list. Such person shall have
Making of valuation-list where none approved.
for that purpose the same powers and duties as overseers.

The valuation-list so made shall be deposited and otherwise
made known to the persons interested in such manner as the court
may direct, but in manner as near as may be as is provided in this
Act with respect to the list originally made.

The costs of making such valuation-list shall be paid by the
assessment committee who failed to approve the list, and shall be
deemed part of their expenses under the principal Act.

36. If any of the parties to the appeal apply to the justices in

---

assessment sessions to direct a valuation of any hereditament with

Assessment sessions may, on application of party to appeal, order valuation.
respect to which any appeal may be made, and if such applicant or applicants give such security as the court think proper to pay the costs of the valuation, the court may, in their discretion, appoint some proper person to make such valuation.

62. Every assessment committee, with the consent of the

Assessment committee and overseers may give security for costs of valuation.
guardians, and every overseer, with the consent of the vestry of his parish, may, for the purposes of any application for a valuation on any appeal, give security for paying the costs of such valuation. An assessment committee may give such

security, and may appear on any appeal by their clerk, and shall indemnify the said clerk against all monies, losses, and costs paid or incurred by him in consequence of such security or appearance.

37. Where the court appoint a person to make a valuation-list

Adjournment to receive valuation-list or valuation.
or a valuation, they may fix some subsequent day, either before or after the day before which all appeals are required by this Act to be heard, for receiving such valuation-list or valuation, and may

adjourn the hearing to that day.

38. The person so appointed to make a valuation shall make his

Valuation to be in writing, person making it to have power to enter.
valuation in writing signed by him, showing the particulars of the hereditaments comprised therein, and the amounts at which he has valued the same respectively.

Such person may at all reasonable times, with or without assistants, enter upon any of the hereditaments directed to be valued, and may do thereon all acts necessary for completing the valuation.

39. The costs of any appeal, including the costs of any such

Costs of Appeal.
valuation as aforesaid, shall be in the discretion of the justices in special or assessment sessions (as the

case may be), and shall be awarded by them to be paid by such parties to the appeal, and in such proportions, as they think just.

Costs (including the costs of making a valuation) so ordered to be paid may be recovered as if they had been awarded by a court of quarter sessions, and when ordered to be paid by parties other than a ratepayer shall be paid as in this Act mentioned.

48. The costs of an appeal awarded against or incurred by any assessment committee or overseers shall be deemed to be expenses incurred under this Act and the Acts incorporated herewith, and shall be raised and paid accordingly.

Costs of appeal, &c.

Any costs or expenses awarded against or incurred by any surveyor of taxes shall be defrayed in the same manner as expenses are directed to be defrayed by the Acts relating to the taxes in respect of which the valuation-list is made conclusive.

49. The Commissioners of Inland Revenue may make such allowances as they think fit for remunerating any person employed by them in the execution of this Act, and for the discharge of any costs or expenses incurred by him.

Inland Revenue may make allowances for expenses of Act.

50. The expenses of the assessment sessions and such remuneration as the Poor Law Board may from time to time allow to the clerk of the managers of the metropolitan asylum district, the clerk of the assessment sessions, and persons appointed to assist the assessment sessions as provided by this Act, and such costs and expenses incurred by such clerks and persons under this Act as the Poor Law Board may allow, after such audit as the Poor Law Board may direct, shall be paid by the receiver of the Metropolitan Common Poor Fund out of any monies for the time being in his hands, and shall be paid at such times and in such manner and upon such precept of the Poor Law Board as the Poor Law Board may from time to time prescribe, and the

Expenses.

Poor Law Board may require contributions for the purpose of raising such remuneration, expenses, and costs.

40. The same proceedings may be had by special case and certiorari or otherwise, for questioning any decision of the justices in assessment sessions, as may be had for questioning any decision of the justices in general or quarter sessions, provided that every such certiorari shall be sued out within three months after the decision is given.

Appeal from decision of assessment sessions on points of law.

At any time after notice given of appeal under this Act to the assessment sessions, it shall be lawful for the parties, by consent and by order of any judge of one of the superior courts of common law at Westminster, to state the facts of the case in the form of a special case for the opinion of any of those courts and to agree that a judgment in conformity with the decision of that court, and for such costs as that court may adjudge, may be entered on the application of either party at the meeting of the justices in assessment sessions next or next but one after such decision has been given, and such judgment may be entered accordingly, and shall be of the same effect in all respects as if the same had been given by the assessment sessions upon an appeal duly brought before them and adjourned; and the justices shall, if necessary, hold a sessions or an adjourned sessions for this purpose.

Notice in writing of the decision of any superior court in pursuance of this section shall be served by the clerk of the assessment sessions on the assessment committee which approved the list questioned on the appeal to such court.

41. Notice of every alteration in the valuation-list, which alteration is made in consequence of any decision on any appeal to the special sessions, assessment sessions, or a superior court, shall, as soon as possible, be sent in writing by the clerk of the assessment committee to the overseers and surveyor of taxes of the parish and

Notice of alteration of list to be sent to overseers.

district respectively to which the list which is so altered relates, and such alteration shall be entered by the clerk of the assessment committee and by the overseers on the duplicates respectively deposited with them.

Notice of every alteration in the total of the gross and rateable value of any valuation-list, which alteration is made in consequence of any decision on any appeal to the assessment sessions or a superior court, shall as soon as possible be sent in writing by the clerk of the assessment committee to the clerk of the managers of the Metropolitan Asylum District, and the clerk of such managers shall send in writing such altered total to every person and body of persons who has power to levy or make any rate or assessment or require any contribution based on such total.

73. Every poor rate made in the metropolis after the fifth of April, one thousand eight hundred and seventy-one, shall contain the particulars specified in the **Form of rate and declaration.** fourth schedule to this Act, together with such other particulars as the Poor Law Board may from time to time by order direct, and the overseers shall sign the form of declaration which is given in that schedule before the rate is allowed by the justices. And the justices shall not allow any rate at the foot of which the said declaration has not been added and signed.

Any overseer who wilfully omits to make the said declaration or makes the same falsely, shall be liable on summary conviction to a penalty not exceeding five pounds.

The Law as Enacted for the Metropolis only.

FOURTH SCHEDULE.

FORM OF RATE.

RATE for the RELIEF of the POOR of the Parish of   in the
Union, and for other purposes chargeable thereon, according to law made
this   day of   in the year of Our Lord 18   , after the rate
of   in the pound, which is estimated to meet all the expenses for the above
purposes which will be incurred before the   of   next.

No.	Name of occupier.	Name of owner.	Description of property rated.	Name or situation of property.	Rateable value.	Rate at in the pound.	

DECLARATION TO BE ADDED TO THE RATE.

WE, the undersigned, do hereby declare that one of us, or some person on our
behalf, has examined and compared the several particulars in the respective columns
of the above rate with the valuation-list made under the authority of the Valuation
(Metropolis) Act, 1869, and now in force in this parish (or township), and the
several hereditaments are, to the best of our belief, rated according to the value
appearing in such valuation-list, and do declare that the total of the above rate
amounts to   pounds   shillings and   pence.

———————————— } Churchwardens.

————————————

———————————— } Overseers.

SECTION 5, ACT 1836.

And be it further enacted, That it shall be lawful for any
person or persons rated to the relief of the poor of
Power to take copies or extracts of rates gratis. the parish in respect of which any rate shall be
made, at all seasonable times, to take copies thereof
or extracts therefrom without paying anything for

the same, anything in any Act of Parliament to the contrary notwithstanding; and in case the person or persons having the custody of such rate shall refuse to permit or shall not permit such person or persons so rated as aforesaid to take copies thereof or extracts therefrom, the **Penalty for refusal to permit.** person or persons so refusing or not permitting such copy or extract to be made shall forfeit and pay any sum not exceeding five pounds, to be recovered in a summary way before any justice of the peace having jurisdiction in the parish or place.

SECTION 70 METROPOLIS ACT.

Where the owner of any hereditament is liable to be assessed to or to pay any rate or tax in the place of the occupier, such owner shall for the purposes of this Act and the Acts incorporated herewith be deemed to be the occupier. **Owner where rated to be in position of occupier.**

71. Any person who feels aggrieved by reason of any clerical or arithmetical error in a rate in the metropolis may apply to two justices of the peace or a magistrate sitting at any police-court in the metropolitan police district, who, after the applicant has given **Amendment of error in rate by two justices.** such notice to the overseers who made the rate and such persons as such justices or magistrates think just, may hear the case in like manner as in the case of summary proceedings, and amend the rate so far as respects such error.

72. Whenever the name of any person liable to be rated at the time the rate is made is omitted from any rate in the metropolis, or if any person is described in any such rate by a wrong name, the overseers **Omissions from the rate.** may, after giving to such person seven clear days' notice of their intention, apply to any two justices or any police magistrate as aforesaid, who may hear the case in like manner as in the case of summary proceedings, and insert the name so omitted, or

The Law as Enacted for the Metropolis only.

correct the name so wrongly entered, and every such insertion and correction shall operate as if it had been part of the original rate: Provided that every person whose name is so inserted or corrected in any such rate may appeal against the same at the general quarter sessions of the peace which is holden next after such insertion or correction, in like manner as he might have appealed against the rate.

SECTION 44, ACT 1862.

All the powers, authorities, provisions, clauses, and regulations now in force relating to the assessment, collection, and levying of poor-rates (save so far as the same are hereby repealed or altered) shall be good, valid, and effectual for the purposes of assessing, levying, collecting, and enforcing the payment of such rate and for carrying this Act into execution.

Provisions concerning the assessment, &c., of poor-rates to be applicable to rates made according to this Act.

Extent of Act.

46. This Act shall extend only to England.

SECTION 12, ACT 1864.

The provisions of the Union Assessment Committee Act, 1862, shall, as far as the same are not contrary hereto, be incorporated herewith, and the terms used herein shall be construed in like manner as in that Act.

25 & 26 Vict., c. 103, incorporated herewith.

Short title.

13. This Act may be cited as "The Union Assessment Committee Amendment Act, 1864."

SECTION 46 OF THE METROPOLIS ACT.
REVISION OF VALUATION-LIST.

46. Every valuation-list shall be revised in manner directed by this Act, and such revision in every period of *five years* (the first of such periods beginning with the sixth of April one thousand eight hundred and seventy-one) shall be conducted as follows:—

Mode of revising valuation-list.

The Law as Enacted for the Metropolis only.

(1.) In each of the first four years of such period a supplemental list shall, if necessary, be made out in the same form as the valuation-list, and shall show all the alterations which have taken place during the preceding twelve months in any of the matters stated in the valuation-list, but shall contain only the hereditaments affected by such alterations. If no alteration has taken place which makes a supplemental list necessary, the overseers shall send a certificate to that effect to the assessment committee in place of such list, which certificate may be in the form contained in the second schedule to this Act :

FORM OF CERTIFICATE WHERE NO SUPPLEMENTAL LIST IS SENT.

We, the overseers of the parish of   , do hereby certify that no alteration has taken place in the matters stated in the valuation-list of this parish which renders a supplemental list necessary.

A.B. ⎱ Overseers of the parish
C.D. ⎰   of

(2.) In the fifth year of every such period the overseers shall make a new valuation-list :

(3.) The same regulations shall be observed and the same proceedings shall be had in the case of a supplemental list and a new valuation-list as are directed by this Act and the Acts incorporated herewith in the case of the valuation-list made in the first year after the passing of this Act :

(4.) A supplemental list and a new valuation-list shall come into force at the beginning of the year succeeding that in which they are respectively made, in the same manner and subject to the same conditions as the valuation-list made in the first year after the passing of this Act :

(5.) In each of the last four years of such period the valuation-list which was in force on the day before the commencement of each such year, together with and as altered by the supplemental list, if any, which comes into force at the commencement of such year, shall be the valuation-list which is in force during that year :

(6.) A new valuation-list when it comes into force shall super-sede the valuation-list which was in force during the fifth year of such period.

47. If in the course of any year the value of any hereditament is increased by the addition thereto or erection thereon of any building, or is from any cause increased or reduced in value, the following pro-visions shall have effect :

Provision for valuing a house built between the time at which the valuation-list is made.

(1.) The overseers of the parish in which such hereditament is situate may, and on the written requisition of the assessment committee or of any ratepayer of the union or of the surveyor of taxes for the district shall, send to the assessment committee a pro-visional list containing the gross and rateable value as so increased or reduced of such hereditament :

(2.) A copy of the requisition shall be sent by the person making it to the clerk of the assessment committee, and if within fourteen days after the requisition has been served on the overseers they make default in sending such provisional list he shall forthwith summon the assessment committee, and the assessment committee shall appoint a person to make such provisional list, in the same manner as is in this Act provided in the case of the overseers failing to transmit a valuation-list :

(3.) On the receipt of the list the clerk of the assessment committee shall serve on the surveyor of taxes for the district a copy of the list, and shall serve on the occupier of any hereditament to which the list relates a copy of so much thereof as relates to that hereditament. Every copy shall be accompanied by a notice specifying a day, being not less than fourteen days after the date of the

———

service of the notice on or before which any objection to the provisional list may be made, and stating the mode in which an objection is to be made. Such copy and notice shall be served in the same way as notices by an assessment committee are served:

(4.) An objection may be made to any such provisional list by the said occupier, and by the surveyor of taxes, or by either of them, by notice thereof in writing being served on the clerk of the assessment committee, on the overseers, on the surveyor of taxes, and on the occupier, or on such of them as the case may require:

(5.) The clerk of the assessment committee, on the receipt of the notice of any objection, shall forthwith summon a meeting of the committee, and give notice of the time and place of such meeting to the overseers, to the surveyor of taxes, and the occupier:

(6.) The committee shall hear and determine on the objection in the same manner as if it were an objection to a valuation-list, and may make such order as they think just:

(7.) If no objection is made, then on the expiration of the time for making objections, or if an objection is made then as soon as the assessment committee have determined on the objection, the assessment committee shall cause a copy to be made of the provisional list, with any alteration made in it by the committee, and shall return the list and the copy thereof, after being dated and signed by their clerk, to the overseers:

(8.) A provisional list, signed as aforesaid, shall have operation from the date of the service by the clerk of the assessment committee of a copy of the list and notice on the occupier, and shall continue in force until the first list (supplemental or other) which is subsequently made comes into force.

(9.) Upon a provisional list coming into operation the overseers
shall make such entries in the rate book for the then
current poor-rate as will bring the same into conformity
with such list, and shall also enter therein the date at
which such list is to come into operation, and shall charge
the occupier of such hereditament with a proper proportion of such current poor-rate, regard being had to the
time which has elapsed between the making of such rate
and the said date and to the rateable value stated in such
provisional list, and such occupier shall be considered as
actually rated for such sum from the said date, and be
liable to pay the same, and the same may be enforced
accordingly :

(10.) A provisional list during the time that it is in force shall
be deemed to form part of the valuation-list for the time
being in force, and shall (so far as is necessary) be substituted for so much of that valuation-list as relates to the
same hereditament, and every rate and tax in respect of
which the valuation-list is conclusive, which are respectively made or charged after the provisional list comes
into force, and the proportion of the current rate charged
as before provided in this section, shall be levied accordingly ; but if when the next revision of the valuation-list
takes place the list as approved and altered on appeal
contains a smaller value for the hereditament comprised
in a provisional list than the value stated in such provisional list, the amount of rate or tax which has been
overpaid in consequence of the larger value having been
stated shall be repaid or allowed :

(11.) Nothing in this section shall affect the value on which any
rate is made or sum is assessed or contribution required
which is made, assessed, or required on the totals of the
gross or rateable value of parishes or unions.

REPEAL OF ACTS.

77. The enactments specified in the fifth schedule to this Act, and so much of any other Acts, whether public or local and personal, as authorizes any valuation of hereditaments to be made for the purposes of any rate or tax in respect of which the valuation-list is by this Act made conclusive, are hereby repealed, where they relate only to the metropolis absolutely, and in other cases so far as they relate to the metropolis: Provided—

Repeal of Acts herein described.

1. That the provisions of the Acts so repealed shall remain in force until the provision or provisions substituted for them by this Act shall respectively come into operation :

2. That this repeal shall not affect the validity or invalidity of anything done or suffered under any of the said provisions while they remain in force, or any right or title acquired or accrued under any of the said provisions while they remain in force, or any remedy or proceeding in respect thereof.

[*End of the Law as Enacted for the Metropolis only.*]

THE foregoing being the principal laws under which the funds requisite for the relief of the poor are raised, it will be the object of these pages to show how the *principle* therein laid down is to be applied to the rating of the various descriptions of hereditament.

The law enacts that the rate shall be founded "*upon an estimate of the net annual value of the several hereditaments*

Principle of assessment to the poor-rate.

rated thereunto; that is to say, of the rent at which the same might reasonably be expected to let, from year to year, free of all usual tenant's rates and taxes, and tithe commutation rent charge, if any, and deducting therefrom the probable average annual cost of the repairs, insurance, and other expenses, if any, necessary to maintain them in a state to command such rent."

The principle herein enunciated is of the most comprehensive character. It is equally capable of determining the contribution of the smallest ratepayer or of the largest; of determining the amount of rate to be paid upon a hereditament of the most trifling annual value, or of a hereditament so great as to require the united contributions of many persons to create it.

In the first place, it will be advisable to consider the various tenures under which property is usually held.

Nature of the various tenures.

These are—First, *on lease.* Under this holding the tenant pays his rent and the rates and taxes, insures, and keeps the premises in repair. Secondly, On a *yearly tenancy.* Under this holding the tenant usually pays his rent, and the rates and taxes, but does not repair; and can either quit, or be required to quit, at the end of any year. Thirdly, A *weekly holding.* Under this holding, the tenant simply pays his rent; the landlord pays all rates, insures, and repairs.

The above are the conditions under which property is usually held by a tenant.

The Parochial Assessment Act has determined (as will be shown hereafter) that the *second* of these shall be the tenure under which property on which a rate is to be levied shall be deemed to be held. It therefore becomes necessary to reduce all tenures otherwise held to this condition.

Tenure of the Parochial Assessment Act.

In the first place, therefore, we will assume the hereditament to be a house held on a repairing lease, and under this tenure the average annual outgoings of the tenant to be as follow:—

Rent under Lease.

Rates and taxes	...	...	...	£20
Repairs...	...	...	...	£10
Insurance	...	...	...	£2
Rent	...	...	...	£68

The question, then, to be solved is, what will be the gross estimated rental and rateable value of such hereditament?

The gross estimated rental will be the rent, *plus* the repairs and insurance, viz.: £80, and the rateable value will be, *not* £68, the rent paid under the lease, *as many suppose*, but such rent reduced by an amount,

Rent under lease not rateable value.

which ought to be set aside annually by the landlord for the ultimate *renewal* or *reconstruction* of the hereditament. This amount will entirely depend upon the life of the building, and will vary from $2\frac{1}{2}$ to 5 per cent. of the rent, and in some cases more.

In some of the metropolitan parishes it is reported that the overseers have, in making their valuation under the Metropolis Act, assumed the rent paid under lease to be the rateable value. The decision, however, of the Court of Queen's Bench, in the case of Queen *v.* Wells (*2 Law Reports, Q.B. 542*) clearly shows this to be erroneous.

In this case two questions were submitted for decision, one of which was:—

"Whether any allowance should be made in respect of any contingent or *future renewal* or *re-construction* of buildings and machinery, or either, or which, and if so, to what amount?"

And the judgment delivered upon the point, by Lord Chief Justice Cockburn, was as follows :—

"The second question submitted to us is, whether any allowance should be made in respect of any contingent or *future renewal* of buildings or machinery? *We are of opinion that such allowance ought to be made.* Farm buildings and machinery are, by the effects of the weather, and of wear and tear, *reducible to a state which will render them unworthy of repair, and necessitates their reconstruction.*

"They cannot at length be kept up but at an expense which renders it practically impossible, because not reasonably prudent, to keep them up. Provision made for a future liability to reconstruct them, involving, as it ought to do, a prudential parsimony as respects all but temporary and indispensable repairs, is an expense which may properly be included among the expenses necessary to maintain a hereditament consisting in part of subjects perishable, in a state fit to command the rent, and which it does in fact while standing, and in use, command."

Under a repairing lease the tenant has merely to do *temporary and indispensable repairs.* He has nothing to do with *future reconstruction,* that burthen falls upon the landlord.

The rent therefore paid by him is *not* "net rental," but "net rental" *plus* "renewals;" deduct for "renewals" and then you obtain the "net rental," or "rateable value."

In the case of houses let by the week, the rent paid includes not only rent in its restricted sense, but also an amount for rates and all other out-goings which are in this case paid by the landlord, and not by the tenant.

Weekly tenements.

To reduce weekly tenements to the conditions of yearly holdings, it is necessary to consider in the first instance what the advantages or disadvantages of such holdings are, as compared with those from year to year. In the first place when property is let from week to week, the landlord has to call *fifty-two* times in a year for his rent, but in the other case he has only to apply *four* times, *i.e.*, the weekly holdings give him thirteen times as much trouble as the yearly. In order therefore to place the two holdings upon a footing of equality with regard to their respective gross earnings it is necessary to make some deduction from the total yearly receipts for the extra trouble of *collection*. This may be taken at about 5 per cent. of the total receipts.

A further deduction again must be made for *rates*, and then we arrive at the gross rental which might be expected on the usual terms of a yearly tenure. From this gross rental, in order to arrive at the rateable value, must next be deducted an amount for repairs, renewals, and insurance, which amount will vary from 20 to 30 per cent., according to the durability of the hereditament.

But since the rateable value of a weekly holding depends upon the amount of *rates*, and these can only be ascertained by knowing what the rateable value is, we therefore at once encounter an algebraical equation, which must be based upon the following reasoning:

That the *rent* is the rateable value *plus* the repairs, &c.; therefore the rateable value is the rent *minus* the repairs, &c. That the repairs be taken at 20 per cent., or one-fifth of the rent, in which case, therefore, the *rateable value* will be four-fifths of the rent. And lastly, that the repairs are one-fourth of the rateable value.

Putting s for the sum of the rateable value, the repairs, and the rates (taken by hypothesis at 6s. in the pound), and x for the rateable value, then we shall have to find r, the rates.

Since the repairs $= \dfrac{x}{4}$

$$r = s - \left(x + \frac{x}{4} \right)$$

And, solving this equation, in which we must substitute the value of x in terms of r,

$$\text{or } \frac{10}{3} r \text{ for } r = \frac{3}{10} x \text{ by hypothesis,}$$

we have $r = \dfrac{6}{31} s$.

And it will be seen that, whatever the conditions may be, r can *always* be expressed in terms of s.

H

These results may appear somewhat difficult to apply, but they are not so actually.

Three or four scales could easily be computed, in each of which the allowance for repairs would differ, and would depend on the durability of the property to be assessed. Thus, one scale would be applicable to *well*-built *brick* tenements, a second to *well*-built *wooden* tenements, a third to *badly*-built *brick* tenements, and a fourth to *badly*-built *wooden* tenements. Overseers of parishes, possessing such scales, would simply have to determine the class of tenement to be dealt with, and the weekly rent paid; and then, from the scale applicable to such case, ascertain its proper gross and net rental.

Upon the question of *tenure*, the following case, to which reference has already been made, was recently brought before the Court of Queen's Bench, and the importance of the judgment pronounced in connection with the principle of rating is so great, that it is deemed advisable to quote it here *in extenso.*

Queen v. Wells, 2 Law Reports, Queen's Bench, 542.

The case found, after setting forth the gross estimated rental, and the rateable value as entered in the rate, that—

"1. The sums which appear in the column headed 'gross estimated rental' are the actual rents paid by the occupiers whose names appear against them respectively, and are fair and *bonâ fide* rents, and represent the rents at which the hereditaments might reasonably be expected to let from year to year upon the customary terms between landlord and tenant: that is to say, in the case of the properties the subject of the present appeal, the landlord paying the insurance, and providing timber, bricks, tiles, and lime, for repairs, and the tenant carting such materials, and providing all other materials for such repairs, including straw for thatching, and paying the cost of the labour for doing such repairs and thatching, and also paying all usual tenant's rates and taxes, and the tithe commutation rentcharge."

2. The case then went on to find that—

"The probable average annual cost of the repairs, insurance, and other expenses necessary to maintain them in a state to command the before-mentioned rents, is—

"1. For dwelling-houses £20 0 0
2. For farms with farm-houses and buildings ... 14 16 7
3. For lands without farmhouses and buildings... 3 10 0
4. For water corn-mills 22 11 6

" 3. Of this total outlay the proportions borne respectively by the landlord and tenant, under the above terms of tenancy, are as follow :—

	Landlord, per cent.			Tenant, per cent.		
"1. Dwelling-houses	£20	0	0	£0	0	0
2. Farms with farm-houses and buildings ...	10	6	7	4	0	0
3. Lands without farm-houses and buildings	1	10	0	2	0	0
4. Water corn-mills	19	11	6	5	0	0

" 4. In the cases of the first, second, and fourth items, the percentages set forth in the above second paragraph include allowances in respect of any contingent or future renewal or reconstruction of buildings and machinery.

"The questions for the opinion of the court were—

"1. Whether, under the above terms of tenancy, any portion of the cost of repairs which is borne by the tenant ought or ought not to be deducted from the rent actually paid in order to arrive at the net annual or rateable value of the premises?

"2. Whether any allowance should be made in respect of any contingent or future renewal or reconstruction of buildings and machinery, or either, or which, and if so, to what amount?

"The judgment of the court (Cockburn, C. J., and Shee, J.) was delivered by Cockburn, C. J.

"Two questions present themselves for our decision in this case, both turning on the construction to be put on that part of the 1st section of the Parochial Assessment Act, 6 & 7 William IV., cap. 96, which provides that in estimating the value at which property is to be assessed, a deduction is to be made from the rent at which the same might be reasonably expected to let by the year, and which is to be taken as the criterion of value of the probable annual average cost of the repairs, insurance, and other expenses necessary to maintain it in a state to command such rent.

"The first question is, whether, where houses or other buildings, either with or without land, are let to a tenant, and the tenant agrees to take upon himself, either wholly or in part, the repairs and other expenses to which the section refers, and which would ordinarily fall upon the landlord, an allowance is to be made in respect of such repairs and expenses, as though they were defrayed by the landlord.

"On the hearing, we were disposed to think that, as the rate when assessed is to be paid by the occupier, the tenant, the repairs and other expenses

H 2

necessary for keeping the property in proper condition, which he has thus taken upon himself, might, as against him, be taken as so much rent, and would not, in his hands, be capable of being deducted. On further consideration, however, we are of opinion that the standard of value adopted by the legislature, is the value of the property to the owner, whether it remains in his own occupation, or is let to a tenant. Now, to the owner, the measure of this value is the rent at which the property is let, or might be let, subject to the deduction which *such owner*, as a prudent man, ought to make from the available income which the rent would otherwise afford, in order to meet the expenses necessary for keeping the premises in a state to command the rent.

"Where, by an arrangement between the landlord and the tenant, the latter takes upon himself to defray these expenses, or any part of them, it is obvious that the rent he can afford to pay will be *pro tanto* less than if such expenses were borne by the landlord. *We cannot think the statute meant to make the rateable value of the premises depend on the terms on which they are actually let, but upon that rent* which might reasonably have been expected if they had *let on the statutable terms.* In order, therefore, to give effect to the intention of the legislature, it is necessary to consider these expenses as *added* to the rent, but then as to be deducted *by the landlord;* thus leaving the rent actually paid by the tenant as the amount on which the rate ought to be assessed We therefore answer the first question by saying that the cost of repairs borne by the tenant ought not to be deducted from the rent actually paid, and that the rent so paid is the rateable value of the premises.

"The second question submitted to us, whether any allowance should be made in respect of any contingent or future renewal of buildings or machinery? We are of opinion that such allowance ought to be made. Farm buildings and machinery are, by the effects of the weather, and of wear and tear, reducible to a state which will render them unworthy of repair, and necessitate their reconstruction. They cannot, at length, be kept up but at an expense which renders it practically impossible, because not reasonably prudent, to keep them up.

"Provision made for a future liability to reconstruct them, involving, as it ought to do, a prudential parsimony as respects all but temporary and indispensable repairs, is an expense which may properly be included among the expenses necessary to maintain a hereditament, consisting in part of subjects perishable, in a state fit to command the rent, and which it does, in fact, while standing and in use command. There seems also no distinction in principle between a sum annually laid by to make good, when it shall become necessary, an inevitable loss by the destructive agency of time, and a fund laid by for an indemnity against a loss by fire or storm, or other peril assured against.

" But although a deduction, in respect of the amount which ought, as a matter of reasonable prudence, to be set aside by the *owner* of property for the reconstruction of buildings or machinery, ought to be made from the rent before the latter is adopted as the test of value, yet, under the circumstances of the present case, the reasoning on which our answer to the first question is founded is equally applicable to the one now under consideration, and we are therefore of opinion that no allowance ought to be made in respect of this head of allowance.

The tenure of the Parochial Assessment Act is constantly ignored by company's witnesses in giving evidence in support of appeals against a poor rate. Of the many estimates which I have heard given in evidence by company's witnesses, I have never heard one framed in accordance with the statutable tenure, nor one in which the rent proved was the rent under the Act.

The amount paid to the landlord under the statutable tenure is the gross estimated rental; and the residue thereof, after the specified deductions have been made, is the net annual value.

The "gross rent" being determined, the next question is, " What deductions are to be made in order to arrive at the 'net annual value?'"

Deductions from the gross estimated rental.

These deductions are—repairs, insurance, and other expenses (if any) necessary to maintain the premises in a state to command such rent.

The first two items require no particular remark here, their nature being self-evident. The third deduction being more comprehensive, it becomes necessary to set forth the allowances which must be made to comply with its requirements.

First come renewals of the subject-matter of the rate. It is evident that many classes of property will, however much they may be repaired, ultimately perish, and must therefore be renewed from time to time. Another deduction, which has recently been claimed and allowed, is the amount of sewers-rate. (*R. v. Overseers of Wennington*, 34 L. J. (N. S.) M. C. 17.) This deduction was allowed upon the following grounds :—

First, although not a "usual tenant's rate," yet the tenant frequently agrees to pay it, in which case the rent he would pay would be less by the amount so paid. If the tenant did not agree to pay it, then, inasmuch as property properly drained will fetch more rent than if it be not drained, the expense of keeping the drains and sewers in proper order must be met, to enable the "premises to continue to command that rent."

The *probable average annual amount only* of each of the above must be deducted. From the allowance of these deductions it follows, that a property is assumed *always* to continue of equal value, so far as condition is concerned. No age is supposed to affect its rent, for allowances are ordered to be made in order *continually* to counteract the effects of wear and tear. Of course no Act of Parliament can provide against a change of value when the change is produced by altered circumstances.

Thus a man has no right to claim a reduction in the rating of, say, his house, upon the ground that it is old and very much out of repair. If it is out of repair, it is his own fault. It is his duty, as soon as the house is finished, to lay by annually a sum for its due repair, when it shall need it.

Having shown what is the principle upon which all properties are to be rated to the relief of the poor, the next **Application of the principle.** step is to consider the various circumstances which would influence a tenant in determining the amount of rent he would give for each of the several classes of hereditaments.

First in order is land, as being the foundation of all other real property. Land may be divided into two divi- **Land in its simplest form.** sions, viz., grazing-land and arable-land. Of these two, grazing-land is the condition in which land *naturally* exists, and shall, therefore, be treated first.

The most elementary condition in which grazing-land could exist would be as unenclosed prairie; the state in which large quantities of land may be found in Australia, America, and in all other partially-occupied countries. The rent that land in this condition would command would be but small, but nevertheless something would be given for the privilege of being permitted to use

such land for depasturing sheep or cattle upon. The amount of
rent so given would depend upon the innate goodness of the land,
the water accommodation, and other matters. But however good
the land, the rent would not be much, because the tenant from
year to year would consider that he would be liable to much
anxiety and loss from the liability of his sheep and cattle to stray,
being stolen, or injured. And he would consider that he would
incur expense in obtaining labour to take charge of his stock.
The rent paid for such land would be both the gross and the net
amount, for there would be no deductions to keep the land in a
state to command such rent, and the landlord would be at liberty
to appropriate to his own use the *full* amount paid to him.

The first improvement that would be made in the condition of
the land would be by its enclosure. For as soon
as this was done, it would, in consequence, com-   Land enclosed.
mand a higher rent; because some of the disadvantages above-
named would no longer exist, and others would be much lessened.
With the enclosure of land would commence its conversion into
arable. For arable purposes land of the best quality would be
chosen, both in order that the least labour should be required to
cultivate it, and that the best crops might be produced. Then, as
population increased, and the demand for the articles produced
became greater, the profit made by producing and selling the
articles would become greater also. But the tenant would not be
allowed to appropriate to himself the whole of this increased
profit, for the landlord would expect to be paid a larger rent for
the use of the land whereby the tenant made his increased profit;
for he would contend that it was by no means due to the personal
exertions of the tenant, but to the improvement in the general
condition of affairs.

As population and capital increased, the land, which we have
hitherto considered as being grazing-land, at first
unenclosed, and subsequently merely *enclosed*,   Land subdivided
would further change its character. The land-   into farms.
lord would find an increased number of applicants for the use of

his land; each of whom would be willing to pay a larger rent per acre for a smaller holding than the tenant, who used the land for grazing, would pay per acre for a larger holding. In consequence, the land would be gradually converted into a number of farms, consisting of arable and meadow-land, let to tenants paying a higher rent than was previously obtained. This conversion would, however, be attended with more or less expense, which expense must in theory be borne by the landlord.

It may be objected that the course of change would be rather by the large tracts of land being broken up into smaller tracts, and then *sold* and not let; and that the purchaser would himself have to pay the expense of roads subdividing the land, and of other incidentals.

The answer to this is, that though in fact such would be the course of things, and that in this, as in a new country, we frequently find the occupier of a farm to be the owner also; yet, for the purpose of this investigation, his tenure, whatever it may be, must be reduced to the condition of a holding *from year to year*.

From whom the tenant holds his property is perfectly immaterial. He may hold it from himself, and so fill the two situations of landlord and tenant; or he may only fill the position of tenant. The Act of Parliament does not say that the premises *are* to be let from year to year, but only that the rent, at which they *would* let from year to year, is to be the basis of the assessment.

In determining the value to rent of enclosed land, it becomes necessary to examine each enclosure, and to determine the yearly value thereof. In so doing, the tenant would be guided by the productive quality of the land, its aspect and situation with regard to the homestead, the ease or difficulty with which it could be cultivated, and by the amount of profit which would remain after expenses were deducted. In determining these things, he would be influenced by considerations of the distance he would have to convey his crops to market, the state of the roads leading thereto, the amount of the rates in the pound, and of other minor matters.

Although land in the condition of a farm would command a higher rent than in its elementary condition, it might be so situate as to be capable of further improvement, either by means of drainage, irrigation, or other alterations. These improvements must be taken to be done by the landlord. When made, the farm would command a higher rent than before, either because it would thereby be rendered more productive, or might be worked at a less expense. It is true that, as a matter of fact, these improvements are frequently made by the occupier. But in that case he has a long lease of the farm, and usually at a rent so low that he can prudently expend his money upon another man's land. But such a tenant would be liable to be rated for the land, not at the rent which he actually *does* pay, but at the rent which he *would* pay if he became the tenant of the farm in its improved condition.

Land further improved by draining, &c.

The most valuable condition in which meadow or pasture land can be placed is that of accommodation land, and when the rent at which it may reasonably be expected to let is so great that the net produce of the land would not even pay the rent; but this is of secondary consideration to the tenant of this class of land. He does not rent it to obtain a direct profit for himself, but for the sake of other advantages which its holding secures to him.

Accommodation land.

Also with regard to arable land, the most valuable condition in which it exists is when it is devoted to growing market-crops. Here, however, the rent paid must always be such as to allow the tenant a profit for himself. Upon consideration it will be evident that the portions of land which can be used for this purpose are limited, on account of the numerous conditions that must co-exist; such as fineness and richness of soil, proximity to large towns, and easy access thereto.

Market garden.

The next transformation which land undergoes is when it becomes the site of buildings. Under this condition it has again greatly improved in value, and commands a higher rent than previously. Then, for

Land built upon. Houses, &c. Shops.

the first time, the element of its productiveness is entirely left out of the calculation of the tenant, when he is determining the amount of rent he is willing to give. In settling this he looks only at the accommodation the house or other premises built upon the land afford, their situation, and the number of houses available for his choice. It matters nothing to him by whom the house has been erected; whether by the landowner, or by a speculator who has taken a lease of the ground. Neither does the tenant inquire into the nature of the tenure upon which the house is held by the person to whom he is willing to pay a yearly rent: whether he owns the house and land, or whether he only owns the house, or whether both the land and the house are mortgaged, such questions matter nothing to the tenant from year to year. Finding a house suited to his requirements, he is willing to pay a certain rent for the use thereof. Whatever subsequently becomes of the rent is immaterial to him. As to the amount of rent paid, it so entirely depends upon situation, that nothing can be said upon that point.

The *land* in this case seems to command no rent for itself; but this is only apparently the case, for the rent paid by the tenant is such as to include a payment both for the use of the land and of the house which stands upon the land. It might sometimes happen that the tenant would have to pay rent to two landlords—one to whom the land belongs, the other to whom the house belongs; but this circumstance would in no way affect the amount; for whether he paid rent to one or to many landlords, the total rent he could pay would be the same. Similar considerations would influence a tenant in determining the amount of rent he could give for a shop, or a house and shop, when the greatest prominence would be given to the question of *situation*. He could afford to give a higher rent for an inferior shop in a good situation than he could for a better shop in an inferior situation.

PUBLIC HOUSES.

A *prudent* tenant before estimating the rent he could afford to give for this class of property, would require to know what the "takings" were, and out of these, his experience would doubtless have taught him what per-centage he could judiciously part with as rent to his landlord.

The amount of this per-centage would in a great measure depend upon whether the tenant could obtain his liquor from where he chose, or whether he would be obliged to obtain it from *one* person—technically speaking—whether it was a "*brewer's*" or a "*free house*."

MANSIONS.

A question which has caused much discussion is in what manner should the rent, which a tenant from year to year would give for a nobleman's mansion or house of a special character, be ascertained?

This question appears somewhat surrounded with difficulty, in consequence of houses of this class very rarely being let, the tenants being almost invariably the hereditary owners. Therefore, the test of comparison which is applicable to ordinary houses is inapplicable here. These houses differ from the ordinary ones inasmuch as the latter are built on purpose to be let, whilst these are built solely for the owners' residence and convenience. In building these houses very little regard is paid to the amount of money expended; the only consideration is to make them suitable for the owners' requirements. In an ordinary house, whether built for the owner himself to dwell in, or for the express purpose of being let, attention, more or less, is paid to the return which may be expected upon the outlay; and generally, although a man occupying his own house will be satisfied if the rent which it would produce, if let, be sufficient to pay him a somewhat less interest for his money than he could obtain if he invested that sum of money in other ways; yet he always will expect that it will produce nearly as much interest. Where houses are built expressly to be let, it is expected that the investment will produce a greater interest than other securities.

But in the case of noblemen's seats, money is expended upon

them without the slightest consideration of the return which the investment would produce.

In settling, therefore, the rent which such places would command, regard must be paid to the following considerations :—

In the first place, the number of tenants available for such places is limited, since the tenant must be one possessing a large income. Living in such a house would of necessity involve a very great expense, entirely independent of the amount of rent paid. But, on the other hand, it must not be assumed that the rent of such houses should be settled at a very low sum as compared with the convenience and comfort they afford. For, in the present flourishing condition of this country, there are persons possessing large incomes who would be willing to pay great rents for such houses; but who, if the houses were not available for them, would not be willing to create for themselves similar ones, because the expense of so doing would be more than they might be willing to incur.

Again, many very large seats have much altered in their value in consequence of a change in the habits of society; much of the accommodation that they afford being unsuited or unnecessary for our present customs.

The rent of this class of property will, therefore, have to be settled by duly balancing these various considerations.

The next class of hereditaments which may be considered, is that in which land is occupied by business premises other than shops.

Business premises, manufactories, windmills, water-mills, &c.

Here again the test of "comparison" to a great extent fails; for it will frequently happen that one hereditament used as business premises occurs in the midst of house property; and there being no other similar premises near, no comparison can be made by which to measure its value. Hence it must be considered what circumstances may be supposed to determine the rent that a tenant from year to year would give for such premises.

It is frequently found that, of premises of this nature, the occu-

pier is at the same time the owner; but for the purposes of this
inquiry the two functions must be entirely separated. It can
readily be conceived that the occupier wanting premises of a
certain description, and finding none to suit him, may agree with .
one who has capital which he wishes to invest, to build for him
such premises as he requires, when he would become a tenant
thereof. The one who agreed to build would have to provide the
land on which to build, and the labour and materials necessary to
construct the premises. He would have to provide the land, either
by purchase or by securing a building lease. First, assume that
he purchases it. Having completed the premises, the tenant
would then pay him such a rent for the use of them as secures to
him not only a fair return upon the capital invested, but also a
yearly amount to cover the expense of repairs, insurance, renewals,
and other matters, if any, necessary to maintain the premises " in
a state to command such rent." In settling this rent, the amount
actually expended would not of necessity be the basis of the calculation, for the creator of the hereditament might have spent money
unnecessarily and injudiciously ; but if no more had been expended
than was judicious, then the amount paid as rent would be such as
to secure to the landlord a fair return upon the money expended,
after the landlord had himself, out of the rent, provided for such
outgoing as he must incur. Again, suppose the creator of the
hereditament had not purchased the land, but had leased it. He
would then have to pay the rent of the land. The capital, therefore, he would have to find would only be that requisite to construct the buildings upon the land. Under this condition of things
the rent paid by the tenant would be the same as before ; for,
whether the creator of the hereditament owned the land or only
leased it, the entire hereditament would be of the same value to the
occupier, because it would in consequence be neither more nor less
commodious. The creator of the hereditament would, out of the
rent paid to him, have to pay the ground rent, and thus leave
himself a less sum than he received in the previous case. But inasmuch as he had expended less in creating the hereditament, he

would get the same rate of return for the money he had expended as in the other case.

The objection may be taken that no one would be found to erect premises for a tenant from year to year. It is quite true that in fact the tenancy would be under a lease for a term of years; but it has already been shown that the conditions of a tenancy under a lease may be reduced to the conditions of a tenancy from year to year. Here, where the occupation really would be for a term, the tenant would not only have to pay the rent, but also to do the repairs himself; but the result would be the same, for having to do repairs, he would pay so much less rent to his landlord, and his landlord, having no repairs to do, would, after he had paid the ground rent, and laid by his annual quota for *ultimate renewal*, be able to appropriate to his own use the whole amount that remained. Neither would the case be altered if the occupier, instead of agreeing with some other person to build the premises for him, were to build them for himself. He would in that case simply pay rent to himself.

It is to be borne in mind that the condition of a tenancy from year to year does not involve a *change of tenant yearly*, although it does allow the yearly readjustment of the rent paid. Instances are continually met with where a holding under a yearly tenancy has continued longer than a holding even under a lease.

MACHINERY IN BUILDINGS.

Again, if the nature of the business carried on by the occupier involves the use of machinery so fixed to the building as to be part and parcel thereof, so long as it continues fixed to the building, the rent that the occupier must be deemed as paying must be such as would include a sum for the use of the machinery, as well as for the use of the buildings. This result will be arrived at by the same considerations as those by which the rent of the building must be estimated—that is, by considering that the machinery has been provided by the landlord, and that when provided the occupier pays rent for it. It is perfectly true that the machinery may really belong to the occupier, but it will usually be found, if that be the case, that he has a lease of the premises, and that, had he not a lease, he would not have put the machinery in, but would rather have rented premises with machinery already attached.

It may be asked whether all machinery in business premises must be rated, regardless as to whether it belongs to the occupier or to the owner. To settle this question, the fact must be determined whether or not the machinery is of such a nature that it must be let from year to year. A few examples will make this clear.

First, let the case of a mill built for a specific business, and fitted with the requisite machinery for carrying on that business, be taken. Such an erection will consist of land, buildings, machinery, and steam-power, whereby the machinery is driven. Such an hereditament as this would have to be taken as being let altogether, for it could only be used for the purposes for which it was erected, and no one taking such a place from year to year would be willing to provide the machinery and the steam-power. The rent paid for such a property would of course be subject to a much larger deduction for repairs, insurance, and renewals, than the rent of an ordinary dwelling-house.

Again, let the case be taken of premises so constructed that they could be adapted to any purpose, and suppose such premises to be fitted with a steam-engine, boilers, and shafting, but with no machinery. They are taken as being supplied with steam-engine, &c., because no tenant from year to year would be at the expense of erecting these, but finding them together with the shafting, he would be willing to pay a rent for the building, and for their use, much larger than he would be merely for the building. He would himself supply the machinery necessary for business, and this he would connect with the shafting. But the machinery thus supplied would not be rateable, because it is not necessarily let with the premises from year to year.

The limits within which machinery is and is not rateable have been very clearly defined by the two following decisions of the court.

First, as to the rateability of machines.

In the case of *R. v. Overseers of the Parish of Lee* (1 Law Reports, Q.B., 241), the question was raised whether certain plant and trade fixtures requisite for the manufacture of gas were rateable. This plant and trade fixtures were fully described in the case. They consisted of steam-engines and boilers, retorts, condensers, exhausters, purifiers, and meters. With regard to the meters, the court ruled that they were tenant's chattels, and therefore not rateable. But with regard to the steam-engines, the boilers, the retorts, the condensers, the exhausters, and the purifiers, the court ruled that they were rateable. Lord Chief-Justice Cockburn said:—

"Whatever doubt hung over the case at the commencement of the discussion has been removed by the arguments. I entirely agree that we must look, not to the position of the particular tenant, as to whether he has had to pay so much money down for the machinery and fixtures which are necessary for carrying on the works, but we must look to see what, as the whole concern stands, would be the rent that an imaginary tenant would give for the thing as a whole, excluding of course from consideration whatever would be mere chattels, and therefore would not pass under demise from the actual to the imaginary tenant. The way being thus cleared, I think the case presents really no difficulty. First, we think Mr. White has failed altogether to show that the meters are anything more than common chattels. The other things, it is plain, fall under one of two classes of articles, which are properly taken into account as enhancing the value of the building. In the first place, with regard to the retorts, Mr. O'Malley's argument has satisfied my mind upon the facts stated in this case, that the retorts are so permanently attached and annexed to the freehold, so fixed to the freehold, as to become part of it, and they must be taken, therefore, not as removable fixtures at all, but as fixtures so connected with the freehold as to become part and parcel of it. With regard to them there is no difficulty: the moment they are found to be part of the freehold, then, of course, they are rateable as the entire freehold would be. The other items seem to me, one and all, to fall under the principle of the decided cases referred to in the argument of *The Queen v. The Southampton Dock Company*, and *The Queen v. The North Staffordshire Railway Company*. In the latter case, the

Court, after taking time to consider, laid down this rule :—That where things which, though capable of being removed, are yet so far attached as that it is intended that they should remain permanently connected with the undertaking, or the premises connected with it, and to remain permanent appendages to it as essential to its working, those must be taken to be things increasing the rateable value of the land, and in respect of which the company were not entitled to have a deduction made. That principle applies directly to the present case. No one can doubt here that the purifiers and the gasholders are part and parcel of the works, which are absolutely necessary for the manufacture of gas, which is the purpose of the undertaking. No one can doubt that it was intended, when those things were erected, that they should remain permanently connected with those premises, that they should remain permanent appendages to it as essential to its working. They therefore fall within the rule laid down by the court in that case."

Justice Blackburn :—

" I am of the same opinion. The rateable value of the premises is to be determined, according to the Parochial Assessment Act, according to the rent that a hypothetical tenant, making the suitable deductions, would give for the rateable property; and the sessions have quite properly proceeded to try to ascertain that. It was disposed of early in the case that the question is, What would a hypothetical tenant give for the whole of the rateable property; and although, in point of fact, as stated in the 18th paragraph of the case, the person who actually did occupy would not pay rent for portions of the property which are fixed to the rateable premises so as to become part of it, which would be capable of removal, because instead of paying rent he would purchase them, yet we are agreed we must look to what a hypothetical tenant, taking a portion of the premises as they stand, would give for them with those portions which were annexed to the property so as to become part of the rateable property. Upon that, so far as that goes, the sessions were wrong. *The rule laid down has been that where the things are attached to the premises so as to be part of the premises, although they are removable afterwards, still they are part of the premises, although there may be a right to remove them.* But if things or chattels be merely fixed to the premises, and so far fastened to the premises as to be still chattels, but fixed and steadied for the purposes of use there, they remain chattels altogether, so that they would not be part of the premises at all —they would never cease, to use the phrase in the case of *Hellawell* v. *Eastwood*, to have the character of movable chattels; although fixed for the purpose of the enjoyment of them, still they remain movable chattels. The common illustration is a mirror which, in the ordinary way, would be screwed to the wall ; still it remains a movable chattel, and is no part of the premises.

I

On the other hand, a grate which is built into a chimney, although it is capable
of being removed by a tenant, would still be fixed to the premises, so that it
would be part of the premises, and therefore part of what would be considered
to be let to the hypothetical tenant and for which he would pay rent. That was
the principle laid down in the case of *R.* v. *North Staffordshire Railway Company*, where the things were similar to those in *R.* v. *Southampton Dock Company*. It was not of course in the precise words, but the same idea is conveyed. The things were cranes, turntables, and a variety of other things,
which were attached to the premises of the railway company, in one sense
screwed down, some of them firmly attached, and some of them not. The
court said that the things which were not attached to the freehold were to be
deducted, and an allowance made for them ; and the things which were affixed
to the freehold clearly enough would not be allowed for. Then the rule laid
down to guide the sessions in what they were to do was this: ' The articles
may be divided into three classes—first, things movable, such as office and
station furniture.' As I have said, all the cases agree in the principle. It is
clear these are not to be included. ' Secondly, things so attached to the freehold as to become part of it.' It is clear on the principle of all the cases that
no deduction is to be made for them, and they are to be considered as part of
what is left. ' Thirdly, things which, though capable of being removed, were
yet so far attached as that they were intended to remain permanently connected with the railway or the premises connected with it, and to remain permanent appendages to it, as essential to its working.' "

Justice Lush :—

" I am of the same opinion. The sum to be arrived at is ' the net annual
value of these premises at which they might reasonably be expected to let from
year to year, free of all usual tenant's rates and taxes, deducting the expenses
necessary to maintain them in that state.' The question is, what is the rateable subject which is comprised within the premises to be rated here? Now I
apprehend that the premises to be rated are to be taken as they are, with all
their fittings and appliances by which the owner has adapted them to a particular use, and which would pass as a part of the premises by a demise of them
to a tenant. It strikes me as expressing what in other words has been expressed in the two cases referred to by my learned brethren—wherever they
have become so far a part of the premises that they would pass by a demise of
those premises, they would form a part of the rateable subject of the inheritance
in the value for the purpose of rating. When we have to apply that test to
any particular footing, the question is not what a tenant might remove, not
what might be taken in execution under a writ against the owner, but what, as
between the landlord and tenant, would pass as a part of the premises which

he was to let, and what the tenant would take. Now, applying that rule, I cannot entertain a doubt that, with the exception of the meters, all the subjects of discussion here would pass as a necessary part of these premises. Without the retorts, purifiers, the steam-engines, and the gas-holders, the premises would be worthless for the purpose for which these things were erected—they would not be a gas manufactory at all. All these things are fixed and so far annexed as to be intended to be permanent, and as really necessary for the use of the premises as gasworks. Therefore, I think, except the meters, that the whole of these items ought not to be allowed in ascertaining the ultimate net annual value. I was struck in the early part of the argument with the finding in the 18th paragraph of the case. It appeared to me to distinguish this from the other cases, and for a time I entertained considerable doubt whether, on account of what was found there, all those items, although forming part of the rateable premises, ought not to be deducted. The finding is that, 'according to the practice and course of business in letting and hiring gasworks, the tenant would have to take to and find capital for all the property comprised under the heads meters, retorts, tenant's fixtures, and utensils, and would have to provide £150,000 for that purpose, and that a deduction in respect of such outlay was to be made in estimating, according to the provisions of the Parochial Assessment Act, what rent a tenant from year to year would give.' It struck me at first that, being so, the tenant would be bound to take these premises, making an outlay by purchasing all these articles, and the rent he would pay would be so much less, and that rent would represent the rateable value. Upon consideration, I quite agree with my brethren, and I am satisfied that that is not the right view, on the hypothesis that all these things, except the meters, do form part of the rateable subject, and ought to be taken into consideration in estimating the rateable value; because if a tenant and a landlord agree, the landlord, before the place is let, agrees that the tenant should pay down a price for part—that is, purchase part of the freehold—to say that the rateable value would be diminished would be absurd. I quite agree with my brethren, therefore, that it makes no difference at all whether the tenant takes the whole, assuming he did, or whether by contract between him and the landlord he purchases the fixed plant, which, if not so purchased, would be a part of the permanent premises, I quite agree that except the meters all the other matters are rateable, and that all of them ought to be disallowed."

Next, as to the non-rateability of machinery, we have the case of *R. v. the Overseers of Halstead* (Justice of Peace, vol. xxxi. p. 873). In this case the parish sought to rate the appellants for certain machinery used by the appellants in their business of silk winders and throwers. These machines, though bulky, were very light, and were fixed to the floor or to the walls for the purpose of being steadied. The buildings in which they were, were ordinary factory buildings, supplied with steam and water power, and could be used either for the purposes of a silk factory, or for any other purposes in which steam or water power was required.

The case, after fully describing the machinery, found that

"The machines are movable at will by being taken down, and put up either for repairs or re-arrangement, or change of use of the building from the silk trade to any other factory purpose, or any other cause, without damage or injury either to the machinery or to the buildings, and are commonly bought, or sold, used, and renewed as chattels."

The question for the court was whether this machinery was rateable.

Judgment was delivered by Cockburn, C.J.: —

"I think there is no difficulty in holding that the chattels and machinery used in this mill are not rateable. They are no doubt fixed to the freehold, but not so as to make them part of the freehold. According to the recent cases, if the chattels are so fixed to the freehold that on a demise they would pass with the premises, then they may be taken as part of the rateable value. But here, *the sessions find they are not so attached to the freehold,* but are merely fixed with a view to steady them. Therefore, the finding concludes the case, and the order of sessions must be confirmed."

J.J. Blackburn, Mellor, and Shee concurred.

In this case an attempt was made to stretch the principle of rating to an unwarranted extent. Since this decision, attempts have been made to unduly contract this principle, and to seek, under the authority of the Halstead decision, to exclude from rating, machinery that really is rateable. The question of the rateability or non-rateability of machinery must be determined by the special conditions of each particular case.

If the machinery is such that, before it can be erected, *special preparations* must be made for it, then such machinery must be rated, for if the premises in which it is erected were let from *year to year*, the machinery would of necessity have to be taken with the premises. Thus, take for example, a five-ton *steam hammer*. It would not be sufficient to place such a piece of machinery on the basement of any ordinary factory, and then work it; since it is absolutely necessary that a special foundation be prepared to receive the hammer, which must be securely bolted down to the foundation. Were this not done, the vibration of the hammer would soon destroy the whole building. Now, it is evident that, were the building in which the hammer is, let from *year to year*, the hammer must be let with it; unless, indeed, it were determined to discontinue using the building as a forge, then the hammer would be taken away, and, by so doing, the character of the hereditament would be entirely changed.

Steam hammer rateable.

On the other hand, take a *sewing-machine*, which is fixed to the wall or to the floor for the purpose of steadying it; since such machine can be readily taken from one building to another building without any *special preparation* being made for its reception, it would be most unjust to seek to enhance the rent which the one or the other building would command from *year to year* by any consideration of the value of the sewing-machine contained therein.

Sewing-machine not rateable.

Having considered the circumstances which should influence a tenant in determining the rent he can give for manufacturing or business premises, either with or without machinery attached, the next step is to see what conditions would determine the rent that should be given for water-mills and windmills.

WATER MILLS.

First, as regards *water mills*. It has already been shown that the rent which can be given for manufacturer's premises, with machinery attached, depends upon the amount required for the land, either as rent or purchase-money, and upon the amount of capital required to erect the buildings and machinery upon it. The principal circumstance which would influence the landlord of the ground in determining the amount he would require for his land, either as rent or purchase-money, would be the quantity of land there might be available for the purpose, and the demand that existed for it. If there were various plots which could be used for the required purpose, all equally available to the person who was going to build the premises, then there would be such an amount of competition between the owners of the plots that any one landlord could not demand any sum he pleased; but if there was but one plot available, the landlord's demand would be limited only by the ability of the tenant to pay the rent demanded; and the tenant's ability would depend, not upon his private resources, but upon the extra advantage which he could secure by occupying the piece of ground in question.

Take as an illustration the case of land in the city of London. There, because almost every available piece of ground is already occupied, the landlord of any piece that may be unoccupied can command a very large rent for such piece. Although the rent which can be obtained may seem to be any sum the landlord may choose to ask, yet such is not actually the case. The persons who will occupy the premises that may be built upon such a piece of land, are persons whose business necessitates their frequent presence in the city. Such persons can afford to pay a very large rent for premises conveniently situate, rather than occupy at a low rent premises inconveniently placed; because, although the rent itself might be low, the expenses the tenants would be put to, in cab-hire and loss of time, would more than counterbalance the high rent paid by them in the city. This circumstance will influence the owner of the ground, when he is determining the rent to be paid to him by the person who is willing to create the premises to be let from year to year; and this circumstance not only influences but limits the landlord of the ground, and also the landlord of the premises; for if the rent asked for the land is so high that, rather than pay such rent, increased as it would be by the rent of the buildings erected on the land, it would be cheaper for the tenant to go elsewhere, and to incur the expense of cabs and the loss of time, then that rent would be more than "the tenant could pay."

Now take a piece of land having a stream of water running through it, which can be profitably employed as a source of power. Then suppose this piece of ground employed as a site for manufacturing premises, either fitted with shafting merely, which is driven by the water-power, or else so built and fitted with machinery as to be adapted for some special use, and let us consider the circumstances which would influence a tenant from year to year in determining the rent he could give. It has already been shown what kind of considerations would influence a tenant in giving a rent for premises fitted with steam-power. In settling this rent he would make allowance for the fact that he would have to find fuel and labour for the engine and boilers. Having supplied these requisites, he would then be able to carry on his business, and to have everything under perfect control.

Then with regard to the premises erected upon that piece of land through which the water runs. The cost of creation may be taken as being the same as that of premises fitted with steam-power; for though, in the latter case, the creator would have to provide an engine and boiler, and in the former no engine would be required, yet an equal expenditure might have taken place in utilising the water-power.

The tenant of the premises supplied with water-power would pay at least as much rent as he would for precisely similar premises fitted with steam-power, for each of the premises is assumed to be equally commodious and convenient. But some further consideration would now have to be taken into account by him. He would, by using the premises supplied with water-power, be free from the expense of providing fuel for the engine, and also free from much of the expense of attending to the boiler. This would enable him to pay a greater rent for the premises, although he would not be willing to pay as rent all that he saved in fuel; for water-power not being so perfectly under control as steam-power, its use would occasion certain inconveniences and drawbacks. It will be clear that a very large share of the extra rent so paid then must be assigned to the owner of the ground, if the land did not belong to the person who erected the premises; for the owner, in letting the land, would be fully aware of the advantages inherent in it.

Again, if the premises built upon the land, having water-power, are fitted up for some special business, the circumstances already considered in the case of ordinary business premises fitted with special machinery would be equally applicable to this case also. But in consequence of water-power being available for driving the machinery, the rent paid in this case would include a sum for the mere use of the land, a sum for the use of buildings, a sum for the use of the machinery in the buildings, and a further sum for the benefit of the water which works the machinery.

In deducing the above principles, all consideration of any *further* rent which the tenant might give in consequence of the premises being so situate as of themselves to command trade, has been omitted. Such a case would be where a mill, say a flour-mill, was so situate that persons wishing to have wheat ground *must* go to that mill, although the charges of the miller for grinding be high. This would happen when there were no other mills near, and when the expense of carting wheat to the more distant mills would be greater than that of paying the higher charge made by the miller.

In such a case, the rent which the occupier would be willing to give would be yet again greater than in the last case. Such a rent, however, might be liable to be much reduced by change of circumstance, such as the erection of another mill near, when the miller, the occupier of the first mill, would become dependent for his business upon the attention which he paid, and not being able *of necessity* to secure a trade as he formerly did, he would no longer pay the large rent which he previously paid, but less, and by as much as was previously paid *as rent for the trade consequent upon the occupation.*

WIND MILLS.

The same principles will influence a tenant in determining the rent he can give for a wind mill; but inasmuch as the capabilities of the best wind mill are but small, the *amount* of rent determined would also be small in proportion.

TITHES.

The next class of hereditament to be considered is the tithe rent-charge. Under the statute of Elizabeth, tithes, amongst other kinds of property, are to be rated to the relief of the poor. Now that tithes have become commuted for a money-payment, the amount so paid, "the tithe rent-charge," being a hereditament for which a tenant from year to year will give a rent, it will be convenient next to investigate the manner in which this rent is to be deduced.

First, it may be remarked that the occupier of land which is subject to tithe, practically pays rent in two portions, and to two persons. One person being the owner of the land itself, the other being the owner of the tithe arising therefrom.

The Parochial Assessment Act evidently considers that the tenant of land subject to tithe shall pay the tithe commutation rent-charge, which is now paid instead of tithes, for the "rent is to be free from usual tenant's rate and taxes, and tithe commutation rent-charge, if any."

When it happens that land is tithe free, then, inasmuch as the tenant has no tithes to pay, he can pay a greater rent.

Hence it will follow, that the full value of the land is the rent *plus* the tithes. And whether the full value of the land be paid by the tenant directly to one landlord, or part of it be paid to one, and the remainder to another, will evidently not affect the real value.

Now, if land be tithe free, and the rent paid to the landowner be therefore greater than would be the case if the land were not tithe free, then also will the amount payable to the parish officers by the tenant for rates be greater. When land is not tithe free, then the rent paid to the landlord being less, the amount paid to the parish officers for rates will be less also.   But inasmuch as the parish officers rate the owner of the tithes for the amount of rent he receives, rates are actually paid upon the entire rent which the land yields.

The tenant pays to the tithe-owner an amount which not only includes the rent he would otherwise give to his landlord, but also the rates he must otherwise pay to the parish officers.   In the act for settling the amount of commutation rent-charge in lieu of tithes, it was specially enacted that such an amount should be arrived at as would include not only the amount of tithes, but also an amount in respect of the rates upon the tithes.

Assuming that the aggregate amount payable to the tithe-owner has been ascertained, the question then arises, what is the gross estimated rental and the rateable value thereof?

The first step in the investigation is to ascertain the total amount which is receivable in the year; for it is on account of the privilege of receiving this amount that the tenant is willing to give a rent. The inquiry as to what are the gross receipts has, in no previous case which has been considered been made, because, in all the other hereditaments, the gross receipts have not been the immediate element in ascertaining the rent; but here, where that which the tenant is supposed to rent is the privilege of receiving a certain amount of money, the question, " what that mount is," must be the first to be settled.   The proposed tenant would base an estimate of the rent he could give upon this consideration, because he would find that the mere fact of his being the holder of the privilege to receive the tithe rent must of necessity bring in an amount of money, a large portion of which he would be willing to pay to the owner in order to receive the remainder himself.   This remainder is the tenant's profit, and is analogous to the profit which a farmer expects to make out of the land, for the privilege of occupying which he is willing to pay a rent to the landowner.

Having determined the total amount the tenant would receive as tithe for any one year, the next question that would arise would be, what expenses he would have to incur in respect of that amount.

The whole question, both as to what should be the basis of the investigation and what deductions should be made from the gross receipts, having been the subject of judicial decision, it will be most convenient to refer to the cases, and to endeavour to set out the deductions as allowed by them. These cases are:—

1st. *R.* v. *Joddrell* (Barnwell & Adolphus, 403).

2nd. *R.* v. *Capel*, 12 A & E. 283.

3rd. *R.* v. *Goodchild*, 27 L. J. (N. S.) M. C. 233.

3rd*a*. Do. do. 27 L. J. (N. S.) M. C. 251.

4th. *R.* v. *Lamb*, 27 L. J. (N. S.) M. C. 233. 251.

5th. *R.* v. *Hawkins*, 27 L. J. (N. S.) M. C. 248.

6th. *R.* v. *Groves*, 29 L. J. (N. S.) M. C. 179.

R. v. *Joddrell* was argued before the Parochial Assessment Act was passed.

The first question raised was, whether the farmers who paid the tithes ought not to be assessed for them, because, if they had not paid them, they would have paid more rent; but it was ruled that they ought not. No such question could have arisen after the Parochial Assessment Act came into force, for therein it is enacted that the rent shall be free of tithe commutation rent-charge.

The second was, in fact, whether or not tenant's profit ought to be allowed to the rector, which the court decided in the affirmative.

The third was, whether land-tax ecclesiastical dues, and a deduction for the performance of the duties, ought to be allowed.

With respect to the deduction of land-tax, it was decided conditionally, and that it should be dependent upon the facts as to whether the other ratepayers paid it themselves, or paid it and deducted it from their rents.

With respect to the ecclesiastical dues, including tenths and synodals, it was decided that they should be allowed.

Lastly, with respect to the allowance for a performance of the duties, it was decided that these being personal, ought to be performed personally by the incumbent.

The next case, that of *R.* v. *Capel*, raised the question of the proportion of the tenant's profits, and the wider one also as to whether tithes were correctly rated upon an estimate of the rent a tenant would give for them, or whether they do not come within the operation of the proviso of the first section of the Parochial Assessment Act?

In this case, the Hon. and Rev. W. Capel, Vicar of Watford, was rated in respect of the small tithes, which amounted, in the year in question, to £660, the average payments for tenant's rates and ecclesiastical dues, being £82. 15s. The tithes were rated at £540, an allowance being made of £37. 5s. for tenant's profits. It was contended that the average profit made by the occupiers of land, being two-thirds of the rent, Mr. Capel was unequally rated, inasmuch as the amount at which he was rated bore a larger proportion to the full *yearly value* of his tithes than the amounts at which the other occupants were rated bore to their entire receipts.

With regard to the question as to the mode of rating, Lord Denman ruled that tithes were one of those hereditaments which are demisable at a yearly rent, and also that the "liabilities" of tithes to be rated are not different from the liabilities of land, nor is the "principle" upon which tithes are rated different, the principle invariably being to endeavour to find the *net annual produce after making proportionable equal deductions (i.e.,* as between land and tithes), and that consequently tithes do not fall within the scope of the proviso. In dealing with the question of the inequality of the profits allowed to Mr. Capel, as compared with those allowed to the farmer or other occupier, Lord Denman quoted from the case of *R. v. Skingle* a sentence in which annual value is defined as follows :—

"Of the whole of the annual *profits* or *value* of the land, a part belongs to the landlord in the shape of rent, and a part to the tenant; and whenever a rate is according to the rack rent (the usual and most convenient mode), it is in effect a rate on *part of the profits only.*"

But Lord Denman denied that this sentence expressed any proposition of law, or any conclusion as to fact from premises stated, and asserted that it was simply an assumption. He said that—

"The net annual value might with as much reason be represented by the *rack rent*, as that consideration which it would be worth while to give, beyond the rates, charges, and outgoings, for the right to occupy and take the actual produce."

This proposition of Lord Denman's does, it is submitted, truly define net value; for the annual value according to the former definition is an amount produced not by property alone, but by property and by *labour*, whereas in Lord Denman's proposition a clear distinction is made between the produce of property merely, and the produce of labour.

The net annual value as suggested by him is the produce of the *property* and the remainder of the total produce is the reward of *labour* expended in producing the whole. If a man possessing property chooses to expend labour also, he receives the whole produce, part of which is for the labour he himself has expended, and the rest is for the use of the property which belongs to him. If he does not choose to labour himself, but allows another man, who is willing to do so, to use his property, then he receives a return merely for such use. This proposition, given by Lord Denman, of net annual value is that adopted by the Parochial Assessment Act as being the *rateable* value of any hereditament.

In the case of *R.* v. *Capel*, the judgment of the Court was that the assessment was free from objection.

The next cases of *R.* v. *Goodchild*, *R.* v. *Lamb*, *R.* v. *Goodchild*, *R.* v. *Hawkins*, were argued upon the same day, and judgment given upon them as a whole.

The following were the points raised in the cases:—

1st. Should an allowance be made for estimated losses by non-payment of tithe?

2ndly.	Do.	do.	law expenses.
3rdly.	Do.	do.	estimated expenses of collection.
4thly.	Do.	do.	land tax.
5thly.	Do.	do.	property tax.
6thly.	Do.	do.	rates other than general rate, tithing rate, and sewers rate.

7thly.	Do.	do.	general rate, lighting-rate, and sewers-rate.
8thly.	Do.	do.	tenths.
9thly.	Do.	do.	ecclesiastical dues.
10thly.	Do.	do.	curate's salary.
11thly.	Do.	do.	amount paid towards the salary of the minister of the district church or chapel.
12thly.	Do.	do.	tenant's profits.
13thly.	Do.	do.	personal services of the appellant as officiating minister.

These were raised in the case *R.* v. *Goodchild* only.

14thly.	Do.	do.	first-fruits.

This additional point in *R.* v. *Lamb.*

15thly. Whether the gross estimated rental was correctly fixed (as was done in all the above cases) at the total amount received?

16thly. Whether an allowance should be made in respect of "certain payments of interest, and repayments of principal to the governors of Queen Anne's bounty," which the appellant had to make out of his tithe income?

These two points were raised in the case *R.* v. *Hawkins.*

17thly. Whether the appellant was liable to be assessed to the general rate, the lighting rate, and the sewers rate?

This last point was raised by the second case of *R.* v. *Goodchild.*

The above is the order in which the points were argued and decided by the court, but it will be convenient to re-arrange them.

Judgment was given by Mr. Justice Coleridge on the 23rd of February, 1858.

After Mr. Justice Coleridge had determined to what extent the questions raised above had already been decided by the cases of *R.* v. *Joddrell,* and *R.* v. *Capel,* and had shown that, in rating tithes, the Parochial Assessment Act must be complied with, he said:

"But as the language of the Act is *literally* applicable, if *all its particulars be looked to,* only to corporeal hereditaments, it is necessary in the assessment of the tithe-owner to proceed by *analogy,* which analogy must be as large and liberal as is necessary to effectuate substantial equality in the assessment, and at the same time be compatible with the maintenance of the principle."

He then proceeded to show that, whilst certain charges and outgoings specified in the Assessment Act could not be allowed, because they did not exist, certain others did exist, and, though not specified, ought to be allowed.

Then the net annual value, or rateable value of the tithe rent-charge, being

" The rent at which the same might reasonably be expected to let from year to year, free of all usual tenant's rates and taxes, and tithe commutation rent, if any, and deducting therefrom the probable average annual cost of repairs, insurance, and other expenses, if any, necessary to maintain it in a condition to command such rent,"

it will be most convenient to treat of the various allowances claimed above in the order in which they would arise in deducing the rateable value.

Arranging them in this manner, they may be collected into five groups, viz. :—

1st. The gross income of the tithe rent-charge, or the actual produce, to enjoy which a tenant is willing to pay rent.

2nd. The necessary outgoings, &c.

3rd. Rates and taxes.

4th. Tithe commutation rent-charge.

5th. Repairs, &c.

Of these groups, the first requires no further remark. The second group will include the following claims:—

(3.) *a. Cost of Collection.*—The deduction of the amount actually paid for this item was, *as a principle*, allowed and admitted in the course of the argument, though some confusion seems to have arisen respecting the amount claimed for tenant's profits, viz., £92, that being stated to be allowed inclusive of this and the next two items.

The amount of the cost of collection per cent. may vary considerably, according as the tithe rent-charge has to be collected from two or three landowners or from a large number of tenants.

(2.) *b. Law Expenses.*—This claim was also allowed, the necessity of the assumed tenant having to consult his lawyer occasionally being admitted.

(1.) *c. Bad Debts.*—These also were allowed.

(10.) *d. Curate's Salary.*—Here the claim of an allowance for the curate's salary was allowed, although in the case of *R.* v. *Joddrell* a claim for providing for the duties of the incumbency was disallowed. Nor are the two cases contradictory, for the circumstances were different. In the latter case the curate acted as a deputy. In the former cases the curate was employed as an assistant. And it was pointed out in the judgment that, in the case of Mr. Goodchild, the bishop could compel him, under the 1 & 2 Vict., cap. 106, to appoint a curate to *assist* him in his duties, and, in the other case, that of Mr. Lamb, although the value of the incumbency and the number of parishioners was below the standard requisite to give the bishop authority, yet the duties were greater than one man could perform ; and it was held, therefore, in both the former cases, that inasmuch as the curate's salary was really a necessary diminution, it ought to be allowed.

In a subsequent case, *R.* v. *the Overseers of Scriven Tenter Gate*, 32 L. J. (N. S.), M. C. 161, where the vicar, in addition to the tithe rent-charge, derived an income from certain glebe lands outside of the parish, Lord Chief Justice Cockburn decided that the true principle was to set the curate's stipend against all the sources of income of the rector or vicar. This ruling as to the allowance of a curate's salary has, however, been reversed in the case of *R.* v. *the Inhabitants of Sherford and Others*, 2 Law Reports, Q. B. 503. And this on the principle (laid down in the Mersey Dock cases) stated by Mr. Justice Blackburn during the argument of this case, viz.,

"The principle of decision in those cases is, that where a person is in the occupation of property capable of yielding a profit, the occupier is rateable in respect of that profit, *and it is quite immaterial to whom* it is paid. If the tithes were rendered in kind, and were rented, the lessee would be rateable in the same amount, whether the whole rent were paid to the incumbent, **or part** went to a curate."

(11.) *e. Claim in respect of a contribution towards the salary of the minister of the district chapel.*—This claim was not positively settled, because the facts stated were not clear enough, but the principles which would determine it were clearly laid down. These were, that if the contribution was merely *voluntary*, and the rector could, if he pleased, withhold it, it could not be allowed as a deduction; but if it was paid in consequence of some formal grant of tithe rent-charge, which could not be revoked, then, inasmuch as it was a necessary lessening of that which was to be let, the claim must be allowed, although it was intimated that the recipient of this portion of the gross amount might be liable to be rated for it.

(13.) *f. Claim for personal services of the appellant as officiating minister.*—This claim was disallowed upon the ground that it was a *duty* growing out of an institution to a cure of souls; for the tithe rent-charge was a property the right to which accrued by induction to the temporalities, and no necessary relation exists between the duties of the incumbent and the amount of tithes.

(12.) *g. Tenant's profits.*—The Court seems to have disallowed this claim, apparently upon the ground that the amount for collection was inclusive of tenant's profit. But the amount for collection, whether it be a large or a small per-centage, has been assumed above to be the amount *actually paid* to a collector for gathering the tithe commutation rent-charge. As the tenant would pay this sum to his collector, there must be some further amount which he himself would receive as a benefit out of the tithes; for no man would place himself under liabilities by taking a tithe rent-charge without some profit to himself; and he certainly would not take the rent-charge merely to secure the collection, for collection would involve labour, and the amount above assumed for collection has merely been such as would pay for labour, and not for labour and liability. All the previous claims (save *d, e, f,* above) must be satisfied by the tenant before he himself would receive one farthing. There will therefore be some allowance under this head as remuneration to the tenant himself.

K

In the case of *R.* v. *Capel* an allowance for tenant's profits was made, and such allowance sanctioned by the Court. Of course the amount of tenant's profits in any case must be determined by the peculiar circumstances of the case. Here, in the argument upon the case of *R.* v. *Goodchild*, certain comparisons were made between the *amount* claimed and that in the case of *R.* v. *Capel;* but no comparisons can fairly be drawn between any two cases.

The sum of the above claims and allowances will complete Group 2. The total amount of Group 2 taken from that of Group 1 will leave the sum which a tenant would give if he had no rates and taxes to pay. But as he is assumed to pay rates, and taxes, and tithe commutation rent-charge; this sum, which is made up of rent, rates and taxes, and tithe, must be separated into its component parts.

GROUP 3.—*Rates and Taxes.*

(6.) *a. Poors rate.*—This was as a general principle admitted, yet it was contended that there were certain special features in this particular case which would influence this principle—viz., that the tithe commissioner, in fixing the tithe commutation rent, had added thereto an amount in respect of poors rate upon the tithe having previously been paid by the parishioners; but the Court decided that this had been done in virtue of a special enactment, and did in no way bar the tithe owner from claiming it as a deduction. The claim was therefore allowed.

(7, 17.) *b. General rate, lighting rate, sewers rate.*—Two questions were now raised—1st, Whether the appellants were liable to these rates at all; 2ndly, Whether, being liable to them, they were entitled to deduct them. The latter point must have been admitted had the Court decided the liability. Then with regard to the general rate and the lighting rate. The Court decided liability to the general rate on account of the construction of the statute imposing it; and the Court decided liability to the lighting rate because the tithe rent-charge fell within the description of property upon which the lighting rate is imposed, and did not fall within the description of property exempted.

Lastly, with regard to sewers rate, the Court found that the tithe rent-charge was not liable to this impost, inasmuch as it was exempt from sewers rate previous to the passing of the Act under which it and the two other rates were levied (18 & 19 Vict., cap 120), and was therefore still exempt therefrom, in virtue of sect. 164.

(5.) *c. Property tax.*—The claim made under this head by Mr. Goodchild amounted to £46. 13s. 4d., the total amount of tithes being £940, and was, therefore, for the property tax upon the entire income. But this income is really resolvable into three parts —viz., the rent a tenant would give, tenant's profits, and necessary outgoings. The tenant must pay income tax upon *his* profits, which income tax he would deduct before he determined the rent he could give. This amount, Mr. Goodchild being his own tenant, he, it was decided, was entitled to deduct. But the rest of the income tax being payable in respect of the rent, he, as tithe owner, received from his tenant, could not, it was decided, in reason be deducted, but ought to be paid out of the net annual value, when ascertained, and this because the income tax upon the rent was not a usual tenant's tax.

(4.) *d. Land tax.*—This claim the Court disallowed, showing that, although allowed in *R.* v. *Joddrell*, it was so because all the other ratepayers in the parish paid it also. And that, since that decision, the Assessment Act had come into force, and that under this Act the only rates and taxes from which the rent was to be free were "usual tenant's rates and taxes;" and further, that inasmuch as this tax was specially required and allowed by the landlord to the tenant, who had to pay it in the first instance, it was not a usual tenant's tax, but a landlord's, and was therefore not to be deducted.

GROUP 4.—*Tithes.*—Of course, as the tithe commutation rent-charge is not subject to tithes, no such deduction can be made. Yet it is subject to certain payments which may be deemed analogous to tithe. These are :—

(14.) *a. First fruits.*

(9.) *b. Ecclesiastical dues.*

(8.) *c. Tenths.*

The whole of these deductions were allowed, and were the subject of these remarks :—First, that first fruits being payable in respect of the first year's occupation, ought to be deducted from the assessment of that year. Secondly, that first fruits and tenths being payable in respect of the whole *annui proventus*, and not of the tithes only, the total amount must not be deducted from the tithes, but only a proportionate amount.

The sum of these two groups—viz.,

GROUP 3. — *Poor rate; General rate; Lighting rate; Tenant's Income tax.*

GROUP 4.—*First fruits; Tenths; Ecclesiastical dues*—

will be the total amount of "tenant's rates, taxes, and tithe commutation rent-charge" to be deducted from that amount which the tenant would pay as rent if he had no rates and taxes to pay.

It has already been shown that that which remains after Group 2 has been deducted from Group 1, is the amount which the tenant would give as rent if he had neither rates nor taxes to pay. We have now seen what rates and taxes it would be necessary to pay. And the problem is to determine their amount. The difference between the amount of Group 2 and Group 1 consists of rates, taxes, and rent. But rent itself includes two things—viz., net annual value, *i.e.*, rateable value, and repairs. It is upon the net annual value that the amount of the rates is computed. Hence, to deduce the amount of rates, we must first deduct from that amount, consisting of repairs, rateable value, and rates and taxes, the cost of the repairs. The remainder will then consist of two parts—net annual value, and rates and taxes. Assume that the rates and taxes, as set out, amount to 5s. in the pound of rateable value. Then the above remainder will be made up of five parts—viz., four parts rateable value, and one part rates and taxes. Consequently one-fifth part of the remainder represents the *amount* of rates and taxes to be paid.

The amount of rates and taxes having been found, and that amount deducted from the difference between the amount of Group

2 and that of Group 1, will give the rent a tenant from year to year would pay for the tithe rent-charge, and which rent is THE GROSS ESTIMATED RENTAL, according to the Parochial Assessment Act.

Of the questions which were raised by the three cases of Goodchild, Lamb, and Hawkins, all have been noticed except two. Of these, one was as to whether "the gross estimated rental had been correctly fixed at the total amount received." But this does not seem to have been noticed by the court. Yet it was evidently wrong to call the total amount of the tithe commutation rent, the gross estimated rental thereof; for it is neither the gross estimated rental as defined by the Poor Law Circular, nor is it the gross estimated rental of the Parochial Assessment Act. It certainly is not

" The rent which would be paid to a landlord who himself undertakes to pay all the usual tenant's rates and taxes with which the hereditaments or premises rented by the tenant are chargeable, together with the tithe commutation rent-charge and the expense of upholding the buildings in tenantable repair, insurance against loss by fire, and other expenses, if any shall exist, necessary to maintain such hereditaments in a state to command such *gross rental;*"

for the total amount of the tithes not only includes all the above items, but others in addition. And it certainly is not the " *rent at which the same might reasonably be expected to let from year to year free of usual tenant's rates and taxes, and tithe commutation rent-charge if any.*" The rent which has been above deduced may be taken therefore as the real gross estimated rental of the tithe rent-charge.

It only now remains to consider what deduction must be made from this gross estimated rental in order to arrive at the rateable value. These deductions must be of the nature of repairs, insurance, and other expenses, if any, necessary to " maintain the premises in a state to command such rent."

Arguing from analogy, so as to determine these deductions in the case of the tithe rent-charge, the first deduction under this head will be the repairs, insurance, and renewal of the chancel, which the rector must himself maintain.

Under this head may be mentioned the last but one of the questions raised by the cases above—viz., Whether an allowance should be made in respect of certain payments of interest, and repayments of principal, to the governors of Queen Anne's Bounty, which Mr. Hawkins made *out of his income*, in respect of monies borrowed by him for the purpose of rebuilding his parsonage house? The Court ruled that he was entitled to an allowance for the probable average "annual cost of repairs, &c.," but that this claim could not be allowed:

" For if a landowner rebuilt his mansion, the expense may swallow up more than the whole income of the estate for the year, but his estate does not thereby become not rateable, and the estate is not the less productive, nor does he the less receive the income because he expends that and more on the building a new house upon it. And so, before the statute passed, if the incumbent rebuilt, as many did, his parsonage-house out of his own means, he must still have been rateable for his tithes. So again, if the landowner had borrowed the money on the security of his estate, he could not have claimed to deduct the interest, or any portion of the principal, which he might repay under agreement, from his poor rate, even if he were tenant for life only. The incumbent who borrows from Queen Anne's Bounty, and mortgages his tithes under the statute, is in exactly the same situation."

The gross estimated rental, lessened by the above allowances for repairs, &c., of chancel, and of the parsonage-house, when circumstances require this allowance, gives the rateable value of the tithe rent-charge.

A reference to one other case is desirable—viz., that of *R.* v. *Grores*, 29 L. J. (N. S.) M. C. 179. In this the appellant was the *lessee* of the rectory tithe rent-charge, and other premises at Herne Hill, which he rented from the Archbishop of Canterbury. The archbishop had granted a portion of the tithe rent-charge, to the amount of £40 per annum, to the perpetual curates of Thorington for ever. This had been done under statutory powers. The appellant, in virtue of the decision in *R.* v. *Goodchild*, claimed that he was entitled to the deduction of the £40 so paid in determining the rateable value of his holding, he, by agreement with the archbishop, paying this portion of the rent of the tithe-rent to the curate. The appellant held his tithe rent-charge upon a lease for twenty-one years, and every seven years surrendered the lease and received a fresh one for twenty-one years, paying a certain fine upon each renewal. The payment of this £40 had only been made since 1848, and the archbishop, in consideration of the appellant paying this sum, demanded and received a less fine on renewal than he otherwise would have done.

In consequence of this condition of things the Court held that the appellant was not entitled to have deducted the £40 in determining his assessment to the relief of the poor; Lord C. J. Cockburn saying, that, in fact, what the appellant had undertaken to pay was so much rent for that portion of the tithe rent-charge paid to the archbishop, and so much for that portion paid to the perpetual curate. He was the *occupier of the whole*.

Mr. Justice Crompton agreed to this, and added, that he might have paid the whole consideration to the archbishop, and that the occupier derived the same benefit from the occupation whether he paid the £40 to the archbishop or to the curate.

This case was simply a payment of rent to two landlords instead of one; for whether he paid rent to one or to two landlords did not in any way lessen the rent he was willing to pay, nor did he pay the rent twice over, for the archbishop took this payment into consideration in determining the amount of fine upon renewal.

It may be here remarked, that, though the tenancy was not from year to year, it was one capable of being reduced to a tenancy from year to year; for the amount of fine paid down, and a certain annual rent, was but the equivalent of a larger annual rent with no fine.

In the next class to be considered, the hereditaments, from their very nature, must at some time or other be exhausted. It has already been shown that the Parochial Assessment Act provides against the effects of wear and tear where possible, but in these properties it is physically impossible to provide for their continued reparation.

On the rateable value of sand and gravel pits, &c.

These hereditaments are sand and gravel pits, clay, chalk, and ballast pits; mines, and similar properties. In this class the produce, for the right to enjoy which the rent is paid, is derived from the *sale* of the *corpus*, and not merely the use of it.

SAND AND GRAVEL PITS.

The considerations which will influence the tenant of the above properties in determining the rent he can give, must be next examined.

The tenant would first ascertain the extent of ground over which sand and gravel might be found in the neighbourhood, in order to see what likelihood there would be of competition. He would also ascertain what demand existed for sand and gravel. Next, what the quality of these was; whether the sand had an extraordinary value in consequence of peculiar fineness, colour, sharpness, or other peculiarity which would create a special demand for it, or whether it was of an ordinary nature; also what the quality of the gravel was. These elements, which, amongst others, would determine the rent, are of an innate character, and entirely independent of external circumstances.

Having satisfied himself respecting the probable quantity of the *corpus* he could dispose of during the year, and the price he could obtain for it, he would then ascertain whether there would be any competition likely to influence either the quantity he sold or the price he could command. If none existed, then he might fairly argue, that inasmuch as a certain demand for sand or gravel existed, he, by the mere occupation of the pit in question, would be able to sell a certain quantity at a certain price. If competition did exist, then either his receipts might be less, or else he would have to expend much additional labour in his business in order to secure those receipts. Next, he would consider what working expenses he would be put to in "getting" the sand and gravel, and in preparing it for sale. Having determined these matters, and also the amount of profit which would satisfy himself, and which would be more or less, according as it was necessary to pay

more or less personal attention to the business, he would be in a
position to determine the rent he could reasonably afford to give.
This rent is usually paid in the form of a *royalty*, the total amount
of which, depends upon the quantity of material sold during the
year. It must be assumed that the occupier of the sand or gravel
pit sells the material to persons who themselves fetch it from the
pit, or if the occupier of the pit delivers it in his carts and horses,
then the estimate of the rent he could pay would be entirely exclusive of any *profits* he made by carting the sand or gravel.

The following illustration may be given :—Suppose a certain
district, in which there is a fair natural supply of sand or gravel.
Suppose also another district some miles off, in which there is a
great demand for these materials, and that the occupier of a pit in
the sand district does a large business in "getting" and carrying
them to the place where there is a great sale for them. Arrived
there, he disposes of the materials at a high price per cubic yard.
It would not be just to ascertain his total receipts, and then
deducting the expenses of "getting," and the expenses of carting,
and a tenant's profits, to call the remainder rent and taxes. For
although the materials fetched a high price when taken into the
district where they were sold, yet a very large proportion of the
price paid would be a remuneration for the trouble of carting, and
the remainder only, which would represent their natural value at
the pit, ought to be taken as the basis of an estimate of the rent.
But if in the district where the great demand exists, there is also
a pit of sand and gravel, of a quality equal in all respects to that
brought from a distance, then a tenant would give a very high
royalty for the privilege of occupying that pit ; for he would know
that the mere occupation would enable him to sell a large quantity
of the material at almost the same price as had hitherto been paid
for the material and the carting. He would sell this with but little
personal trouble and anxiety to himself, and he would therefore be
willing to pay a large proportion of the entire profit as rent for the
privilege of appropriating to himself the remainder.

Here, of course, as in all other hereditaments, it will frequently be found, as a fact, that tenants occupy sand and gravel pits upon conditions other than the payment of a royalty based upon quantity sold, such as a fixed rent for a term of years. *But in such cases the fixed rent ought not to be taken as the basis of the assessment.* But an inquiry should be made as to what would be the rent paid by a yearly tenant. Or, again, a tenant may hold under a royalty of so much per yard, the total amount varying with the quantity of material sold during the year; such royalty, however, having been settled some years back. In this case, again, the royalty must not of necessity be made the basis of the assessment. For the very condition of a tenancy from year to year involves the yearly re-adjustment of the rent paid, and a royalty agreed upon some years back might be too high or too low, and that in consequence of an imperfect appreciation of the value of the material sold, or from a change of circumstances, or other cause.

Having, with a due regard to the above circumstance, and to the amount of rates to which the tenant is liable, determined the rent he could pay, the next consideration is as to what deductions must be made from that rent, in order to arrive at the rateable value?

A simple case may be assumed—viz., where a gravel pit is situate in a field having a frontage to a public road. The field will have a fence separating it from the road, and a private road or cart track leading from the road into the pit. This shall be taken as the condition in which the pit was when the tenant took it. Then, as to the deductions for "repairs, insurance, and other expenses, if any, necessary to maintain the premises in a state to command such rent." First, a deduction must be made for the expenses of maintaining the fencing, the gates, and the private road. As to insurance, none would be required. Having made these deductions, the question arises, What deduction, if any, must be made from the rent in consequence of the fact that the gravel must at some time be exhausted? Now, the words of the Act which would justify any deduction under this head are, "to *maintain the premises* in a state to command such rent." But, from the very nature of this class of premises, it is a physical impossibility to "maintain them in a state to command such rent." They must at some time or other be exhausted, and then must go out of the rate. It is quite true that the landlord, by laying aside each year, out of the rent paid, a sum of money to accumulate at compound interest, would, when that which yielded him rent was exhausted, be in possession of such a sum as to enable him to buy another field of gravel, either in the same parish, if he could get one, or, failing in this, have a sum of money which he could invest in some other way, and so derive for himself a revenue from other sources in lieu of that revenue which ceased, in consequence of that which produced it being exhausted. But the words of the Act are not, to "maintain the premises in a state to command such rent, or else to provide fresh premises to command some other rent;" but they are simply "to maintain such premises in a state to command such rent." If the premises cannot be so maintained, then it would seem that no deduction ought to be made on account thereof. The parish would be recompensed for a future failure of rate in respect of this particular hereditament by levying a greater present rate. Possibly it would be prudent in the landlord to lay aside each year such a sum as would enable him to derive continually an income from his capital. But that income would not of necessity be derived from the rent of an hereditament. He might choose to invest his capital in the funds.

BALLAST PITS.

A similar course of reasoning to the above will determine the rent a tenant could pay for ballast pits. There are pits so situate, that the occupiers of them can obtain an income by the sale of ballast to ships which have come into port with cargoes, and make the return voyage in ballast. Here there must be a special combination of circumstances necessary to the existence of such pits; they must be near navigable water of such depth as to enable ships to come in to obtain the ballast, and there must be land so close to this water, on which land again there must exist such a superabundance of earth as will permit of its being sold without detriment to the remainder. The very combination of conditions requisite are such that in but few sites can they exist; therefore competition will be almost entirely out of the question. It is not enough that the navigable water exists, or that the land possessing a superabundance of earth exists. These must be so situate that communication can readily be kept up between them, and not only that, but, in addition, there must exist a demand for ballast. As, in the last case, the rent the tenant could give would depend upon the quantity of material he could sell during the year, the expenses he would incur in "getting" the same, and upon the amount of profit he could reasonably expect to realise by the occupation. In determining this profit, he would have to consider that the total receipts were almost entirely dependent upon the natural situation of the pit, and not upon *his personal exertions*. He would be in receipt of an income as a *necessary consequence* of the occupation of the premises. Such being the case, he would reasonably expect to give to the owner of the property a large share of the entire net produce; for the owner would not be willing to let the pits from year to year unless he did receive such a share; he would feel that he could, if he kept them in his own hands, and bestowed the requisite amount of labour upon them, which would be small, himself secure, not merely such large share of the net profits, but the whole of them. In this, as in all other cases, the supposition must be made that the pits, with the entire conveniences for shipping the ballast, are ready to the occupier's hand when he takes the hereditament, and that he has not to expend any money in developing the capabilities of the property. As in all other cases which have been noticed, it frequently happens, as a matter of fact, that the occupier has himself expended money in developing and improving the property leased.

In one case that came under my notice the occupier not only held his premises from two or three persons, but had paid a large premium and spent much money in creating the hereditament. The land whereon the superabundance of earth existed was separated from the river into which the ships came for ballast by a public high road, and by land belonging to another person, whilst the land immediately abutting upon the river belonged to the owner of the ballast land.   This being the situation, the occupier had leased the ballast land and the river frontage from one landlord, paying a heavy rent for the same.   He had also leased the intervening land from a second landlord, and then upon the river frontage had built a wharf, and connected the ballast land with the wharf by a tramroad passing under the public road.   In addition to this, he had incurred expense in obtaining the remissions of certain restrictions previously in force.   Having done all this, he carried on an extensive business in the sale of ballast.   The question then arose, what was the gross estimated rental and rateable value of this hereditament?   In deducing these, the fact that the occupier had spent so much money on the hereditament was entirely ignored; no regard was paid to the rents which he paid to the landlords; it was simply considered what rent he might have reasonably expected for the entire holding from a tenant from year to year.   This was determined upon the principles already laid down, and a certain gross estimated rental deduced, and then a rateable value.   Out of the rateable value it was necessary to pay the various rents to which the premises were liable.

The difference between the rent which the occupier in this case might have expected to receive, had he sublet, and the rents which he had agreed to pay, would be the return he would get for the money he had expended to benefit other persons' property.   But, inasmuch as he was himself the occupier, he received, in addition to this difference, the amount of tenant's profits, which were his reward for the labour he continued to expend; the other receipt being in respect of the capital he had expended.

The question with reference to the deductions which ought to be made from the gross estimated rental to arrive at the rateable value in such a case as this will be of interest.   To determine this, a review of the various circumstances affecting the property is requisite.   The entire hereditament consisted of the ballast-yielding land, the land on which the tramway was built, and the land upon which

the wharf was built.   These various plots were held upon various
leases by the occupier, as lessee; each of the leases would terminate
at a different time.   Then, is the occupier entitled to any deduction in respect of his leases expiring.   The only deductions authorised by the Parochial Assessment Act are for "repairs, insurance,
and other expenses, if any, necessary to maintain the premises in a
state to command such rent."   Is, then, a deduction in respect of
an expiring lease a deduction "necessary to maintain the premises
in a state to command such rent"?

To determine this, the case of a house built upon leasehold ground
may be considered.   In that case would the mere expiration of the
lease lessen the rent which the house might reasonably be expected
to let for?   It would appear not.   For the occupier, instead of paying rent to one landlord, as owner of the house, would simply pay
rent to another landlord, as owner of the land; and in consequence
of the expiration of the lease, the now owner of the house; whether
the house were owned by one man or another would not affect the
rent it would let for.   Next, let us suppose that part only of the
house is built upon leasehold land; then, out of the total rent paid
to the owner of the house and of part of the land, the rent of the
other part of the land would be paid.   When the lease of the latter
part expired, then so much of the house as stood upon the leasehold
land would become the property of the owner of that land.   But
whether the house was owned by one or by two persons, still it
would command the same rent.   But the owner of the leasehold
land would then have a greater share of the entire rent than he had
before.   It may be said that, on the expiration of the lease of the
ground, the lessee might choose to pull his portion of the house
down (a case that I have actually known), and that, therefore, the
house would cease to "command such rent."   It would have that
effect.   But the only way to prevent this would be for the owner of
the one part of the land to buy the remainder and the house upon
it.   But there is no power to compel the owner of the other part to
sell; nor could any deduction from the rent, towards providing a
fund for the purpose of buying, be rightly made, for by such a

purchase property would be increased. No deduction is authorised to provide for the increase of property, but only for the conservation thereof.

It may, therefore, be stated that no deduction should be made from the gross estimated rental of the ballast pits to provide for the expiration of the various leases. For the expiration of the leases would not of necessity cause the destruction of the hereditament, since it would still, as a whole, command the same rent, whether one man owned the ballast-yielding land, another, the tramroad and the land on which it stood, and a third the wharf and the land on which it stood, or whether one man owned the entire property.

The next question is that with regard to the ceasing " to command such rent," which result is inevitable when the ballast is all sold. What deductions, if any, must be made to provide for this ? As to the provision against the exhaustion of the ballast, that has already been considered. But here the entire hereditament consists of other parts besides the ballast-land, and these are of such a nature as they can be continually kept in a state to "command such rent," viz., the tramroad and the wharf. Inasmuch as they require repair, and the wharf insurance, a deduction for these must be made. Inasmuch as mere repairs would not keep them in a condition to "command such rent," a deduction must also be made towards a future renewal of those parts which will require renewal. But in addition to these, another question arises. The rent commanded is in consequence of the joint action of the three parts—the wharf, the tramway, and the ballast-yielding land.

It will be evident that it is by the joint operation of the three parts, that the hereditament as a whole commands the rent which it does. Apart from the tramway and the wharf, the ballast-pit would command but little, if any rent; and, apart from the ballast-pit, the tramway and the wharf, again, would also command but little rent. It has already been shown that the whole hereditament consists of various parts; one part, which must of necessity be destroyed at some future time, and other parts, which may, by continual repairs and renewals, be always maintained. But it has also been shown that the whole rent is commanded by the joint operation of each of these parts. Hence, when the time arrives when one part can no longer act, the other two parts will of necessity cease to command the rent which the whole did. They may cease to command any rent at all. In the latter case they would become valueless, and they might become so before they were worn out. Then the question is, must any deduction be made from the gross estimated rental of the whole, in respect of the recoupment of the capital invested in the parts? We have seen that a deduction must be made both for repair, insurance, and renewal, yet the probable average annual amount of such deduction would not be sufficient to recoup the loss that would arise from those parts becoming valueless before they were worn out. Of course, if they, *per se*, could command any rent, then such a question would not arise, for, from the rent they could command, a deduction would have to be made for their maintenance. It would seem, however, in the case of their becoming valueless, that a deduction for the recoupment of the capital invested in them could not be made, for no such deduction is authorised by the Parochial Assessment Act. It would appear that the same arguments which apply in the case of the expended gravel or sand, apply here also. No injustice is done thereby, for the parish officers would, while the premises as a whole continued in existence, rate them at a higher sum in consequence of the rent being subject only to a deduction for keeping *part* of them in a state " to command such rent," than they otherwise would do; and with regard to the owners, the rents which they would receive would be so much greater than average property of an equal total value commands, that they could, out of the rent, afford to make provision for the time when the rent of the property might either entirely or in great part cease.

It so happened in the above case, that the whole of the property was situate in the same parish. Had the centre of the road mentioned been the boundary of two parishes, a very complicated question would have arisen as to the apportionment of the entire rent be-

tween the two parishes. As this question must be considered hereafter, it is not necessary now to notice it.

CHALK QUARRIES, CLAY PITS, AND
BRICKFIELDS.

Chalk and clay pits differ from sand, gravel, and ballast pits inasmuch as the occupier of them does not always derive his profit
from the sale of the material which the ground yields, but from its
manufacture. The occupier of a chalk pit in many instances does
not sell the chalk, but burns it into lime, and the occupier of a
clay pit does not sell the clay, but manufactures it into bricks,
tiles, or pottery. Under these circumstances, the rent which
such properties command is determined, as in the previous cases,
by an inquiry as to the quantity of material yearly obtained, and
the amount of *royalty* which ought reasonably to be paid thereon,
having regard always to the particular quality of the material
produced. In estimating the *royalty*, reference will be had, as in
the other cases, to the circumstance of there being a great or small
quantity of chalk or clay producing land in the neighbourhood.
But the inquiry must not be extended to the profits made by the
occupier out of the business he carries on as a manufacturer of the
raw material. In determining the rent of brickfields or potteries,
no notice must be taken of the profits made from brick-making or
pottery-making, for these arise as a consequence of the personal
skill required therein, and not as a necessary consequence of the
occupation of the ground.

It is true, that only a single piece of ground producing clay fit
for bricks, or for some special kind of bricks, may be situate in a
neighbourhood in which there is a demand for them, and this circumstance will be taken into account in determing the *royalty* to
be paid upon the raw material. All the profit made by carrying
on the business of brick-making, lime-burning, &c., is essentially
due to the ability of the tenant ; for out of the same premises, one
man, being master of his business, will make a fortune, while another, through ignorance, will lose money. If, however, the con-

ditions are such, that the mere occupation of the premises *will of
necessity involve* a large business in the manufactured article, then
in that case the rent a tenant may be expected to give will be proportionately increased. Such a case occurred in one of the parishes
which the late Mr. Penfold valued. The hereditament in question
was a lime-kiln, situate in a part of the country which consisted of
one mass of chalk. The rateable value of this property was fixed at an
almost nominal sum, because anybody acquiring land could readily
have procured chalk and made lime; but it subsequently transpired
that, in the neighbourhood, although chalk could be had anywhere,
those who required lime were, by a peculiar regulation of the
manor, compelled to buy at this particular lime-kiln. Upon these
facts becoming known, Mr. Penfold fixed the rateable value of the
property at a high amount, nor was his rating appealed against.

The decision of the Court of Queen's Bench in the following
cases of *Westbrook* and *Everest* clearly establishes the principle
upon which those properties, where the "corpus" is being annually
exhausted, should be rated.

Queen v. *E. Westbrook* (10 Q.B. 178, and 16 L.J. Ref (N.S.), M.C. 87).

"On an appeal by *E. Westbrook and others* against a rate for the relief of the
poor of the parish of Heston, in the county of Middlesex, the quarter sessions
for the said county of Middlesex confirmed the rate, subject to the opinion of
the Court of Queen's Bench on the following:—

CASE.

"The appellants are brickmakers by trade, and for the purpose of carrying
on that trade they occupy various plots of land in the parish of Heston, in the
county of Middlesex, amounting altogether to 123a. 2r. 36p. or thereabouts.
They were rated by the rate or assessment appealed against in respect of their
occupation of such land in several sums, amounting in the whole to £177. 7s. 7d.,
that rate being laid at the sum of 1s. 6d. in the pound on the amount of
what the respondents contended was the right estimate of the annual value to
let of the land in question. The only dispute between the parties at quarter
sessions was as to the amount of the annual value in respect of which the rate
ought to be laid on each of the appellants.

"The following facts were agreed upon by the parties, and found by the
sessions.

"In all previous rates the appellant had been rated on an estimated value of about one-eighth only of the sum which is inserted in the rate appealed against, and former rates having been laid with reference to the value of the land for any purposes of agriculture to which it might be applied; but in laying the rate appealed against, the respondents calculated the number of bricks which, on the land in question, were capable of being made in the manner hereinbefore mentioned, and the result was the large increase above stated in the amount of the rates. In the business of brick-making the following things are necessarily done:—The superficial soil being removed, the clay or brick earth is dug out, various foreign raw materials are purchased and brought to the brickfield by the brickmaker—for instance, chalk, breeze, sand, ashes, and straw; some of these materials are always added to the clay or brick earth—sand and breeze are always so used, and in the parish of Heston are obtained by water and land carriage, the former from Woolwich, in the county of Kent, and the latter from London, a distance of about fourteen miles. The quantity of chalk, ashes, and breeze required to be used depends on the quality of the clay—sometimes the clay requires to be washed, and for the purpose of washing it a steam engine is erected and used in many cases, but does not happen to be so on the field in question.

" The clay has also to be ground or mixed in a mill, called a pug mill, each pug mill is worked by one horse, and one is necessary for each stool—a stool being a frame or table at which the bricks are moulded, and a gang, consisting of a moulder, a temperer, an off-bearer, a walk-flatter, two pug boys, and a barrow boy. Each stool is capable of making about 700,000 bricks in a year.

" The amount of capital required to enable the brickmaker to work each such stool is about £900.

" The appellants severally hold under such leases, and E. Westbrook holds the field above mentioned for a term of seven or fourteen years, or till the earth is dug out, and is liable to pay to his landlord £20 per annum as rent certain for the same, being a trifle under the sum of £2 per acre, without any reference to the kind of use which he may make of the land; and he is also liable, in addition thereto, to pay his landlord a separate sum, called a royalty or realty, of 1s. 6d. for every thousand bricks moulded on such land in any one year. The rent, per acre, for the above-mentioned 10a. 1r. 32p. which on so taking a lease thereof, with liberty to consume the soil and clay or brick earth and without any liability to pay any royalty in respect of the number of bricks made), any tenant would have been willing to pay, would have been the sum of £10 per acre.

" If the Court of Queen's Bench should be of opinion that the respondent's mode of rating was correct, the order of sessions was to be *affirmed*, otherwise that order to be quashed, and the rate to be amended, and any such other order to be made in the premises as to the Court of Queen's Bench should seem to be just."

The Queen v. Henry Everest (10 Q.B. 178, and 16 L.J. Ref. (N.S.), M.C. 87).

"Upon an appeal by Henry Everest against a rate for the relief of the poor of the parish of Frindsbury, in the county of Kent, the sessions confirmed the rate, subject to the opinion of the court on the following:—

CASE.

"The appellant is the occupier of a piece of land in the parish of Frindsbury, containing brick earth, on which he makes and burns bricks. He entered on the occupation by virtue of the following agreement, and has since continued to occupy upon the same terms, without any formal renewal of the contract:—

"Memorandum of an agreement entered into the 3rd July, 1835, between John Batten, of, &c., of the one part, and H. Everest, of, &c., of the other part. First, that the said J. Batten agrees to let to the said H. E. a certain piece of land as a brickfield (which is now, and has been for the last   years, in the occupation of the said H. E.), as marked out, &c., containing, &c., together with the cottages thereon, to make and burn bricks for three years certain, from Christmas, 1834, to Christmas, 1837, on the following terms:—

"To make or pay for one million of bricks, at least for each year of the above period, at the rate of 2s. 3d. per thousand, and so on for every thousand beyond the said million, to be considered and estimated by and between the parties hereto, to be the same number as the duty to the King is actually paid for.

"Such payment to be considered due and payable as a rent, and to be made on the 25th of March and the 29th of September in each year, during the said term hereby granted, and in each year of the said H. E.'s occupation," &c. Then followed an agreement to pay at the rate of £3 per acre for land not used for brick-making, and for levelling the land broken up, &c.

"The appellant appealed against this rate, on the ground that he was over-rated in respect of the annual value of the land in his occupation. The clay dug in the land in question is never sold as such by the appellant, and is only *one* of the materials used in the manufacture of bricks. The other materials used in the manufacture of bricks are *chalk, ashes, sand*, and *breeze*—all of which have to be brought to the brickfield from other places. The manufacture is attended with great risk and uncertainty, and in the process of making, the bricks are exposed to considerable damage from rain and other accidental causes, for which, however, an allowance of one-tenth from the gross number is made by the Excise in charging the duty. When the rate appealed against was made, the appellant had twenty-two stools for the purpose of brick-making upon his brickfields. The sum of £800 per annum is necessary for the proper working of each stool. The sum paid by the appellant to Mr. Hankey, under the memorandum of agreement, at 2s. 3d. per 1,000 bricks made, amounted in the year 1840, to £1,010. 9s. 6d.; in the year 1841, to £928. 1s. 4d.; in 1842, to £960. 7s. 2d.; in 1843, to £953. 13s. 3d.; and in 1844, to £1,321. 4s. 9d.

"The question for the opinion of the Court was, what was the net annual value of the land in question?

"If the sums paid by the appellant under his agreement, were to be considered in the nature of rent, and as such ought to form the basis of the rating, the order of sessions was to be confirmed. If either of the modes contended for by the appellant should be considered correct, the case was to be sent back to the sessions, that the rate might be adjusted accordingly."

Lord Denman, C.J. :—

"These were cases sent from the sessions respectively of Middlesex and Kent, which may properly be considered together, being intended to procure a decision on the same question, the proper mode of rating the occupiers of brick-fields to the relief of the poor. The material facts found in both cases are nearly the same. In both it is stated that much expense, and the introduction of foreign matters, are necessary in order to make the occupation productive and profitable, and the result is liable to much risk. It is understood, therefore, if not made legally certain, that the tenancy shall be of some years' duration, and the rent is in part only fixed, in part made to depend, in the nature of a royalty, on the number of bricks made. The material, the brick earth, is not in its nature renewable, and in both cases will be consumed, according to reasonable calculation, within no great number of years. In both cases, the basis of the rate has been the supposed total amount paid to the landlord, considering as well the royalty as the fixed sum to be rent, and to be the proper criterion within the Parochial Assessment Act, of the rent at which the land may reasonably be expected to let, from year to year, free of such charges, and making such deductions as the statute specifies.

"In the case of Westbrook, however, the session found ' the rent per annum, which, on taking a lease, with liberty to consume the soil and clay, or brick earth, and without any liability to pay any royalty in respect of the number of bricks made, any tenant would have been willing to pay, would have been the sum of £10 per annum only.'

"No finding, correspondent to this, appears in the case of Everest. The question which we have to determine is, whether the principle on which the parish officers have proceeded is correct, with reference to the statute before alluded to?

"We must assume the amounts to be correct, both as to the royalty and the deductions made; and no question involving any difficulty in principle was raised as to the nature or number of these last. It will be convenient, in the first place, to consider the question, without reference to the special finding in Westbrook's case, and then to see whether that finding makes any difference in the decision of that case.

"It is objected by the appellants, in the first place, that it is a fallacy to infer from the fact that there are so many stools on the ground, from which so many thousand bricks may be made in each year, that so many will in fact be made and paid for; or, secondly, from the fact that so many have been made and paid for in one year, that the same, or an equal number will be made and paid for in the following year and years; and, without doubt, the conclusions do not follow with certainty from the premises. But the answer to the first of these questions is, that it is rather a question of amount than of principle: it does not touch the question, of whether the royalty is in substance a rent. Considered *as a question of amount only, the parish officers having to make a prospective rate, may well look to see what it is probable the land will be made to produce in the current year:* they may well proceed with a brickfield as they would with land used for agriculture.

"They cannot, in that case, tell for certainty how much will be tilled, nor with what grain, still less how much will be produced, or at what price sold. Yet, supposing the tenant to occupy at a rent, to be ascertained in each year by the actual produce and price, as it well might be, they may reasonably beforehand, from such premises as the nature of the land, its usual mode of cultivation, the preparations actually made, if any, and other such circumstances, infer what will be the rateable value in the given year. In the present case, we cannot say that the nature of the occupation does not afford rather safer premises for drawing the conclusion as to amount. The preparations are somewhat of a more permanent nature. It is not unreasonable to infer that the stools would not be erected but with the intention of making bricks, and that more would not be erected than the quantity of bricks to be made would require, and that more bricks would not be made than were expected to be sold, especially as the duty to Government, and the royalty to the landlord, are to be paid, not on the sale, but on the making. These premises raised at least a *primâ facie* case; *and if they led to an exaggerated conclusion, it was in the power of the appellants to have shown the error by actual proof.* As to the second objection, the answer is, that the rate is made but for the year, and any falling-off in succeeding years would, of course, operate in reduction of the rate for those years.

"But the next objection is a more important one: *that it is altogether wrong in principle to consider the royalty as rent:* and this appears to be founded mainly on this, that it is a sum paid not in respect of the

THE PRINCIPLE OF RATING.

renewing produce of the land, but of a portion of the land itself and that not consumed by slow degrees, and to be exhausted at the end of a long period, as is the case with a coal mine, under which circumstances it was admitted that it might be treated as produce, but in such large proportions that the whole in a *few* years would be exhausted. It does not appear to us that the circumstance of a *more or less rapid consumption* can make any difference in the principle. The rate is always imposed with reference to the existing value, whether temporary or enduring is immaterial. A case was supposed of a brickfield worked out in less than a year, to meet the demand of some enormous contract for a public work, the consequence would be, that the land would have a very much increased rate for that year; in the following year its value might *sink almost* to nothing, and the rate ought to fall proportionately, *even to nothing, if the brick earth being exhausted, the land, like an exhausted coal mine, should become entirely unproductive. If this were not so an obvious injustice would be done to the ratepayers. Suppose two brick fields of the same size, which, if worked, so as to be consumed in ten years, and by equal working in each year would produce £1,000 each, on which the rate should be ten pounds in ten years, each will contribute one hundred pounds to the parochial authorities; let one be exhausted in the first year, the produce will have been £10,000, but the rate only ten pounds for that year, according to the appellant's argument, and it may be nothing afterwards, but, whatever it be afterwards, it is clear that there will have been a valuable occupation in one year, escaping as to nine-tenths the rate entirely. But no injustice would be done if in every year the occupier could be assessed according to the actual value in that year, and it is the duty of the overseers to arrive as nearly at this as they can.* The case of *King* v. *Mirfield* was mentioned in the course of the argument, the facts of the case are wholly unlike the present, the saleable underwoods there produced no profit, except in the twenty-first year, here there is nothing to show that equal profits may not arise in every year of that tenancy; long or short, the term of tenancy is fixed on that assumption: the principle of that decision, however, is in accordance with what will be our conclusion.

" We come then to the bare objection, that the royalty is paid, not for the renewing produce of the land, but for several portions of the land itself, mixed up with foreign matter. *The expense, however, must of course have been cast off before the royalty itself was fixed.* That was a sum, which, after all such expenses were paid, the occupier could afford to render to the landlord. When the case is thus laid bare, *there is no distinction between it and that of the lessee of coal mines, of clay pits, of slate quarries;* in all these the occupation is only valuable by removal of portions of the soil, and whether the occupation is paid for in money or in kind, is fixed beforehand, by contract, *or measured afterwards by the actual produce; it is equally in substance a rent;* it is the compensation which the occupier pays the landlord for that species of occupation which the contract between them allows. This would not admit of an argument in an agricultural lease, where the tenant was to pay a certain portion of the produce, that would be admitted to be in all respects a rent service, with every incident to such a rent, and in *Daniel* v. *Gracie* we held the same with regard to a *marl pit* and *brick mine*, as the parties termed it, where the render was of so much *per cubic yard* of the *marl dug*, and so much per thousand of the bricks made.

"*We are brought, then, to the conclusion that the parish officers have done right in considering the royalty as a portion of the rent, and we see no objection to the mode by which they arrive primâ facie at the conclusion, that the amount of royalty reckoned in the rate will be paid in the year for which the rate was made.*

"Still, it must always be remembered, that the ultimate question is that propounded by the statute, and therefore the amount which has been paid, or what is reasonable to infer will be paid, is only evidence, not the fact itself to be ascertained. When, therefore, the case came to the sessions, it was open to the appellants to prove such uncertainty in the market, or such circumstances affecting the process of making, as showed that the parish officers had done wrong in concluding from such a quantity made or expected to be made, that the land might reasonably be expected to let, at a rent measured by that quantity; such evidence would have raised a question of fact for the sessions, and they would have had upon the whole to sustain or reduce the amount of the assessment. It may well be, that although at the end of the year the lessee has made so many bricks, that he can afford to pay one hundred and fifty pounds in royalty to his landlord, he could not prudently at the beginning of the year contract to pay more than one hundred pounds, and if so, the latter, rather than the former, will be the sum at which the land may reasonably be expected to let from year to year. And this is what we understand the sessions mean in *Westbrook's case*, by the special finding. The parish officers estimate the rent at a supposed amount of bricks actually made, and the royalty then payable on such amount; from this they make such deductions as reduce the rateable value to one hundred and fifty-nine pounds ten shillings, but the sessions say, that, placing the tenant exactly on the same footing as to the incidents of his occupation, but calling on him to say beforehand, what rent he would pay per acre for it, he could not be expected to give more than ten pounds per acre, which, on the whole, would amount to a little more than one hundred pounds. This latter appears to us to be the true criterion rather than the former, and the rate must be amended accordingly.

"It is not so easy to deal with *Everest's case*. The sessions ask us, what is the net annual rateable value of the land? and ad 1, if the sums paid are to be considered in the nature of rent, and as such, ought to form the basis of rating, their order is to be confirmed ; if either of the modes contended for by the appellant be correct, the case is to be sent back, that the rate may be adjusted accordingly. Now, *neither of the appellant's modes are correct, nor were contended so to be ;* they were in effect to rate land occupied in one mode, as if it were occupied in another, the modes producing different rates of profit, and commanding different amounts of rent, than which nothing can be more unreasonable. But, on the other hand, although the sums paid are in the nature of rent, it does not follow that they must form the basis of the rate in the sense of fixing its amount. The true question is that which the sessions ask, but which they must answer for themselves, by finding, upon evidence according to the principles laid down, what, in the words of the statute, is ' the rent at which the land may reasonably be expected to let from year to year,' remembering the purposes to which it is to be applied, and the privileges which the tenant will enjoy under his contract and by reason of his occupation, and after making all the deductions specified in the statute. It by no means follows that this mode of examination will produce so great a change in *Everest's case*, as it has in *Westbrook's*. The circumstances may be such as to risk, or market, or competition, as to make the difference little more than nominal. The market may be so sure, the competition so little, as to make the risk almost nothing. Still this is the question to be tried, and for the purpose of trying it, this case must go back to the sessions. Both orders should go back to the respective sessions, that the rates may be amended according to the principles laid down."

The orders were sent back to the sessions accordingly.

Although the above decision was pronounced by the Court more than thirty years ago, yet, even at this present time, very few *chalk pits, brickfields, gravel pits*, and other occupations of a like character are properly assessed.

It is only a short time ago that many properties of this class, situate in various parts of the country, came under the notice of our firm. Some were chalk pits, having lime kilns or cement factories attached, others were chalk pits used solely for ballasting purposes, and others were pits from which was being extracted either sand, gravel, or clay.

The following comparative amounts having reference to the *old* and *new* rating of some of those hereditaments, will illustrate how very little could have been known about applying practically, the principles laid down in the above judgment :—

				Old Rateable Value.			Rateable Value finally settled by A. K. & M.
1	.	.	.	£250	. . .		£470
2	.	.	.	50	. . .		110
3	.	.	.	300	. . .		1130
4	.	.	.	413	. . .		1108
5	.	.	.	212	. . .		906
6	.	.	.	120	. .		500
7	.	.		80	. .		330
8	.	.	.	135	. .		500
9	.	.	.	36	. . .		68
10	.	.	.	70	. .		300
11	.	.	.	280	. . .		1397
12	.	.	.	1685	. . .		3980
13	.	.	.	331	. . .		742
14	.	.	.	200	. . .		588
15	.	.	.	0	. . .		110
16	.	.	.	120	. . .		354
17	.	.	.	480	. . .		900
18	.	.	.	21	. . .		470

Other instances might be given, but it is simply intended here to show what parishes lose annually by their officers not properly seeing after this exhaustible class of property.

Case No. 18 was a sand and gravel pit, in the occupation of a railway company, from which they were extracting large quantities of ballast for their permanent way, and had been for several years. The parish officers knowing nothing of the *principle of rating*—nor can they be expected to—had assessed it as ordinary agricultural land. We were called in to value the whole of the company's property in the parish, and rated the pit at the above amount, *which was never even appealed against.*

It would be well for ratepayers if their representatives would bear in mind the words pronounced by Mr. Gladstone in his great

Budget Speech of 1853—viz., that "The exemption of one man means the taxation of another."

MINES.

The rent which a mine would let for from year to year may be ascertained upon the principle already considered in reference to ballast pits. The total annual produce would have to be ascertained in the first instance, and also the total working expenses in respect of "getting" the produce. An amount for tenant's profit must be determined, and this amount, in the case of mines, should be made upon a liberal scale, because, from the very nature of the work, there will always be a certain liability to accidents which, with the utmost possible care, cannot be avoided. The difference between the gross receipts, and the working expenses and tenant's profits, will give a certain rent in respect of the total annual production, if the tenant had not rates and taxes to pay. Making allowance for these, the residue is the amount of rent a tenant could pay, and which may be reduced to a fair *royalty per yard, per ton*, or *per chaldron*. With regard to the deductions to be made from the rent in order to arrive at the rateable value, the principles upon which they must be made have already been noticed when considering the question of ballast pits. For a mine, like the ballast pit, will, as a whole hereditament, consist of parts which of necessity must some time become exhausted, and of other parts which will cease to yield rent in consequence of the exhaustion of those parts. With regard to the tenure of mines, they in very many cases are occupied by persons who have spent much money in converting them from land with a certain quantity of minerals contained beneath, into collieries from which the minerals are in process of being extracted. The rent or royalty paid by the occupiers in such cases is by no means a necessary criterion of the rent the mine, in its *present* condition, would let for from year to year ; for, in addition to paying a certain rent or royalty per annum, they may have expended large sums in sinking shafts, erecting engines and various kinds of machinery to work the mine. By doing this they have created a hereditament which will let from year to year at a certain ascertainable rent.

It very often happens that the *workings* of a mine extend into several parishes; in such a case a careful survey would require to be made and the parish boundaries accurately laid down, the surveyor could then, after ascertaining the *total yield*, approximate sufficiently close by an inspection of the workings, to enable him to apportion to each parish its respective share of the rateable value of the whole.

It does not follow that because the shaft of a colliery happens to be situate in *one* parish that the rateable value of the whole mine is to go to that particular parish. If the workings extend into other parishes, then the value of each of the portions in those parishes must be ascertained distinctly. Such was the decision of the Court of Queen's Bench, in the case of the Queen *v.* Foleshill, 2 A. & E., 593.

In the following case, many of the principles which have been already discussed, are so clearly stated, and authoritatively confirmed, that it is desirable to quote, not only the judgment, but also the case and the arguments :—

The King v. John Attwood, Esq., and others (6 B. and C. 277).

"On the 29th of March, 1825, the churchwardens and overseers of the parish of Rowley Regis, in the county of Stafford, made a rate for the relief of the poor, in which the above John Attwood was assessed as owner and occupier, and Thomas Davey Wightwick, John Jones, Joseph Fereday, and Josiah Parkes, were assessed as lessees and occupiers of certain coal mines then at work.

"Upon an appeal to the Midsummer General Quarter Sessions for the county of Stafford, the rate was confirmed, subject to the opinion of this Court upon the following case :—

"The appellant, John Attwood, was the proprietor and occupier of the coal mine upon which the above rate upon him was made (which mine is situate in the parish of Rowley Regis, in the county of Stafford), and had expended upwards of £10,000 in planting the mine and setting it to work. The mine had been at work one year and a quarter. The value of the whole of the coals which had been raised from the mine did not exceed £5,000. The full value of the annual produce of the mine in question, after deducting the current expenses of working the same, amounted to the sum of £128. 9s. Upon that amount the appellant was rated.

"The appellant, T. D. Wightwick, had been for five months prior to the said 29th day of March, 1825, lessee of the coal mine upon which the rate upon him was made, and which is situate in the said parish of Rowley Regis; and during the five months he had been lessee he had paid £785. 14s. in royalties for coals raised; he had also expended in the purchase of the lease and setting the mines to work, £5,020. During the five months that he had occupied the mine he had raised coals to the amount of £3,825. 2s. 8d. The appellant, T. D. Wightwick, was rated upon the sum paid for royalties, the sum of £785. 14s. being considered by the respondents as the annual value of the royalties paid by him.

"The appellants, John Jones and Joseph Fereday, were the lessees of the coal mines upon which the rate upon them was made, and which are situate in the said parish of Rowley Regis. Sir Horace St. Paul, the owner and lessor of the mines, sunk the pits, and made preparations requisite for working the mines, and then let them to the appellants, Messrs. Jones and Fereday, at a certain fixed royalty, not a specific proportion of the amount of sales: £192. 12s. 8¾d. was the amount of royalties paid to the lessor during the last year. The lessees had expended £600 in permanent erections on these mines. The appellants, Messrs. Jones and Fereday, were rated upon the supposed amount of the annual sums paid for royalties.

"The appellant, Josiah Parkes, had been eight years lessee of the mine upon which the rate upon him was made, and which is situate in the said parish of Rowley Regis, and had expended £2,500 in planting the mine and setting it to work. During the last year he had raised coals to the value of £2,500, and, during that period, had paid £585 in royalties, and was rated upon the supposed amount of the annual sums paid for royalties.

"The questions for the consideration of the Court are—first, whether under all the circumstances of this case, Mr. Attwood was properly rated at the sum of £138. 9s. in respect of the said coal mine, such sum being the full value of the annual produce of the mine, after deducting the current expenses of working the same; and, secondly, whether the said T. D. Wightwick, John Jones, Joseph Fereday, and Josiah Parkes, were rateable in respect of their occupation of the said coal mines to the full amount of the sums paid for royalties upon the coals raised from such mines?'

"Campbell, Shutt, and Holroyd, in support of the order of the sessions. Two objections are made to the rate in this case: first, that the rate should have been not upon the annual value of the produce, but upon the interest of that value; secondly, that in making the rate, allowance should have been made for the expense of planting the coal mines. The words of the statute 43 Eliz. c. 2 are decisive on the first point; the occupiers of coal mines are thereby made rateable in respect of the mine; that is, the capital, when occupied by the owner; the coal raised is the annual value, and for that the occupier is rateable, whether the adventure be profitable or not. *And when the mine is in the hands of a lessee, he is liable to be rated upon the full amount of the royalty or rent which he pays, so long as he continues to work the mine. R. v. Parrott* (5 T. R. 593). *R. v. Bedworth* (8 East, 387). Then as to the second question, the argument on the other side must go to the length of saying, that no rent can be made upon the mines until the expense of planting them has been repaid, for no proportion of those expenses can ever be fixed as proper to be deducted before the rate is made. But *R.* v. *Mast* (6 T. R. 154) shows that the property is rateable for the improved value, without taking into consideration the expense of making the improvements. If a canal is cut, the whole of the produce of the toll is immediately rateable; so, if a house is built, it is rateable as soon as occupied.

"The same principle applies whether the premises be in the hands of the owner or occupier. The rent is the value after deducting the outgoings. *R.* v. *Hull Dock Company* (3 B. & C. 516). Here the tenants agree to pay a certain proportion of the produce as royalty or rent, for that sum they are rateable. Attwood, who occupies his own mine, *is said to have made a certain clear profit, after deducting expenses; that, therefore, would be the amount of royalty if the mine was in the hands of a tenant, and he is, therefore, rateable for that sum.*

"The Solicitor-General, Oldnal Russell, and Whately, *contra.* The important question for consideration is, whether the mode of rating coal mines which generally prevails, has been well considered. All the other things mentioned in the 43 Eliz. c. 2, as the subject-matter of rating, are of a permanent nature; but the coal in the mine is the capital, it is the soil and freehold, and the sum produced by the sale of it must be considered as the purchase-money of a part of the estate.

"The rate, therefore, should not be upon the whole sum produced by the sale of the coals, but upon the interest of that sum. *R.* v. *Parrott* and *R.* v. *Bedworth* are the only cases upon the rating of coal mines, and in neither of them was the attention of the Court called to the circumstance that the subject-matter of the rate was part of the realty, and, not being renewable, would, in a few years, become exhausted. But, on the other ground, Attwood was not rateable at all; the moneys expended by him had never been repaid, and therefore the mine had never become productive. Now, it is difficult to find any difference between the case of a mine which has never become productive, and one that has ceased to be so; and, in the latter case, it is not rateable. *R.* v. *Bedworth*, and in *R.* v. *Dursley* (6 T. R. 53), it was held that stock in trade was not rateable, because not proved to be productive. At all events, Attwood is rated too high in proportion to the other appellants; the rate upon him is in respect of the full value of the annual produce of the mine; now, that includes both the landlord's and the tenant's profit; the rate certainly cannot be good if imposed upon more than the estimated value to let. As to the other parties, the rate upon the royalties cannot be supported. If the owner is to be considered as the seller of part of the realty, the lessee is the purchaser, and the royalty is the purchase money; the rate, therefore, should be, not on the royalty, but on the sum at which the mine could be let subject to the royalty.

Abbott, C.J. :—

" We are all of opinion that the owner and occupier of a coal mine should be rated at such a sum as it would be let for, and no more. As to the other points, the first was, that the rate should not be imposed upon the coals produced, because that was part of the realty. It is the first time that such a proposition has ever been submitted, although many coal mines, in various parts of the country, have constantly been rated; and the argument in support of it is wholly untenable. The legislature has expressly made coal mines rateable, *and they must be rated for what they produce—viz., the coals. Slate quarries and brick earth are also exhausted in a few years,* but, nevertheless, *the rate is always imposed upon that which is produced.* The other argument was, that the rate could not be imposed until the expense of planting the mine had been recouped. But I cannot discover any distinction between expenses incurred in bringing a mine to a productive state, and building a house. The attempt to distinguish them is perfectly novel; and if a house is to be rated as soon as built and occupied, it must follow that a coal mine is rateable as soon as it is set at work and produces coals, although it may happen that the expense of sinking it may never be recovered. *If the tenant of a mine expends money in making it more productive, that is the same as expending money in improving a farm or house, in which cases the tenant is rateable for the improved value.*

" Order of sessions amended as to the rate upon Attwood, and confirmed as to the residue of the rate."

The next case brought before the Court of Queen's Bench, having reference to the principle of assessing mines, was that of

The King v. *Lord Granville* (9 B. & C., 188).

The defendant appealed against a rate made the 22nd day of February, 1828, for the relief of the poor of the parish of Stoke-upon-Trent, whereby he was

rated for a colliery, including engines and railway, at £61. 17s. 5d., being a
rate made upon the sum of £989. 18s.   The court of quarter sessions confirmed
the rate, subject to the opinion of this Court, on the following case:—

  "The defendant is the lessee and occupier of a colliery in the parish of Stoke-
upon-Trent.   In the year ending on the 31st of December last (1827), he paid
to his landlord, for royalty, a mine-rent upon the coals raised from the said
colliery, viz., the sum of £802. 1s., which sum is a *fair mine-rent* for a tenant
to pay upon the quantity of coal raised in that year.   The sum of £802. 8s.
forms part of the sum of £989. 18s., upon which the defendant is charged.
The defendant, some time since, erected several steam and other engines in
the colliery, which are used solely in draining the mines, and in raising the
coal to the surface; and he also laid down a railway, which is solely employed
in facilitating the carriage of the coals.   These form the machinery with
which the mines are worked, and without which they could not be worked;
and there would be no mine-rent at all unless such machinery were used.   The
sum of £187. 10s., which is the remainder of £989. 18s. on which the defendant
is charged, is a charge over and above the amount of the mine-rent introduced
into the assessment in respect of the engines and railway.   And it is calculated
that if the colliery were now to be let by the defendant to a sub-tenant, along
with the engines and railways, the total sum of £989. 18s. would not be more
than a fair rent for such sub-tenant to pay.   If the Court should be of opinion
that the defendant ought to be rated for his engines and railways, in addition
to what he ought to pay as mine-rent to his landlord, then the rate was to
stand; but if not, then the rate was to be reduced to £50. 3s."

  Bayley, J.:—

  "*I have no doubt that the defendant ought to be rated for his engines and
railways.* Whether the sessions have made proper deductions we are not to
decide.   The only point for our consideration is, 'Whether the defendant
ought to be rated for his engines and railways.'   *If the owner had occupied
the mine he would have been liable to be rated according to the improved
value of the property, and where the owner of a mine fixes an engine, or otherwise, by expenditure of his capital, raises the value of his property, he will be
rateable for the value of that property so improved by his expenditure.*   If it be
leased to a tenant, who is to incur the same expenditure of erecting an engine,
the owner will receive a less (rent or) royalty, but as a greater quantity of coal
will be raised the tenant will be thereby remunerated for his expenditure, and,
I think, the tenant being the occupier, *is liable to be rated for such improved
value.*   The order of sessions must therefore be confirmed."

  Littledale, J.:—

  "The question is, 'Whether the defendant be liable to be rated at the increased amount mentioned in the case, by reason of the engines and railway he has erected? Generally speaking, the rate is to be in proportion to the rent. Here the tenant has erected an engine, which renders the mine more productive. It is immaterial, with reference to rateability, whether the landlord or tenant erect an engine, or lay down a railway. The bargain between the landlord and tenant may be varied on that account, *but the occupier of the property is rateable in respect to its improved annual value.* I think, therefore, that the lessee of this mine, being the occupier, was properly rated for the improved value."

Mr. Justice Parke says—

"The question left to us is, 'Whether the defendant be liable to be rated for improvements?' I think he clearly is." Concluding as follows :—"The only question for us, however, is, 'whether it be right in principle to rate the lessee in respect of an annual value, *increased by reason of improvements made by himself.'* I think he was properly rated for the *improved* value."

Order of sessions confirmed.

The above decisions clearly establish the principle upon which the net rental or rateable value of *coal mines* shall be arrived at.

In reference to *other* mines, which at present are not rateable, it is reported that a Bill has been prepared, and will probably be introduced and passed next Session of Parliament, which will place them in the same category as *coal mines*.

See Appendix.

GAS AND WATER WORKS.

The organisation of such properties as *gas and water works* is much more complicated than that of any of the properties hitherto considered; instead of the hereditaments having been created by one person and being occupied by another, it is generally found that the entire hereditament has been created by the joint contributions of many persons acting as a corporate body, and who themselves (by their officers) almost invariably occupy the hereditament, and fill at once the two positions of landlord and tenant. But it will be evident from what has already been said, that the interest of the tenant may easily be separated from the interest of the landlord by an application of the principle of "*What rent may the hereditament reasonably be expected to let for from year to year?*" The hereditament itself is frequently situate in many parishes, there being in some parishes works, reservoirs, conduits, mains, &c., and in other parishes mains and pipes only. When property is so distributed, it may seem to be a difficult question to determine the rent which a tenant would give for each of the various parts; but when, instead of inquiring what rent a tenant would give for the portion situate in any given parish, the question proposed is, "What rent a tenant would give for the whole hereditament?" and then, "What share of that rent is due in respect of the part situate in that parish?" the problem assumes a phase which can readily be discussed.

Those who have been affected by the preceding questions, having at various times joined issue upon the point of how the rent is to be determined, the necessity for frequent appeals to the Court of Queen's Bench has arisen.

The leading decisions affecting these properties are :—

1st. *R. v. The Cambridge Gas Light Co.*, 8 A. and E. 73.

2nd. *R. v. The East London Water Co.*, 10 Q. B. 208.

3rd. *R. v. The West Middlesex Water Co.*, 28 L. J. (N. S.), M.C. 135.

. 4th. *R. v. The Sheffield Gas Co.*, 32 L. J. (N. S.), M. C. 169.

5th. *R. v. The Overseers of the Parish of Lee (The Phœnix Gas Case)*, 1 Law Reports, Q. B. 241.

Although the cases were argued in the order in which they are enumerated, yet, inasmuch as the points raised by them may be more conveniently noticed in the order in which they would actually arise in deducing the rent a tenant would give, it is not proposed to consider them chronologically.

The questions to be considered are divisible into two principal classes—viz., first, questions affecting the rateable value of the whole hereditament ; and, second, those affecting its apportionment.

The first question raised as to " the circumstances which ought to be taken into account in determining the rent a tenant would give for the whole," is the most important. **Principle of ascertaining the total rent.**

On the one side, it was contended that a tenant about to take either gas works or water works would base his estimate of the rent he could afford to give upon the receipts and expenses connected with the whole undertaking.

Upon the other side, it was contended that the tenant would simply take into consideration the amount of capital invested in the works and mains, and pay as rent an amount sufficient to afford good interest upon that capital.

The argument in favour of basing the estimate of the rent upon the receipts was that, inasmuch as that for which the tenant is willing to pay rent, is the right to occupy and take the actual produce, and inasmuch as the actual produce of gas or water works is ultimately measured by the gross annual receipts, the gross receipts alone should be the basis of the calculation of the rent which the tenant would give. It was further contended that gas and water works are of that class of hereditaments in which a trade, more or less profitable, is a necessary consequence of the occupation; that, from the very nature of the properties, there exists, more or less, a monopoly of trade in either of those articles. It was also contended that any persons requiring either gas or water must, in the case of gas, either make gas for themselves, or, in the case of water, possess a well of water of their own, or, in each case, must purchase that which they require from the gas or water company which happens to supply the district. Upon the other hand, it was argued that the rent deduced from the gross receipts as a basis, is not the rent at which the premises might *reasonably* be expected to let from year to year; that any inquiry into the gross receipts earned is an attempt to rate profits in trade; that no inquiry is made into the gross receipts of the ordinary trader; and that the rent deduced from the gross receipts is not the rent the hereditament would command from year to year, but that which the hereditament and the *goodwill* of the business together would command. That, inasmuch as if the owners of the premises had neither works nor mains, they could have works erected and mains laid by paying as rent a certain per-centage upon the capital required; the amount that would be so paid is the true measure of the rent which might be expected from year to year for the occupation of this class of hereditament.

In reply it was contended, that no goodwill need be rented by the assumed tenant, because the mere occupation of the premises, without the slightest consideration of the goodwill, would of necessity command a trade; that the case is not similar to that of a shop which may be let, and then afterwards the lessor of the shop open a similar one immediately opposite, and so, although he lets his shop, still retains his trade; for in such a case it must be clear, that unless the lessor not only lets his shop, but also agrees not to trade within a certain distance, the occupier of the shop would not of necessity have any of his landlord's trade. Further, it was contended, that the rent which a gas or water company

might pay for the use of premises erected for them, would not be
the same as they themselves could obtain for the use of the
premises by a tenant from year to year.

This question was raised and finally decided in the case of *R. v.
The Sheffield Gas Company;* for although cases had been before
the Court in which secondary questions were raised, yet, inasmuch
as in those cases the total amount of rent was agreed upon,
the Court were not called upon to decide whether the total amount
of rent had been ascertained upon correct principles.   The Sheffield
case, which was most carefully drawn, set out at length the method
adopted by the respondents, the parish officers of the township of
Sheffield, in determining the rent of the whole hereditament.   This
they did by taking the gross receipts and deducting therefrom the
working expenses.   They then deducted a sum for tenant's profits,
a sum on account of rates and taxes which are payable by the
tenant, and also sums on account of repairs, renewals, and insurance
of buildings and mains.   The residue, after all these deductions
had been made, amounted to £21,072, which, according to the
case, was taken to be the rent at which the works might reasonably
be expected to let from year to year, and to be the true estimate of
the net annual value thereof.

To this mode of ascertaining the rent the appellants objected,
and contended, that

"The respondents should have first ascertained the quantity of land, and
the size and class of the buildings and fixed machinery, if any, at each of the
different stations of the company in the respondent township, and the class of
station of each in the town of Sheffield; and then as to each station used for
manufacturing, they should have considered it as land and buildings, with
machinery affixed, employed in a first-class and lucrative manufacture in the
prosperous manufacturing town of Sheffield; that they should then have ascertained whether there were any, and if any, what other localities than the one
in question, available for such a station for this company as the one in question; that they should then have ascertained the actual rental of other stations *
consisting of land and building, and machinery employed in the large manufactories in Sheffield; that then, having regard to the quantity of space occupied
by the station in question, and to the size and class of the buildings and

machinery, and to the possibility, if thought expedient, of obtaining a competing locality, and to the fact of such station being fit for and used as the manufacturing station of a first-class manufactory in such a manufacturing town as Sheffield, the respondents should have fixed the rental of the station in question by comparing it with the other manufacturing stations above mentioned, and the actual rental paid for them; and the respondents should then have made from such rental the deductions pointed out by the statute, and should so have obtained the rateable annual value of each such station."

Upon this statement, the first question put to the Court was—

"If the Court of Queen's Bench should be of opinion that the method above applied by the respondents of fixing the net annual value of the appellant's rateable property in the respondent township is not according to the Parochial Assessment Act, and is contrary to law, then the Court is prayed respectfully so to declare."

To this Mr. Justice Blackburn, who delivered the judgment, replied :—

"As to the first—viz., the mode in which the respondents have arrived at the value of the entire subject—it seems to us that if the proper allowance for expenses, and for tenant's profits and interest on capital, has been made, and the proper value is put upon the stations, and works, and buildings, &c., a proper mode has been adopted for obtaining the rateable value of the remaining property."

Here the correctness of the principle upon which the rent of the whole had been ascertained by taking the gross receipts as the basis, is, for the first time in the case of gas or water works, distinctly affirmed ; for although in the West Middlesex case such a definition of " rent "—viz.,

"Profit remaining after all deductions have been taken from the receipts"—

had already been given so as to imply that the rent of the whole must be based upon the receipts, yet, inasmuch as this question was not then before the Court, the extent to which the definition could apply was open to argument.

The *principle*, that the rent of the whole is to be ascertained by taking the gross receipts and making certain deductions from them, being thus authoritatively stated, the next question which arises is with reference to

Deductions from the gross receipts.

" The proper allowances for expenses and for tenant's profits and interest on capital invested."

Whether the hereditament rated be in the form of water works or of gas works, there are of necessity certain expenses incurred by the occupier, whether he be owner or not.

These are the actual working expenses incident upon the occupation. If the property be gas works, these expenses will be :—

Coals; materials for purification; supervision and labour; wear and tear of tools and other implements; salaries to secretary and clerks; collectors' commission and pay; stationery, printing, &c.; salaries of inspectors; wages to lamplighters; bad debts—this being more strictly a non-receipt of part of the entire income.

If water works, they will be :—

Coals, oil, tallow, yarn, &c.; wages; wear and tear of tools and other implements; salaries to secretary, engineer, clerks; collectors' commission; law charges; bad debts.

Besides these items, which are actual payments by the occupier, there must in either case be deducted a sum in respect of the tenant's own personal remuneration.

This sum represents the amount of benefit he will expect to reap in consequence of his occupation of the premises.

The amount of this profit, inclusive of interest upon the tenant's capital, i.e., of the capital which he, as a prudent man, must be able to command before he takes the premises, must depend in each case upon its own merits. But two things are equally certain—first, that the tenant must have such an allowance made to him as will induce him to occupy the property; and, secondly, that the allowance to the tenant must not be so exorbitant that it represents nearly all the difference between the receipts and the necessary expenses.

I have known cases in which the rateable value of most flourishing undertakings was reduced to an almost nominal sum, in consequence of the amount assigned as tenant's profits having absorbed all the profits of the undertaking. This is in effect saying that the profits were due to the personal skill of the tenant, and not, as was actually the case, to the innate value of the hereditaments. The mode of effecting this was by making the tenant's capital (the amount upon which the tenant's profits are usually calculated) much larger than any tenant from year to year would require.

In the case of the *Phœnix Gas Co.* and *Lee Parish*, already noticed (1 L. R. Q. B. 241), it was argued that the tenant's capital should be such as to enable him to provide not only for the working expenses, but also for the purchase of what were called tenant's fixtures.

It may be remarked, that the works, as distinguished from the mains, consist of land, buildings, and plant. The plant consisting, in the case of gas works, of the gas holders, condensers, scrubbers, purifiers, station meters, retorts, steam engines, and governors, &c., &c., the whole of which are essential to the existence of the gas works; and of the meters which are used for the *distribution* of the gas, although they are *not absolutely indispensable* for that purpose. In the Phœnix case, the whole of these were classed under the head of tenant's fixtures. The amount claimed by the company's witnesses, and allowed by the Sessions as tenant's capital, was such as to include their purchase, it being shown in evidence, that if the works had been constructed upon leasehold land, all of them could be removed when the lease expired. But surely it must have been forgotten that the estimate of the rent was to be such as the hereditaments would command from "*year to year*," and that consequently no tenant from year to year would have to provide these "fixtures." Without these "fixtures," the hereditament in its unfinished state would command no rent from "*year to year*," although upon a long lease a tenant might be found who, seeing this part of a hereditament, would be willing to give some rent for it, and afterwards to complete the hereditament, and convert it into a state to command a rent from "year to year." But the rent given under such circumstances would certainly not be the rent the premises would command from "year to year." It may further be remarked, that the proprietors of gas or water works would not allow their tenants to receive interest and profit upon an amount of capital invested in the purchase of things for which they ought to be paying rent to them, and by thus retaining to themselves so large a share of the total profits, only pay to them some almost nominal sum for the use of the remainder of the hereditament, and this the largest portion of the whole.

The decision of the Court of Queen's Bench was taken upon the question as to whether the retorts, the exhausters, the steam-engines and boilers, the condensers, the scrubbers, the purifiers, the gas holders, and the meters were to be deemed tenant's property, and, therefore, not liable to be rated, or to be deemed part of a hereditament that is to be let from year to year?

The case, which is fully given in 1 Law Reports, Q. B. 241, and carefully describes the above apparatus, found that—

"18. It was proved on the part of the appellants, and found, as a fact, by the court of quarter sessions, upon the evidence before them, that, according to the practice and course of business in letting and hiring gas works, the tenant would have to take to and find capital for all the property comprised under the heads meters, retorts, tenant's fixtures, and utensils, and would have to provide £150,000 for that purpose; and that a deduction in respect of such outlay was made in estimating, according to the provisions of the Parochial Assessment Act, what rent a tenant from year to year would be willing or reasonably expected to pay.

"19. They found that 17½ per cent. was a fair percentage to allow on 'tenant's capital,' for interest of money, for his own trouble and skill, and for provision against risks and casualties: and allowed a deduction at that rate not only on £50,000, which they found to be the amount of working capital which a tenant would require, but also on the further sum of £150,000.

" The question for the opinion of the Court of Queen's Bench was, whether it was competent for the quarter sessions to allow a deduction by way of tenant's profits in respect of any, and if any, of which, of the matters and things comprised under the heads meters, retorts, tenant's trade fixtures, and utensils, the nature of which is above more particularly stated; and if the Court of Queen's Bench should be of opinion that in any of the above-mentioned cases it was not competent for the quarter sessions to allow a deduction, they were to amend the rate accordingly."

The decision of the Court was as follows :—

Lord Chief Justice Cockburn :

" Whatever doubt hung over the case at the commencement of the discussion, has been removed by the arguments. I entirely agree that we must look, not to the position of the particular tenant, as to whether he has had to pay so much money down for the machinery and fixtures which are necessary for carrying on the works, but we must look to see what, as the whole concern stands, would be the rent that an imaginary tenant would give for the thing as a whole, *excluding of course from consideration what would be mere chattels*, and therefore would not pass under demise from the actual to the imaginary tenant. The way being thus cleared, I think the case presents really no difficulty. First, we think Mr. White has failed altogether to show that *the meters are anything more than common chattels*. The other things, it is plain, fall under one of two classes of two articles, which are properly taken into account as enhancing the value of the building. In the first place, with regard to the retorts. Mr. O'Malley's argument has satisfied my mind upon the facts stated in this case, that the retorts are so permanently attached and annexed to the freehold, so fixed to the freehold, as to become part of it, and they must be taken therefore, not as removable fixtures at all, but as fixtures so connected with the freehold as to become part and parcel of it. With regard to them there is no difficulty ; the moment they are found to be part of the freehold, then, of course, they are rateable as the entire freehold would be. The other items seem to me, one and all, to fall under the principle of the decided cases referred to in the argument of *The Queen* v. *The Southampton Dock Company*, and *The Queen* v. *The North Staffordshire Railway Company*. In the latter case the Court, after taking time to consider, laid down this rule :—*That where things which, though capable of being removed, are yet so far attached as that it is intended that they should remain permanently connected with the undertaking, or the premises connected with it, and to remain permanent appendages to it as essential to its working, those must be taken to be things increasing the rateable value of the land*, and in respect of which the company were not entitled to have a deduction made. That principle applies directly to the present case. No one can doubt here that the purifiers and the gas holders are part and parcel of the works which are absolutely necessary for the manufacture of gas, which is the purpose of the undertaking. No one can doubt that it was intended when those things were erected that they should remain permanently connected with those premises; that they should remain permanent appendages to it as essential to its working. They therefore fall within the rule laid down by the Court in that case. If you look at the equity and justice of the thing, there can be no doubt that if the company proposed to abandon this undertaking and to let these premises because they found it did

not answer, or that they had realised so much money that they did not want
to carry it on any longer, or were desirous to shift their premises to somewhere
else, and they proposed to let to another company, or individual or individuals,
the gas works, of course what a man would propose to take and pay rent for
would not be the land independent of all these articles, all of them essential
to the manufacture of the article called gas, because the retorts, purifiers,
and gas holders are all as essential to the taking of these premises,
and the using and occupying these premises as gas works, as any
other thing that can possibly be suggested, however permanently they
may be attached to the freehold.   They seem, therefore, clearly to come
within the principle laid down in that case.   There is another rule
which is applicable here, that is, the principle on which the Court
proceeded in the case of *Walmsley* v. *Milne*, in the 7th Common Bench Reports,
New Series, page 115.   There the owner of land mortgaged it, and afterwards
erected certain buildings thereon to and for the more convenient use of the
premises in his business of an innkeeper, brewer, and bath proprietor; he affixed
a *steam engine* and *boiler*, a *hay cutter*, a *malt mill*, or *corn crusher*, and a
pair of *grinding stones*.   The lower grinding stone was fixed into the floor of
part of the premises by means of a frame screwed thereto, the upper one being
fixed in the usual way, and the steam engines and other articles, except the
boiler, were fastened by means of bolts and nuts to the walls or the floors, for
the purpose of steadying them, *but were all capable of being removed without
injury either to themselves or to the premises*.   It is possible that some of the
articles here, like the steam engine and this boiler which is fixed to the
freehold—it is possible that the steam engine, the purifier, and the gas holders
may be removed without injury to themselves or the premises.   What said the
Court?   They first say, upon the facts it appears that, as a matter of fact, all
those articles were firmly annexed to the freehold for the purpose of improving
the inheritance, and not for any temporary purpose; then they go on to say
' But the man who was the owner, who had mortgaged the premises after
having attached these things to them in the way described, proposed to take
them away as belonging to him, and not as having parted with them under the
mortgage.' The Court says : ' When the mortgagor, who was the real owner of
the inheritance, after the date of the mortgage annexed them to the inheritance
and for the better enjoyment of his estate, he thereby made them part of the
freehold which had been vested by the mortgage-deed in the mortgagee ; and
consequently the plaintiffs, who were the assignees of the mortgagor, cannot
maintain the present action.'   So here we cannot doubt, as a matter of fact
that when these purifiers, and when these gas holders, when this steam engine
and this boiler, which are absolutely essential to the working of the manufacture, were erected, it was with the view to their remaining permanently there

for the benefit of the inheritance, just as much as when a man puts up the various things referred to in this case of *Walmsley* v. *Milne.* I therefore think, on both grounds, these must be considered as forming part, if not of the freehold (the latter things), still as so far connected with it as to be intended to be permanently attached to it, and therefore they may be taken into account in determining the rateable value of the land and the premises in question, and that no deduction can be allowed in respect of them. I think, therefore, that the sessions were wrong in allowing those deductions, and that those deductions must be disallowed and the rate increased *pro tanto*."

Justice Blackburn :

" I am of the same opinion. The rateable value of the premises is to be determined, according to the Parochial Assessment Act, according to the rent that a hypothetical tenant, making the suitable deductions, would give for the rateable property, and the sessions have quite properly proceeded to try to ascertain that. The property in this individual parish is a portion of a much larger property which the gas company possesses in this parish and in others. The first thing the sessions had to do was to ascertain the rateable value of the entire thing which the company possessed, and afterwards to see what portion of it belonged to this parish. Now, in proceeding first to get at the value of the entire property, as it was not a thing which in practice is let, you cannot ascertain it by finding what people would give in the market, and they had, as is common in these cases, to proceed to ascertain it for themselves, looking at the elements which a tenant would take into consideration on taking it from year to year. I think we are all agreed upon this. It was disposed of early in the case that the question is, what would a hypothetical tenant give for the whole of the rateable property? and although, in point of fact, as stated in the 18th paragraph of the case, the person who actually did occupy would not pay rent for portions of the property which are fixed to the rateable premises so as to become part of it, which would be capable of removal, because instead of paying rent he would purchase them ; yet we are agreed we must look to what a hypothetical tenant, taking a portion of the premises as they stand, would give for them with those portions which were annexed to the property so as to become part of the rateable property. Upon that, so far as that goes, the sessions were wrong. Then comes a question which is important if considered with respect to other matters. I take it that it is quite clear that the principle established by the cases is this: to take an illustration of the principle, it would be applied in this way :—If you are letting a house furnished, you would ascertain what was the rent given for it, and what was the rent for the furniture and the fixtures, so as to ascertain how much it would be rateable for. The way to do it would be to ascertain how much was paid for the furniture and the things in no way forming part of the rateable premises; and deducting that from the rent paid for the furnished house, the remainder would be the rent given for the house itself. The question then would arise, and must arise, whether the things for which you are to make an allowance and deduction are in themselves part of the premises, or are, like the furniture, not part of the premises. Now there are some things fixtures that are attached to the premises, and part of the premises, although as between the landlord and the tenant, and the heir and executors there is a right to remove them. Clearly no allowance is to be made for those. There are other things—such as movable furniture in the supposed house—which are manifestly not part of what is let, and for which allowance must be made. But there are intermediate things with respect to which it is sometimes very difficult to determine, and as to which a question may arise whether they are made part of the premises or not; and upon those the question mainly arises in the present case. The rule laid down has been that where the things are attached to the premises so as to be part of the premises, although they are removable afterwards. still they are part of the premises, although there may be a right to remove them. But *if things or chattels be merely fixed to the premises, and so far fastened to the premises as to be still chattels, but fixed and steadied for the purpose of use there, they remain chattels altogether*, so that they would not be part of the premises at all—they would never cease, to use the phrase in the case of *Hellawell* v. *Eastwood, to have the character of movable chattels;* although fixed for the purpose of the enjoyment of them, still they remain movable chattels. The common illustration is a *mirror,* which, in the ordinary way, would be screwed to the wall; *still it remains a movable chattel,* and is no part of the premises. On the other hand, *a grate* which is built into a chimney, *although it is capable of being removed by a tenant, would still be fixed to the premises,* so that it would be part of the premises, and therefore part of what would be considered to be let to the hypothetical tenant, and for which he would pay rent. Now comes the difficulty of applying it to the present case. We find in the case of *Hellawell* v. *Eastwood* the Court of Exchequer were dealing with machinery that was fixed and screwed, and attached to the premises, and they laid down the rule as being a matter of fact, depending upon the circumstances of each case, but principally on two considerations—first, the mode of annexation to the soil or fabric of the house, and the extent to which it is united to them; whether it can be easily removed, *intégré, salvé, et commodé,* or not without injury to itself or the fabric of the building; secondly—this is what I am calling attention to —on the object and purposes of the annexation, whether it was for the permanent and substantial improvement of the dwelling—in the language of the civil law, *perpetui usus causa*, or in that of the year book, *pour un profit del inheritance*—or merely for temporary purposes, or the more complete enjoyment and use of it as a chattel. In that case the Court of Exchequer thought the things were only put up and fastened in a way for the temporary use and enjoyment as a chattel; but they did put it clearly and distinctively that two important elements to consider are, *first, the degree of annexation;* and, *secondly, if it be in fact annexed, the object of the annexation*—whether it was for the improvement of the inheritance that it was attached to a part of the inheritance, and whether it was for the enjoyment only of the thing itself. In the case that my lord referred to, of *Walmsley* v. *Milne*, in the 7th Common Bench, New Series, page 115. which was very nearly a similar case, as far as the facts went, to this of *Hellawell* v. *Eastwood*, the Court of Common Bench laid down the same rule, and came to the conclusion that the machinery and things were firmly fixed to the freehold, for the purpose of improving the inheritance; and, taking that view, they thought it attached to the inheritance, so as to become part of it. That is the rule laid down there, and their definition as to when the thing ceased to be a chattel, so as to become part of the inheritance, although it might be removed. That was the principle laid down in the case of *R.* v. *North Staffordshire Railway Company*, where the things were similar to those in *R.* v. *Southampton Dock Company*. It was not, of course, in the precise words, but the same idea is conveyed. The things there were cranes, turn-tables, and a variety of other things, which were attached to the premises of the railway company, in one sense screwed down, some of them firmly attached, and some of them not. The Court said that the things which were not attached to the freehold were to be deducted, and an allowance made for them; and the things which were affixed to the freehold clearly enough would not be allowed for. Then the rule laid down to guide the sessions in what they were to do was this: ‘The articles may be divided into three classes— first, things movable, such as office and station furniture.’ As I have said, all the cases agree in the principle. It is clear these are not to be included. ‘Secondly, things so attached to the freehold as to become part of it.’ It is clear on the principle of all the cases that no deduction is to be made for them, and they are to be considered as part of what is left. ‘Thirdly, things which though capable of being removed, were yet so far attached as that they were intended to remain permanently connected with the railway or the premises connected with it, and to remain permanent appendages to it, as essential to its working.’ I think that that phrase, as it seems to me, contains the same idea identically as is stated in the case of *Hellawell* v. *Eastwood*, citing it from the year book, where they say if it be fixed *pour un profit del inheritance;* and again, as in the case in the Common Bench Reports, where it was said the question was, whether they were for the enjoyment of the inheritance. The

idea is throughout the same: if the things are annexed, though but slightly,
but with a view to the enhancement of the inheritance, and the permanent improvement of it, they may be considered as part, for which a hypothetical
tenant would be considered rateable. Now, that being so, and applying that,
I was inclined at first to take an opposite view as to some of them. Look at
the various matters put here; they all, with the exception of the meters, on
which I shall say a word afterwards, are, although but slightly, attached to the
premises: nevertheless, I think it is clear they all are, in fact, attached to the
premises, and equally clear they all are, in fact, attached to the premises with
the view of enhancing the benefit of the premises, so as to come within the
principle laid down in the three cases I speak of. Then, with reference to the
meters, it is a different matter. The meters are chattels themselves, except so
far as they are attached to the houses in which they are put up. They are
attached to the house, as a pipe comes in through the wall and is attached to
the meter. That is attached to a house, so as to render it part of the house to
improve it. Then it would become fixed property. Then, in fact, it is obvious
that the meters are kept as the company's meters, to be used as their chattels
for measuring the gas, and were never intended to be for the benefit of the
house to which they are attached at all. They are no part of the inheritance
of the company, and cannot be said to be so. Mr. White endeavoured to argue
so as to make out that a meter occupies part of the space of the house, and
therefore the company did, by occupying by the meter, occupy part of the house.
That is not so. Although the meter is firmly fixed to the house, steadied by
being fixed, that does not make the company the occupier of any portion of the
house, just as in the case I put in the course of the argument, of a person who
has hired out or let a chattel which is not fixed to the house, but enjoyed as a
chattel. He cannot be said to occupy by means of his pianoforte, if it be a
pianoforte, part of the premises. For that reason I think the meters are properly matters of deduction, and the rest are the other way. Therefore, the
result will be that the amount on the rateable value of that entire chattel—
the proportionate sum, I think, £8,000—will be deducted, as rateable value of
that portion of the premises: that amount ought to be deducted. The figures
will have to be rectified, and I do not go into the question of figures now. I
believe there will be no great difficulty in finding out and rectifying them when
the facts decided by us are taken as the basis to go upon."

Justice Lush:

  "I am of the same opinion. The sum to be arrived at is 'the net annual
value of these premises at which they might reasonably be expected to let from
year to year, free of all usual tenant's rates and taxes, deducting the expenses
necessary to maintain them in that state.' The question is, what is the rate-

able subject which is comprised within the premises to be rated here? Now, I apprehend that the premises to be rated are to be taken as they are, with all their fittings and appliances, by which the owner has adapted them to a particular use, and which would pass as a part of the premises by a demise of them to a tenant. It strikes me as expressing what in other words has been expressed in the two cases referred to by my learned brethren—wherever they have become so far a part of the premises that they would pass by a demise of those premises, they would form a part of the rateable subject of the inheritance in the value for the purpose of rating. When we have to apply that test to any particular footing, the question is not what a tenant might remove, not what might be taken in execution under a writ against the owner, *but what, as between the landlord and tenant, would pass as a part of the premises which he was to let, and what the tenant would take.* Now, applying that rule, I cannot entertain a doubt that, with the exception of the meters, all the subjects of discussion here would pass as a necessary part of these premises. Without the retorts, purifiers, the steam engines, and the gas holders, the premises would be worthless for the purpose for which these things were erected—they would not be a gas manufactory at all. All these things are fixed, and so far annexed as to be intended to be permanent, and as really necessary for the use of the premises as gas works. Therefore, I think, except the meters, that the whole of these items ought not to be allowed in ascertaining the ultimate net annual value. The meters are on a different footing, and in no sense a part of the gas works ; they are not upon the land occupied by the company, and are not fixed in such a way as to be a part of the freehold. I was struck in the early part of the argument with the finding in the 18th paragraph of the case. It appeared to me to distinguish this from the other cases, and for a time I entertained considerable doubt whether, on account of what was found there, all those items, although forming part of the rateable premises, ought not to be deducted. The finding is, that '*according to the practice and course of business in letting and hiring gas works, the tenant would have to take to, and find capital for, all the property comprised under the heads meters, retorts, tenant's fixtures, and utensils, and would have to provide £150,000 for that purpose, and that a deduction in respect of such outlay was to be made in estimating, according to the provisions of the Parochial Assessment Act, what rent a tenant from year to year would give.* It struck me at first that, being so, the tenant would be bound to take these premises, making an outlay by purchasing all these articles, and the rent he would pay would be so much less, and that rent would represent the rateable value. Upon consideration, I quite agree with my brethren, and I am satisfied that that is not the right view on the hypothesis that all these things except the meters do form part of the rateable subject, and ought to be taken into consideration in estimating the rateable value; because if a tenant and landlord agree — the landlord before the place is let — agrees that a tenant should pay down a price for part—that is, purchase part of the freehold—to say that the rateable value would be diminished would be absurd. I quite agree with my brethren, therefore, that it makes no difference at all whether the tenant takes the whole, assuming he did, or whether by contract between him and the landlord he purchased the fixed plant, which, if not so purchased, would be a part of the permanent premises, I quite agree that, except the meters, all the other matters are rateable, and that all of them ought to be disallowed."

It will be seen the Court ruled that, with the exception of the *meters*, all the other apparatus was part and parcel of the hereditament, and as such was rateable, and was not to be deemed to be provided by the tenant from year to year.

The broad question whether this apparatus was landlord's or tenant's, whether it was rateable or non-rateable, is noticed here, because on the answer to that question would depend the amount of the rateable value of the entire undertaking. After the tenant's working expenses, the rates and taxes payable, and the proper amount for repairs, insurance, and renewals have been deducted from the gross receipts, there remains a clear amount divisible between landlord and tenant. This amount represents two things —first, remuneration to the tenant for the labour and responsibility he incurs, and for the return on the capital he invests in working the concern; secondly, remuneration to the landlord, or the return he gets as interest on the money which he has expended in creating the hereditament.

These two sums, in ordinary cases, make up the dividend paid to the shareholders, who themselves (when the works are not actually let) fill the position of both landlord and tenant.

Now, it will be seen that, since the "net results of working" are divisible into two parts, the greater the first part is made, the less will the remainder, the second part, become, so that if the first part be made so great as to amount to the "net results of working," then the second part will become nothing at all—that is, if the tenant be allowed the whole, the landlord receives nothing.

N

If, on the other hand, the tenant is entirely ignored, then the landlord takes all. In the one case, the "rent that may reasonably be expected" is unduly diminished; in the other it is unduly increased. Now, the tenant's remuneration depends upon the capital he would have to invest in working the business. If this be unduly increased by assuming that he would have to purchase things which he, in fact, would really rent, then his profit is unduly increased, and *pro tanto* the landlord's share is unduly diminished. Had the Court in the above case ruled that all the apparatus described in the case was rateable, then the tenant would only have had to find £50,000 instead of £200,000—viz., £50,000 for working capital, and £150,000 to purchase the "tenant's fixtures." Consequently, his profits would have been very much less than the Court of Quarter Sessions allowed; and, therefore, a much larger sum would have remained for the landlord.

The Court, however, ruled that the meters were to be considered as belonging to the tenant, and were therefore not to be rated. The case had found that

"The meters in all cases are placed on the premises of the consumers: they are not in any way connected with the manufacture, *nor are they indispensable though used for the distribution* of gas and the earning of profits. They are maintained in their position by being soldered to the service pipes, which are made of lead. If the service pipes were not required to be flexible, soldering would not be necessary, for the meters might be so placed as to remain in a position without being fixed in any. Meters are taken off when they require repair and renewal, or for other causes, and replaced by others, and when repaired are frequently placed in a different house, and in a different parish."

The latter finding is equally true of *mains*, which are frequently taken up and replaced by others, and these again relaid in a different parish.

In the above it is admitted that the meters, though used for the *distribution* of gas, are not *indispensable*.

Imagine, therefore, a gas works complete in all respects except that it possesses no meters. Now, imagine this gas works let to a tenant *from year to year* (i.e., on a tenure determinable at the end of any one year). Since the meters are not *indispensable*, the tenant may be assumed to work the concern without meters. He would therefore have to supply his consumers by contract. In the early days of gas lighting, consumers were thus supplied. Having these contracts to perform, he would have to make a sufficient quantity of gas to enable him to carry them out. Making this quantity of gas would involve certain working expenses. These expenses being deducted from the gross receipts, certain net receipts would remain. These would be divisible into two parts—tenant's profits and landlord's rent.

At this point a proposition is advanced, viz., that provided the tenant can obtain a certain profit for himself, it is immaterial to him what rent he pays to the landlord.

If the hereditament is, for example, a fertile farm, the tenant will give a large rent for it: for if any tenant wants too much for his own profits, there will be plenty of others to be found, who, knowing what the land will yield, will be content with a reasonable share of the produce as profit, and to give the remainder as rent.

If, however, the hereditament is a very poor farm, the tenant, since he must have his profit, will give but a poor rent, and no competing tenant will reasonably give more, for every tenant must have his reasonable profit.

Reverting to *gas works:* the tenant, out of the net receipts, can afford to pay to the landlord a certain rent. Under these circumstances the tenant might be satisfied, but the landlord might not. Now, it is submitted that a tenure from year to year involves the yearly readjustment (if necessary) of the rent paid. The landlord being dissatisfied with the rent he receives, and being assumed to be a prudent man, would consult an engineer, who would advise him that the gas works, in their present condition, could command no more rent, for, owing to the system of supply by contract, the gross receipts are not earned in the economical manner in which they might be. But he would point out that if the works were supplied with meters, the whole concern could be more economi-

N 2

cally worked, and the net receipts increased—that is to say, the *hereditament could be improved.* Now, whose business is it to improve an hereditament—that of the landlord, or that of the tenant from year to year?

When I read the report of the Phœnix case, it occurred to me that if the above argument had been advanced, the decision of the Court might have been different.

The Court of Quarter Sessions found "that 17½ per cent. was a fair per-centage to allow on tenant's capital." This was made up thus:—Interest, 5 per cent.; trade profits, 10 per cent.; risks and casualties, 2½ per cent.

This was the first time in the history of the rating of gas works in which a claim for risks and casualties had been made, although I had previously heard the claim (to the extent of 5 per cent.) made in the case of railways.

Although the discussion of this claim, so far as railways is concerned, is somewhat anticipatory, yet, as the point

Risks and casualties.

occurs here naturally in the case of gas and water works, it may as well be now discussed once for all.

The claim is justified in the case of the tenants of gas works, on the ground of risks to which, as experience has shown, gas works are exposed. In the case of railways, I have heard it claimed on the ground "that a bridge might fall down;" and I have heard it claimed on the ground, "that, as in rating the other occupiers of a parish, a deduction for insurance is allowed to them before arriving at the rateable value, so, when rating a railway company, a similar allowance should be made. And as the railway company is its own insurer, the amount which ought to be allowed to it is not merely that which it does pay, but that which it would have to pay if, like the other ratepayers, it insured with some office which made a profit out of the transaction." This proposition is perfectly fair and true; but when it is advanced in support of the claim made for risks, it is improperly used.

The claim for risks is made on behalf of the tenant for the

risks he incurs in carrying on his trade. That is, in the case of the tenant of a railway, for the risks he incurs in carrying passengers and goods on the railway which he is assumed to have rented from year to year, and in the case of a tenant of gas works, for the risk he incurs in the manufacture and distribution of gas at the works and through the mains which he has rented from year to year.

In the case of a railway, experience has shown that the risk of the trade is on the average 1 per cent. of the gross receipts per annum, which is the amount usually paid and set out in the printed accounts. The printed accounts also usually contain a payment for insurance, which is but small when compared with the payment for accidents, &c.

Now, when a railway company seeks, in addition to the claim for tenant's profits, to be allowed a further amount on the ground above stated, for risks and casualties, they seek to unduly diminish the rent; and they seek to do so by endeavouring to establish a false analogy. An ordinary trader is not allowed a deduction from his rent to provide against any trade risks which he may incur. No deduction is authorised by the Act to be made from the rent "for trade risks and casualties."

The claim made in the Phœnix case, of $2\frac{1}{2}$ per cent. for risks, was justified by the accidents which, during the last few years, have happened rather frequently to gas works. There was the fire in Wood Street, for which the Great Central Gas Company were made responsible. There was the explosion at the London Gas Works, by which two large gas holders were wrecked. There was the fire at Leicester Square, by which Saville House was destroyed, and for which it was sought to make the Gas Light and Coke Company responsible.

But the misfortunes which happened to these companies, happened to them in their *capacity of landlords.* The fire in Wood Street arose through an alteration in the service pipe. A tenant from year to year has nothing to do with altering service pipes, or with any other repairs. This is made quite clear by the case of *R. v. Wells,* already noticed. The explosion at the London Gas

Works arose through carelessness in plastering the governor house, the works being used before they were properly finished.

But a tenant from year to year has no business to plaster governor houses. He has no business to do anything by which the hereditament is either increased or diminished in value.

It is quite true that a tenant may undertake to do things he is not assumed to do by the Parochial Assessment Act; but is he to claim allowances, which have the effect of lessening the rent he can give, to compensate him for the risks he may incur in undertaking to do that which he is not called upon to do?

The above considerations equally affect the claim for risk made by a tenant of a railway from year to year, on the ground that a " bridge may fall down."

The late Mr. Penfold was employed in valuing the Sheffield water works. While the valuation was being prepared, the dam of one of the large reservoirs, which was being constructed, burst, and in consequence great destruction both of the company's and of other person's property, and much loss of life ensued. But did this catastrophe in any way affect the rent a tenant would give? It was no business of the tenant. Had the reservoir been constructed, the whole hereditament would have produced more, and would therefore have commanded a higher rent. Had the dam which burst been that of a reservoir, on which the working of the concern did at the time depend, the consequence would have been that the whole concern would have gone out of rating until such time as the dam was reconstructed. But when that was done, the rent the concern would then command would (all other things being equal) be the same as before. Nor would the cost of rebuilding this dam have been any deduction from the rent. If a house falls down, it goes out of the rate, when it is rebuilt the rate on it is resumed; nor is the rate in any way lessened by the cost of rebuilding the house. This clearly appears from the judgments that have already been noticed.

Of course such risks and casualties as the tenant necessarily incurs in carrying on his trade must be provided for. These, in the case of a railway, are the chances of damage to rolling stock, to the lives and limbs of passengers, and of loss of, or damage to, goods carried. These risks occur year by year, and the loss occasioned thereby is charged in the accounts.

In the case of a gas or water works the risks are unlooked for —rise in the price of coals or labour, or from decreased consumption of gas owing to bad trade. But seeing that the rent is assumed to be adjusted from year to year, any loss occasioned by these risks is at once shown by the accounts, which form the basis of each successive assessment.

In all trades there is more or less risk, and it is t) provide for such risk, and to remunerate the tenant for his personal trouble, that money invested in trade produces 10 per cent., $12\frac{1}{2}$ per cent., 15 per cent., or 20 per cent., according to circumstances, instead of from 3 to 5 per cent., a return which is secured when capital is invested so as to be free from risk, and when no personal trouble is involved.

In addition to the expenses already enumerated, there are sometimes found in the accounts of gas and water companies items of deduction which, though actually paid, ought not to be allowed in deducing the rent a tenant will give. They ought not to be allowed, because although actually paid, they are not such payments as a tenant from year to year would be required to make. It is quite true that the items may be correctly charged when the directors are accounting to their shareholders for monies paid and received. The first of these items is "interest to bankers for loans," or "interest upon debentures." These loans have been contracted or the debentures issued by the company, not in their capacity of tenant, but in their capacity of landlord, and these expenses must be discharged out of that income which they as landlord should receive. This income is the balance, after all authorised deductions have been made, of the *rent* paid, or, in other words, the "net annual value." Out of this landlord's income the landlord's liabilities ought to be discharged. This is reasonable, for the money raised by debentures (for example) has been raised

to finish the hereditament, the capital of the company not having
been sufficient for the purpose.   But if, instead of issuing debentures, they had called up more capital, it is evident that the money
now paid as interest would then have been paid as dividends upon
the capital ; and it is also evident that the dividend is not a charge
to be met by the tenant before he arrives at an estimate of the
amount of rent he can give.

Again, "rent" is not a charge that must be deducted.   This
outgoing arises from the circumstance of the land, upon which
the works are built, not being freehold.   It will be evident from
what has already been said upon this matter, that such a deduction could not be made before arriving at the rent.   This is the
same as in the case already noticed, where a hereditament is
created upon land belonging to another, and the whole hereditament, *when created*, let to a tenant from year to year.   It is the
same in the case of the ground rent of a house, which, as is well
known, is not deducted in ascertaining the rateable value.

One case in which Mr. Penfold was concerned was peculiar in
this respect.   A gas company, A, originally existed upon a very
small scale.   Subsequently another gas company, B, was formed
which acquired the interest of the first, not, as is usual, by a lump
sum payment, but by the payment of an annual amount as dividend
upon the A shares.   But in making an estimate of the rent of the
property belonging to the B company, no deduction was made on
account of the dividend paid to the A company, because this payment was not one which a tenant from year to year would have to
incur.   In deducing the rent of the hereditament as it was, it was
no concern of the tenant through what stages it had passed in
arriving at its present condition, nor was it any concern of his
what expenses or what liabilities had been incurred.   However
created, the hereditament existed; existing, it yielded a certain
annual produce, and to enjoy the benefit of this produce a tenant
would be willing to give a certain rent without regard to any
liabilities or incumbrances to which the rent might be subject.

Again, such an item as "payment to fund for redemption of

lease," or any item of similar effect, ought not to be deducted in deducing the rent. When such a charge as this appears, it is because the works, or some part of them, are erected upon lease-hold land, and such a payment is towards providing for the loss that must accrue to the shareholders when the lease expires. But, as has already been shown, such a circumstance would not affect the tenant from year to year, nor would it affect the premises in continuing "to command such rent." For assume that the time has arrived when the lease has expired, then, as in the case of the householder, the hereditament, as a whole, would not thereby be in any way depreciated, or rendered less able to command the rent ; but the case would again be, that of the total rent paid, a *larger* share would be taken by the owner of the land, and also of the works erected upon the land. It is quite possible that, as a matter of fact, the shareholders, who would still be possessed of the mains and pipes laid in the ground, might not continue to occupy the leasehold land, but rather would have secured a piece of freehold land and have erected *fresh* works thereon. In such a case the old works would not cease to command the share of rent due to them, in consequence of having become valueless, but because the owner of the land and the owners of the remainder of the apparatus had not agreed among themselves.

Neither can such a charge as "rent of springs" be deducted before ascertaining the rent of the premises of a water company. For here again the rent of the springs is only paid because the water company have not been able to purchase the land in which the springs are situate. Had they purchased them, this item would not appear in the revenue accounts of the company, but their capital account would be greater.

An instance of such a charge occurred in another case in which Mr. Penfold was concerned. A water company whose supply of water was insufficient, having heard of a piece of land in which was a spring, secured a lease of the land, paying for it a heavy yearly rent. They then on this land erected an engine and pumps. Having done this, they were enabled to increase their yearly rental

largely, and consequently so to improve their entire property that
it could command a greater rent from year to year than previously. But the land in which the spring was, was held upon a
somewhat short lease ; consequently the company not only charged
in their accounts the annual rental paid for the spring, but also a
sum in respect of the recoupment of capital invested in buildings
and machinery upon the land. But neither of these charges could
be allowed in deducing the estimate of the rent a *tenant* would give.
For, as regards the rent, it is evident that it stands in the same category as the ground rent of a leasehold house, and must therefore be
paid out of the rent of the entire hereditament when that is ascertained, and must not be deducted as an outgoing before deducing
the rent. As regards the redemption funds: here, as in the case of the
leasehold ground of the gas works, it is evident that the redemption fund is not a charge which in any way concerned the tenant
from year to year, nor, as regards the landlord, is it a deduction
necessary to maintain the premises in a "state to command such
rent ; " for, as in the case of the house on leasehold ground, so here
the whole hereditament would continue to command such rent,
even though one part of the hereditament be owned by one landlord, a second part by a second, and another by a third.   For the
whole, so long as the various parts are used in common, will continue to command such rent; and if owners of individual parts, by
disagreeing amongst themselves, prevent the parts being worked
together, and so commanding the given rent, the result is simply
a wilful destruction of the rateable hereditament for which no
Act of Parliament has made provision.

The sum of the expenses and allowances having been determined,
the difference between it and the gross receipts is the rent which
a tenant could give if he had no rates nor taxes to pay. But as he
is supposed to pay the taxes, their amount must be deducted before
the rent can be deduced.

The principle upon which this is done has already been noticed.

Having thus deduced the rent or gross estimated rental, the

requisite statutable deductions must be made to maintain the premises in a state to command such rent.

The nature of these deductions having already been noticed, it only remains to be remarked here, that *only* such deductions are required to be made as are necessary to *maintain* the premises in a state to command *such* rent. The accounts of gas and water companies frequently contain not only disbursements for these purposes, but also further disbursements which really are for the *extension of the premises*, the result of which is, that they are thereby put into a condition to command a *greater* rent. As between the shareholders and the directors, this extension of the premises out of the revenue is not only perfectly legitimate, but exceedingly prudent, and is more or less adopted; but such expenditure must not be allowed in determining the *rateable value* of any hereditament.

The rateable value being determined, there would remain nothing further to be done if the hereditament were all in one parish. But in the case of gas and water works this rarely happens. Consequently, there **The mode of apportionment.** arises the exceedingly difficult question of how the entire rateable value is to be apportioned among the various parishes. To determine this question, the Court of Queen's Bench has been frequently appealed to.

The first case that must be referred to is that of *R* v. *The Cambridge Gas Light Company*, 8 A. and E. 73.

Of the points raised in this case, some had only a local interest, but others involved a universal principle.

The property of the company comprised works and mains situate in several parishes clustered around the works. Some portion of these mains were situate in the grounds of certain colleges which are extra-parochial. It had been found by the sessions that the whole property would let for a rental of £2,400 per annum, and the main point was as to how the rateable value should be apportioned among the various parishes. Other questions were raised which require only a brief notice. The first was whether the company should not be rated upon the actual productive value of the works, &c., the amount of which should, it was contended, be ascertained by a calculation based upon the company's total receipts and expenditure. But the Court decided that the £2,400 *rent at which they would let* must be the basis of the estimate. The case set out

that the total annual receipts of the company were . . £5966

That the *expenses*, including rates and taxes, were . 3596

Leaving a net receipt of only £2370

It would seem, therefore, that the rent of £2,400, as stated by the case, was too high; for, arguing in the absence of more particular information, from the above premises, no tenant would give as rent the total net receipts, inasmuch as he would then get no benefit for himself. It may, however have been that there were other considerations existing, and not stated in the case, such as would induce a tenant to pay that amount as rent. But as the case had found that a tenant would give a rent of £2,400 for the premises, the Court, therefore, acting in accordance not only with the Parochial Assessment Act, but with all the previous decisions, determined that that *rent* must be the basis of the assessment.

It was no part of the duty of the Court to inquire whether £2,400 correctly represented the rent for which the premises would let; but such rent being determined, they could only make that *rent* the basis of the rate. It is to be remarked that the case did not find that a tenant *was* paying, or *had* paid, a rent of £2,400 a year, but that a tenant *would* pay that rent.

Next, assuming that the company were bound by this rent, they claimed to make from it the following deductions—viz., for the annual cost of the renovation of the buildings, mains, gas meters, and other perishable articles, £500; for the annual value of their mains, pipes, and apparatus, within the colleges and halls, which were not rated to the relief of the poor, £350; for the profits in trade of the company, £600.

The last of these claims the Court disallowed, pointing out that the very fact that a tenant would pay a rent of £2,400 involved the fact also that tenant's profits had already been deducted.

The claim for £500 for renovation of buildings, mains, &c., was allowed, both upon the authority of a previous case, *R.* v. *Lower Hutton*, and also in virtue of the special enactment,

"Deducting therefrom the probable average annual costs of the repairs, insurance, and *other expenses, if any,* necessary to *maintain them in a state to command* such rent."

With respect to the claim of £350, the judgment was:—

"It remains only to consider whether the deduction of £350, being the annual value of that part of the apparatus which lies within the colleges and halls, ought to be made; and we purposely reserved the consideration of this point to the last, because it is connected with the principle which regulated our answer to the last question. For, inasmuch as the rate is imposed upon land used for the apparatus, and as none can be imposed upon that part which lies in those extra-parochial places, the amount which would otherwise have arisen therefrom (the aforesaid sum of £350), must, we think, be deducted."

Having thus noticed the secondary questions which were raised, the main question of

"Upon what principle ought it *(the total rateable value)* to be distributed amongst the several parishes in and through which the mains and pipes are laid, after deducting £150 for the value of the buildings and works in St. Andrew-the-Less,"

must be considered.

Here it is first to be noticed that in this case no question was raised as *to the principle* upon which the "works" were to be rated, but an amount was agreed upon as their rateable value. After the rateable value of the works had been deducted from that of the whole, the remainder of the rateable value would have to be apportioned amongst the parishes concerned.

In dealing with the question of apportionment, it would be proper to consider first the principle upon which the rateable value of the station works ought to be determined; but it will be more convenient for the present to accept the fact, that their rateable value has been deducted from that of the whole hereditament, and not to make special inquiry into the principle upon which that rateable value has been ascertained; for the principle will be found to be developed in the course of the inquiry of "how the whole rateable value is to be apportioned?

At the hearing before the sessions it was, as appears from the case itself, contended on behalf of the parish, that this apportionment should be made in proportion to the gross amount received for the sale of gas in each parish.

In giving judgment upon this point, Lord Denman first proceeded to determine " in respect of what " the company were rateable according to previous decisions in analogous cases. He showed that the effect of the decisions was to determine that the company were rateable as occupiers of land for the " *improved value of the land* from the gas pipes being laid in it." And he then went on to show that, this being the acknowledged principle, the mode of apportionment adopted by the sessions was, as a consequence, incorrect ; for if such, as a principle, were adopted, it would follow that in case the land was occupied in any parish by mains and pipes, and *no receipts* accrued from that parish, then no rateable value could be apportioned to it.

" Suppose (adopting their own rule) the value of the whole works to be £2,400 per annum, minus certain deductions, and the quantity of apparatus in the soil of each of the several parishes to be equal, but the sale of gas and the receipts for it to be confined to one, the case of *R.* v. *The Corporation of Bath*, before referred to, and *R.* v. *The New River Company*, and *R.* v. *Foleshill*, are express authorities to show that a rate upon the company in that particular parish where all the profits are received could not be sustained. . . . . Since, therefore, in the present case, the land occupied by the apparatus in each parish through which it passes contributes to the whole value to let, it follows that the company must be rated in *respect of its occupation in each parish.* And if so, we are aware of no rule which can be laid down as to the amount, except that it must be in proportion to the *quantity* of *apparatus* situate in each parish."

No explanation was given of how the *quantity of apparatus* was to be measured. Whether it was by the quantity of *tons* of pipes in the ground, or the quantity of cubic feet the pipes contained, or the quantity of money represented.

It may be noticed here, that the main principle settled by this judgment was, that the company must be rated in respect of *its occupation in each parish.*

In the subsequent case of *R.* v. *Mile End Old Town*, in which also Lord Denman pronounced judgment, he, after settling certain points which were raised, said—

"This apportionment is not at variance with the *grounds* of the judgment in *R.* v. *Cambridge Gas Light Company.* There the Court decided that the parishes in which profits are received are not entitled *to all* the amount produced by the rate; but that the parishes in which parts of the apparatus indirectly conducing to produce profit are situate, are entitled to a proportion."

The effect of this judgment was doubtless to effectuate substantial justice between the various parishes concerned in this particular case, and also in other cases where the circumstances are similar, *i.e.*, where the area in which the gas or water is distributed is clustered around the station works. For, whether "quantity of apparatus" is represented by the "quantity of tons," or the "quantity of cubic feet," or the "quantity of money" possible, the three terms may be pretty nearly equal, either for equal areas or equal receipts.

As the experience of *this method* of carrying out the principle of *rating the company in respect of their occupation in each parish* became greater, some very anomalous results were found to be produced. Thus it would happen in one case, that the land in a parish was very closely built upon, and consequently the receipts therein were large, compared with the quantity of apparatus in that parish (however measured) used in the supply of gas or water; but in another parish, in consequence of the houses and other buildings being further apart, a much greater "quantity of apparatus" was required to distribute a quantity of gas or water, for which the receipts were much less. This being the case, the consequence of apportioning the rateable value in proportion to the " quantity of apparatus," would be to assign the largest share of that rateable value to the parish in which the largest "quantity of apparatus" was situate.

But it is evident that in such a case the *extent* of a company's occupation is not at all proportionate to the *value* of the occupation; for since, on the one hand, a very extensive occupation might be of but little value, a much smaller occupation might be of much greater value.

When this method of apportionment was adopted in the case of a property consisting of works, of large trunk mains passing through parishes in which *no* receipts were taken, and of distributing mains and pipes in parishes where receipts were taken, then the effect was to produce a certain amount of inequality between one parish and another. For, after the rateable value of the station works was provided for, as in the Cambridge case, the remainder of the rateable value, which was due in respect of the mains and pipes, was distributed "in proportion to the quantity of apparatus."

In those parishes through which the main trunk mains pass, the quantity of those mains, whether measured in cubic feet of capacity or in tons weight, is usually a very large proportion of the total quantity of mains; consequently a very large proportion of the remainder of the rateable value would by this mode of apportionment be assigned to such parishes, while for those parishes in which the receipts arise, and from which the whole hereditament is rendered valuable, but a small share of the rateable value would remain. And, inasmuch as the quantity of apparatus does not necessarily bear any proportion to the *value of the occupation*, the effect may be to take some of that value from the locality to which it really belongs, and to give it to a locality which has no claim to it.

The next case which came before the Court of Queen's Bench was that of *R. v. The Inhabitants of Mile End Old Town*, wherein the East London Water Company were the appellants. The case was argued in 1847, and judgment given by Lord Denman. In this the circumstances were as follow:—The entire property of the company was situate in several parishes. In some there were simply

"Buildings, reservoirs, conduits, canals, bridges, mains, yielding to the company no other profit than as being conducive to the earning of water rates received in other parishes." "The annual value of these may be assumed, for the purposes of this case, to be £6,500, as mere land and buildings, with their fixtures and machinery attached, and deriving some *additional value* from their capacity of being applied to such purposes as that of a water company.

"In the hamlet of Mile End Old Town, there are no works except mains and pipes for the supply of the inhabitants. The quantity of mains and pipes, and of land occupied by them in the different parishes in which water rates are received (excluding from the calculation all land, reservoirs, buildings, and the other permanent works above mentioned, rateable merely as such without regard to the profit derived from water rates), may be taken in this case to be in the *direct ratio of the gross receipts in each parish.*"

No question was raised with respect to the method in which the rateable value of the whole was to be ascertained, but a total amount was found in the case, viz., £30,000, which amount was deduced upon the principle of taking the gross receipts as a basis.

Neither was any question raised as to the *principle* upon which the rateable value of the station works was to be determined, though the case stated that on which it had been. An amount was found in respect of them, and of some portion of the apparatus in addition to them, viz., £6,500.

This case differs from the Cambridge case in this: that while in the Cambridge case an amount was found in respect of the *works* only, in this an amount is found in respect of the works and of some portion of the *apparatus* beyond the works, i.e., of *some portion* of the mains and pipes. And for this reason: it was argued that the works, and such portion of the mains as was classed with the works, only yielded profit *indirectly*, whereas the remaining portion of the mains and pipes, namely, those used for distributing the water, was said to be *directly* conducive of profit.

Provision having thus been made for the works and for a portion of the apparatus, the remainder of the rateable value was

apportioned by the case among the parishes in which the remainder
of the apparatus was situate in proportion to the *gross receipts*
which accrued from each parish :—

" The result gives an annual value in Mile End Old Town, which will
support the rate. So if this net value be apportioned among the parishes in
which the water rates are received in the ratio of the quantity of mains, pipes,
and lands occupied by them in each, the result will be nearly the same, and
will support the rate, inasmuch as those quantities are (as above stated) to be
taken, in the present case, to be in the ratio of the gross receipts."

The points raised were :—

" On the part of the company, it is contended—First, That the *net receipts*
do not represent the *earnings* in each parish, the water rates being in fact
earned by all the works of the company employed to collect and to distribute
the water from its sources.

" Secondly, That the deduction in respect of tenant's profits should be ascertained by a percentage on the gross receipts of the company, and they claim a
deduction of 10 per cent. on such gross receipts. As to this point, I find as a
fact that the tenant's profits bear no definite proportion to the gross receipts,
and cannot be ascertained solely by reference to such receipts, but are governed
by other extrinsic considerations.

" Thirdly, That some allowance should be made for goodwill ; such goodwill
being the pecuniary value of the advantages which a lessee or assignee of the
company derives from his enjoyment of an established business with customers
already secured.

" Fourthly, That assuming £36,000 to be the net value of the whole works of
the company, and the basis of the entire rate on them, the amount ought to be
distributed among the parishes in proportion to the quantity of fixed capital or
property of the company in each : that the proportion of such fixed capital or
property being fairly represented by the sums invested in works in each, the
rateable value of the hamlet may be ascertained by the following proportions—
that is to say, as is the whole fixed capital to the whole net receipts, so is the
fixed capital in the hamlet to the proportion of net receipts in the hamlet.

" As to the last point made by the company, I find, in absence of proof to
the contrary, that the relative *quantity of fixed capital* or property of the company in each parish (including not only mains and pipes, but also their extensive permanent works of every description throughout the district) is fairly
represented by the sum that has been invested in works in each parish.

Of these, the last only was noticed in the judgment, and was
decided against the company, Lord Denman saying :—

"The rule of law laid down by Act of Parliament for ascertaining the rate-able value of any subject refers to an estimate of the *rent* it should yield. The outlay of capital might furnish no such criterion, since it may *have been injudiciously expended*, and what was costly may have become worthless by subsequent changes."

Having thus decided against an apportion in proportion to the fixed capital, the remainder of the judgment was devoted to a comparison of the various methods of apportionment submitted—viz., by "gross receipts," or by "quantity of apparatus."

But in making this comparison, a mode of apportionment was named by Lord Denman which the case did not suggest—viz., in respect to the *service pipes*. What the case did was to separate the *apparatus, i.e.*, the mains and pipes, into two parts—viz., the large mains through those parishes where no water was distributed; and the smaller sized, but exceedingly numerous mains from which the water was distributed into the *service pipes*, leading from these mains into the houses. The whole property may be compared to a tree; the works, under which term is included the engine and all the apparatus upon the site of the works, being the root; the large trunk main, the trunk (timber) from which the branches grow; and the rest of the mains, the smaller branches (the top and lop). But the Court introduced the further distinction of the service pipes, which may be likened to the *foot stalks* of the leaves.

Having done this, a comparison was instituted between apportionment by "gross receipts," by "net receipts," or by "quantity of apparatus," with a view of establishing a principle of apportionment in those parishes in which the receipts were *not* in the same ratio as the quantity of apparatus. And here it may be remarked that the introduction of the *service pipes* as an element of apportionment produces a more equitable result than if apportionment by "quantity of apparatus" had been made the rule. For it has already been shown, that the quantity of apparatus in two different parishes might be very different for equal gross receipts, in consequence of one parish being densely built upon, and the other but sparsely. Although the apparatus may thus vary, a much closer

relation will exist between the gross receipts and the number of
the services. For although there may be a large quantity of pipes,
yet, in consequence of there being few houses, the pipes would
have but few services leading from them, and it is the number of
occupied houses in any parish that really determine the *value* to the
company of their occupation in the parish.

In pursuance of the comparison between gross receipts and net
receipts, Lord Denman said—

" It is clear that the *net profits* in each parish would be the best criterion of
such rent, and they, therefore, would give the proper ratio.

" It is also clear that the ratio of the *gross receipts* or earnings in the several
districts to each other, will be the same as the ratio of the *net profits* in those
districts to each other, in all cases where the total of expense is taken to be
common to the whole apparatus, and is deducted from the total of receipts in
the progress of ascertaining a rateable value. For in such case the net profits
in each district would be ascertained by distributing the expense among the
several districts, and it would be distributed in the ratio of the gross receipts
in each; the ratios of the remainder to each would be the same as the ratio of
the gross receipts. *As any attempt to ascertain the net profits in each district
in any other way would lead to minute and inconvenient inquiries in practice, the
ratio of the gross receipts should be adopted as being an index of the net profits
when the rateable value is ascertained in the way stated in the case.* We think
that an apportionment in this sense, according to *gross receipts*, is in accordance with the decisions which have apportioned the sum of rateable value from
a railway or canal, according to the length of line in each parish. (*R. v. Kings-
winford, R. v. Woking.*) When the profit arises from transit, the line of the
canal or railway is directly productive of profits, and the reservoirs, warehouses, stations, &c., indirectly conduce to such productions.

" Each portion of the line earns an aliquot portion of the profits; and if
equal portions of one line carrying at *one* rate could be conceived to be let
separately, no one portion would be let at a higher rate than another, and an
apportionment of a sum of rateable value according to the length of line in
each parish is according to the rent to be expected for that part of the line. In
the case of water companies, where the profit arises from the delivery of water
at a given place, the previous transit being immaterial to the consumer, the
service pipes immediately produce the profit, and the agency by which the
water reaches those pipes indirectly conduces to such production.

" If the service pipes in each parish could be let separately, the water being
assumed to be sold at the same price throughout, the *criterion of the rent* would

be found in the *gross receipts*, which would depend on the number, and diameter, and level of the service pipes in each parish ; and an apportionment according to the gross receipts in each district would be according to the *rent* to be expected from the part of the rateable subject situate in such districts.

"This apportionment is not at variance with the grounds of the judgment in *R. v. The Cambridge Gas Light Company*. There the Court decided, that *the parishes in which the profits are received are not intitled to all the amount produced by the rate, but that the parishes in which parts of the apparatus indirectly conducing to produce profits are situate, are entitled to a proportion*. The Court also declared that the principle upon which the sum of rateable value from the rates of all the parishes should be apportioned is the same as that which has been applied to canals. By the method adopted in this case, the rateability of the portion of the apparatus indirectly conducing to produce profit is provided for, and the residue of the sum of rateable value is apportioned to those parts of the apparatus directly producing profit in analogy to the mileage proportion for canals and railways. We have thus endeavoured to show that the rule for ascertaining the value for separate rating ought to be applied, as far as practicable, to apportioning among separate districts a sum of rateable value *arising partly in each*."

The effect of this judgment, it will be seen, is to reconcile an apportionment either by "net receipts," "gross receipts," or "apparatus." But to do so an assumption has to be made, the absolute truth of which may well be questioned, viz., that the gross receipts " would depend upon the number, and diameter, and level of the service pipes in each parish."

Although it must be admitted that there is a *much greater necessary* ratio between the gross receipts and the number of the service pipes than between the gross receipts and the *quantity* of apparatus, yet a certain number of service pipes *may produce* the same amount of gross receipts which a larger number of service pipes does in another parish ; either because a greater use is made of them in one parish than another, or because a greater charge for the same use is made, *i.e.*, for the same quantity of the article sold.

It would appear, in the first instance, that this judgment is contrary to that in the Cambridge gas case, for in this an apportionment by "gross receipts" is sanctioned, while in that such an apportionment was not only repudiated, but an apportionment according to "quantity of apparatus" required.

But it will be found that each of these is only used as means. So far as the result is concerned, the two cases agree. That is, that wherever there is a beneficial occupation there must also be a rateable value in respect of that occupation, which rateable value, moreover, must be such as *will fairly measure the value* of the occupation : and that consequently the whole profit in respect of the entire occupation must not be assigned to the locality in which it arises, but out of the said profit the rateable value of all parts must be provided for. But it was nowhere laid down that the *value of the occupation* was in proportion *to the extent thereof;* and when it became evident that an apportionment according to the "quantity of apparatus" would practically apportion the rateable value upon such an assumption, then the *mode* only of apportioning was, by this judgment, modified, yet the result to be achieved left the same.

In the next case, that of *R. v. The West Middlesex Water Company,* questions were raised which resulted in a fuller development of the principle laid down in the Mile End Old Town case, and in the settlement of the *principle* upon which the station works and the indirectly profit yielding apparatus is to be rated.

In this case, as in that of the Mile End Old Town, the whole of the company's property consisted of works, reservoirs, trunk mains, and distributing mains, situate in various parishes. The company's principal station was at Hampton, where they drew their supply of water from the Thames. The locality in which the water was sold was a part of London, and was situate some miles from the principal works. The source of supply and the locality wherein the water was consumed were connected by a large trunk main lying partly in the parish of Hampton, but no water rates were received in that parish.

"The company derive no *direct* profit whatever in the parish of Hampton, nor have they any freehold or leasehold interest in the soil of the highway through which the main is laid; but they could not supply the water so raised to their customers without using the main in question for its conveyance.

"The questions for the consideration of the Court are, whether and upon what principle the buildings, works, and mains of the company are rateable in the parish of Hampton.

"The company contend that they are not rateable at all in respect of this main, and that the company's works in Hampton are to be rated as ordinary buildings, without reference to the profit earned by the company; and if the Court should be of opinion that the company were liable to be rated in respect of their main, the company then contend that they are only liable to be rated in respect of the land actually occupied by the mains, and not in respect of the profits derivable from the other parishes which they supply.

"The parish contend that the whole works and mains are rateable, and that they are to be rated in reference to the profits derived in the other parishes to which the water is conveyed by their agency.

"The questions for the opinion of the Court are:—1st. Whether the company are rateable for their main? and 2nd. On what principle the company are to be rated?"

Judgment was delivered by Mr. Justice Wightman. The question of rateability for the main was decided against the company, the Court saying:—

"In this case, the first question is whether the company are rateable for their mains which are laid under the surface of the highways, without any freehold or leasehold interest in the soil thereof being vested in the company? We think they are. These mains are fixed capital vested in land.

"The company is in possession of the mains buried in the soil, and so is *de facto* in possession of that surface in the soil which the mains fill for a purpose beneficial to itself. The decisions are all uniform in holding gas companies to be rateable in respect of their mains, although the occupation of such mains may be *de facto* merely, without any legal or equitable interest in the land where the mains lie by force of some statute.

"To the second question, requiring the principle to be stated on which the company is to be rated in respect of their plant, engines, houses, cottages, buildings, wharves, mains, lands, and premises, we answer, in the language of the Mile End Old Town case, 'that it is to be rated as for mere land and buildings, with the fixtures and machinery attached, and deriving some additional value from their capacity of being applied to such purposes as that of a water company.' And, we add, such additional value is derived from the increase of demand beyond supply, according to the principle regulating exchangeable value, and not by reference to receipts earned in another parish, beyond assuming that they are sufficient to pay for all outgoings.

"If an apparatus occupied by one occupier, consisting of several parts, lies in one parish, the rate is on the whole, and is received by that parish. If such an apparatus lies in several parishes, the occupier is liable for the same amount of rateable value, and no more : but that amount is to be apportioned among the parishes in which it lies ; and the question then arises (as in this case), what is the principle which regulates such apportionment? It is clear that each parish must rate the part which lies within it, as such part becomes a separate rateable subject in that parish, and must be rated according to the Parochial Assessment Act, upon the estimate of the rent which that part would yield after proper deductions. In practice the tenant of the parochial portion of a canal, railway, gas works, water works, or the like, has rarely if ever been known : but a hypothetical tenant must be assumed, and the terms of such tenancy are not difficult to be conceived. But in the hypothesis some necessary incidents are also assumed to be involved, such as: First, that each part of the apparatus is to continue in joint co-operation, no one tenant of an essential part being able to stop his part ; secondly, that the title to the required land is permanent, so that there is no risk of being compelled to move fixed capital ; thirdly, that there is land in the required quantity, and capital to be invested therein, and occupants ready to take and work plant yielding profit as tenants at rack rent ; *and parts not yielding profits as contractors for remuneration, provided any greater profits can be obtained than ordinary in such relations.*

"If the tenancy of each parochial part be assumed according to this hypothesis, then although each parish rates separately upon its own estimate of the value of the land lying within it, and the law gives no power of making all the parishes co-operate in rating the several parts lying in each, nevertheless this Court is bound to protect the occupier of such an apparatus from being rated beyond the rateable value of the whole taken together ; and it is with reference to this protection that the Court must take into its consideration at once all the separate rates as so many claims upon one common fund, and must apportion that fund, bearing in mind that every addition to the rateable value assigned to one parish must be a subtraction from the rateable value which might be given to some other parish.

" Supposing then the apparatus to be apportioned to several tenants according to the parts in several parishes, the tenants of the lands directly earning net profits in a parish would be rated by that parish for all the profits earned therein, this being the parochial principle of apportionment, which has been unanimously upheld hitherto in respect of all canals, railways, water companies, gas companies, and bridges. But the tenants of the lands directly earning no profit would not be liable to be rated in respect of any rent in the ordinary sense (which is profit remaining after all deductions have been taken from the receipts), but as these parts of the apparatus *directly earning nothing,* but *indirectly conducing to such earnings elsewhere* are assumed to continue in operation. the company to whose interests such continued co-operation is essential, *must be assumed to pay adequate remuneration to a contractor for land and fixed capital vested therein*, together with the labour and skill requisite for the effectual continuance of such operation: and these contractors with the company would stand in relation of occupying tenants in the parish, and the part within the parish would be the rateable subject, and the *local rateable value would be such a sum as would pay the rent of the land and the profit on the fixed capital therein*.

" It is said in the Mile End case, that the parts indirectly conducing to produce profit are to be rated as mere land, &c., with some additional value from their capacity of being applied to such purposes as those of a water company.

" The meaning of these words would be exemplified in this case, if it be supposed that the bank of the Thames and the underground of the highways in Hampton were heretofore of no rateable value; but that when a work on the bank was required to raise water from the Thames, and when the underground of the highways was required for the laying mains giving transit to such water, the owners of the soil of the bank and that of the highways could get some payment for allowing the use of their soil.

" Thus, land which before produced nothing. would produce something, and so have a rateable value, which would be an addition arising solely from its capacity, for being used for a water company. Value is derived entirely from the relation of demand and supply; and if a water company comes into competition with a mere agriculturalist for land for water works, an addition is made to the value of such land by the additional competition.

" This principle might raise land worth nothing into being worth something, as above supposed, and land worth something into a higher value in the case of a site for a steam-engine, with yard, and shed, and cottages attached: or a site for a reservoir, a filtering bed, and the like;—upon the common principles regulating value, it is enhanced in proportion to the scarcity of the thing in demand, so that if a few levels only were suitable for the required transit, or a few sources of water alone were accessible, the price would be higher. In this sense the words cited above, from the Mile End Old Town case, are applied to the mains in Hampton in its ordinary meaning, and in the meaning in which they are applied to stations. warehouses, yards, workshops, and the other premises appertaining to railways and canals, rated on the principle of indirectly conducing to the direct earnings of railways and canals.

" On this principle the company contended that the rateable value of the part of the apparatus in the parish of Hampton is to be ascertained, and we are of opinion that the company is right. The parish contended for a higher rateable value, and it remains to consider on what ground.

"First, Mr. Lush argued that every part of the apparatus was equally essential for the delivery of water from Hampton to the consumer in other parishes, and that, therefore, the rate should be on the quantity of apparatus in Hampton.

"The answer is twofold. In the first place, all the apparatus is not equally essential. The subject of purchase by the consumer is *water* delivered at the required place; it matters not to him whether the water is from the east or the west, or been raised on the spot from a well.

"Transit of water is not the subject of demand, as in the case of goods or passengers to be conveyed by railway and canals, but the water itself brought to the service pipe of the consumer; the junction of such pipes with the main being the source of profit, such delivery is the one indispensable requisite for purchase, whereas the course of transit might be varied in manifold directions, according to convenience, without affecting the value of the water to the purchaser.

"In the next place, no definite meaning was, and, as it appeared to us, could be given to 'quantity of apparatus' for apportionment of rateable value. Quantity must be ascertained by some measure, lineal, superficial, or solid, and if any of these measures were applied to steam-engines, reservoirs, filtering-beds, cottages, mains, and the like, and the rate upon the sum total of earnings apportioned accordingly, the sum total would be disposed of upon a principle not more rational than a lottery.

"The cases relating to the apportioning of rateable value on water companies are worth considering. In *R.* v. *The New River Company*, in Maule and Selwyn, the question was whether Amwell should rate Chadwell Mead at £5 or £300.

"The case stated that no profits arose in Amwell; that the land alone, without the spring, was of the value of £5, but if the advantages which the company derived from the use of the spring may by law be included in the rate upon the land, the land and the spring together are of the annual value of £300. The judgment is for the rate on £300. This case has been supposed to sanction the notion that the parish of Amwell was entitled to rate land in Amwell by reference to profits made in Islington and elsewhere. Probably the parish officers and sessions may have included a reference to those profits in the amount; but the Court entirely ignores any such reference, and takes the question to be, whether the rate is to be on two acres of mere land, according to the value of the land of that kind in Amwell, or with reference to its value in the occupation of the company, with the power of using it for their purposes, and with capital laid out for making it fit for those purposes.

"Lord Ellenborough confines his judgment expressly to the local value in Amwell, for he says, 'the water has a certain ascertained value at the fountain

head.' 'And if it has, it is rateable for that value, irrespective of profits
which may or may not be derived elsewhere from distribution through pipes.'

"In *R.* v. *The Mayor of Bath*, 14 East, the question of apportionment was
again approached, but left undecided. There the corporation had collected
springs in the parish of Lyncome and Widcombe into reservoirs, and distributed the water there and in Bath, making £50 profit by the sale of water in
the parishes, and £350 in Bath. The parishes rated for £600, claiming the
whole profits because all the water was derived from the fountain head: but
the rate was quashed because a large portion of the apparatus and the soil in
which the pipes are laid, and eleven-twelfths of the water rent are situated in
Bath: therefore, Lyncombe and Widcombe is wrong in rating for the whole
water rent, the source of the water not being rateable for all the profits of the
supply. The Court decides that the profit from the water ought to be *apportioned*, but gives no rule for apportioning it.

"In *R.* v. *The Mile End Old Town*, the principle of apportionment above
mentioned was adopted. It has been said to be inaccurate in laying the rate
for the direct source of profit on the service pipes which belong to consumers,
as the rate must be on the property in the occupation of the party rated. The
principle of the judgment is, that the direct source of profit from water or gas
is the delivery of the article to the consumer, and that the instrument of the
delivery should be rated for the net profits; and that if the service pipe belongs
to the consumer, the *junction of the service pipe with the main* is in the
occupation of the company and is rateable. Our judgment here is founded
upon that case, and we have thus endeavoured to apply the principle there
laid down to the rating of the premises here in question.

"I may here observe, speaking for myself alone, that from this judgment, in
which Lord Campbell, my brother Erle, and my brother Hill concur, I do not
dissent, as it is founded upon the principle laid down in the case of *R.* v. *The
Mile End Old Town*, which is the leading case as well as one of the latest
cases upon the question before us, and it is most desirable to preserve uniformity of decision, if possible.

"There appears to me, however, so much difficulty in satisfactorily applying
the parochial principle of rating by estimating the rent which the tenant would
give for the subject-matter in such a case as the present, as practically to amount
nearly, if not entirely, to an impossibility of doing so satisfactorily. I may also
add, that I am not quite satisfied that the distinction which has been taken
between *direct* and *indirect* sources of profit applied to the mains and pipes of a
water company running through different parishes is well founded, and more
especially in cases where the mains only belong to the company and not the
service pipes. Indeed, the whole subject-matter appears to me to be involved in
so much difficulty and uncertainty, that I cannot but hope that the legislature

may interfere or make some provision adapted to the rating of the property of such companies as that in question, and which may declare the principle upon which such companies are to be rated, and establish some uniform and practical mode of carrying that principle into effect."

From this judgment it will be seen that the Court was evidently of opinion that the whole rent, which, as has already been shown from the Sheffield case, must be founded upon the gross receipts of the hereditament as a basis, is to be considered as being made up of the rents of the various parts.

In effect, the entire hereditament which is occupied by the tenant (who may be also the owner of it) is to be deemed as being occupied by one tenant who pays a rent for it as a whole, which rent is then to be split up into the rents of the various parts. And the assumptions which the Court makes as to the manner in which the whole hereditament is constituted, viz., by the united action of various owners of property, is not inconsistent with our experience, at least in other properties, if not in those of gas and water companies. The ballast pit already described is a case in point, and although at present the sum of the various rents paid by the actual occupier of *that* property may not be such as fairly represent the sum of the values of each part, yet, when the leases expire, it may be readily imagined that out of the rent of the whole, determined from the gross receipts, the rent of the various parts necessary to the joint action of the whole would be paid ; and, further, that if the occupier had to pay such rents, he would be influenced in determining their amount by considerations similar to those used by the Court in the West Middlesex case.

It will be evident, from the previous pages, that various circumstances may influence the tenant in determining the amount he can give for any property ; and it will have been seen that the rent of the various properties considered, viz., of land, dwelling houses, manufactories, tithes, gravel pits, &c., has been determined either by a consideration of the " accommodation afforded," or by a consideration of the "actual produce." But in this case *both* these considerations are brought to bear in determining the rent of the whole and of the parts : a consideration of the actual produce in determining the whole, and a consideration of the accommodation afforded in determining the rents of the parts.

It may be observed that the "contractor" assumed by the Court is not a "contractor" in the ordinary usage of the term ; that is, one who undertakes to execute a certain work, and upon the execution thereof receives again the amount he has expended, and, in addition, a further sum as profit upon the transaction ; but the "contractor," as used in that judgment, must be regarded as a capitalist who wishes to invest his capital, and not, like the ordinary contractor, to increase it. The Court then assumes that such capitalist, finding that by investing money in providing certain accommodation which is required, he can secure a greater interest upon his capital than if he invested it in the ordinary securities, undertakes to construct and maintain such accommodation. And, on the other hand, that one who has the privilege of supplying water or gas in certain localities, will pay a rent to such investor, for the necessary accommodation, to enable him so to supply gas or water. It by no means follows as a necessary consequence that the privilege of supplying gas or water involves the command of the requisite capital, nor that the command of capital involves the privilege of supply; although our general experience of such matters is, that they are co-existent in the same hands : the companies who have the privilege, having also the capital to provide the requisite accommodation. But abroad, we continually find that "concessions" are made to individuals or corporate bodies, who then seek the aid of a capitalist to carry out the concession. To the capitalist who thus invests his money it matters nothing in what description of property he invests, for the return he may receive will be such as, *after allowing him continually to renew his property,* will pay a rate of interest greater than is usual ; and it will be remarked that the judgment assumes not only that the rent of the whole is sufficient to pay all outgoings, such as the rent of the various parts, but that the investment also will take place under such circumstances as will secure the contractor from loss.

The possessor of the *privilege* of supplying gas or water will be willing to pay such rent as will render his privilege a valuable one. The mere privilege, until exercised, is valueless, and it might be that the possessor of the privilege is unable to exercise it for want of the necessary accommodation. That being provided, the privilege *in conjunction with the apparatus*, may or may not constitute one whole and more than usually valuable hereditament; but the *extraordinary value* of such hereditament, if any exists, is due to the *existence of the privilege or monopoly*, and, consequently, the rating in respect of the occupation of such privilege, ought to be made where it exists. Such rating, the judgment declares, would be for all the "profits" earned by such occupation, and subsequently defines "rent in the ordinary sense to be profit remaining after all deductions have been taken from the receipts," and that consequently, in determining the profits of the "privilege of supply," the rent paid to the creators of the necessary accommodation must be included among the deductions.

Nor is this inconsistent with what has already been stated respecting the proper allowances to be made from the gross receipts, when it was shown that rent paid was *not* among those proper allowances. In that case, the object was to ascertain the *rent of the whole*. Here, where the object is to ascertain the *rent of one part*, it is evident that the rent which is paid for the other parts must be one of the deductions; for the rent of the other parts must be paid so as to enable any one part to earn a profit at all. It is the same here as in the case of a house built upon leasehold ground. Before the rent of the *house* alone can be ascertained, the rent payable for the ground must be one of the deductions. But when we are ascertaining the rent of the whole hereditament, of the *house and the ground*, no deduction is made in respect of the *ground-rent* payable.

The last case in connection with gas and water works is that of *R. v. The Sheffield Gas Company*, which has already been partially noticed. The remainder of the case raised a second time the question of how the rateable value in respect of the *mains*, whether they be directly or indirectly yielding profit, is to be apportioned. This was done in order to enable the Court of Queen's Bench to review the decision given in the West Middlesex case.

In the Sheffield case, where there were no trunk mains situate in a parish in which the receipts were *nil*, the proposition was made to apportion the rateable value in respect of the mains and pipes according to their *lengths* in each parish. But the Court declined to allow such mode of apportionment.

"It is very true that the mode they propose of dividing according to the portion in each township has the great advantage of simplicity; and when applied to such a homogeneous subject as the present, it probably brings out a result not far from the true one." "But we cannot say that this is the rule given by the Parochial Assessment Act." "We think we must refer to the judgment in the case of the *Queen* v. *The West Middlesex Water Works*, as giving the last exposition of the Parochial Assessment Act, to which, as already said, we must adhere, and require these parties to apply the rule as there laid down, as well as they practically can."

"If this is found not practically possible, as it certainly seems not *strictly theoretically right*, application must be made to the legislature to interfere and relieve the parish officers and justices from the obligation to apply the Parochial Assessment Act to such cases as these, which we agree with my brother Wightman in thinking it practically impossible to do satisfactorily."

It is to be noticed that the impossibility of the "satisfactory application of the Parochial Assessment Act" refers only to the mode of *apportionment* of the rent of the whole when ascertained, and not to the ascertaining of the whole rent. But it certainly seems difficult to devise any method which shall more *justly* assign a fair share of the whole rateable value to each parish, than the method arrived at from the considerations employed in the Mile End and West Middlesex cases. For whichever of the other methods which have been proposed is adopted, it can be shown that, among the numerous gas and water companies' properties, many cases peculiarly situate will arise, in which much greater injustice would be done to one or another parish by the application of some peculiar mode of apportionment founded upon expediency, than can ever be done by the application of the mode of apportionment laid down by the West Middlesex case—a mode founded upon the *principle* that the *rent* in any parish must be measured by the *value* of the occupation—a proposition which is most just.

RAILWAYS AND CANALS.

The principles that have already been considered will be of service in determining the rent which such extensive properties as canals and railways may be expected to command.

It will not be necessary to consider these two descriptions of hereditaments separately, inasmuch as the same considerations which determine the rents of railways will also determine the rents of canals, in all cases where the rateable value of the latter depends upon the rent. For in many of the canal acts a special clause states in what manner the particular canal in question is to be rated. When such is the case, it has been determined that the proviso in the first section of the Parochial Assessment Act comes into force. It will not be expedient to consider any of the questions involving a judicial decision which have arisen under these special acts; since such decisions have but a local interest, and merely depend upon the special wording of a clause in each particular act, they are without general interest.

Before proceeding to consider the principles which determine the rent a railway, or a part of a railway, will command, it will be well first to review the various conditions under which railways exist. In doing so, we will trace the successive changes that have occurred in railway property.

The conditions under which it was first intended that railways should exist were that, the owners of the railway having bought the land forming its site, and having constructed it, it should be open to any person to run engines and carriages upon it by paying toll to the proprietors. The railway was to be simply a road made in a special manner and by private persons.

Though this was the original theory, it hardly existed as a fact,

P

for the owners themselves ran their engines and carriages upon it, and the public did not ; but whoever required to use the railway did so by using both the railway, the engines, and the carriages of the proprietors. As the railway system increased, either the owners of the original railway extended it and made branches to it, or else other persons made and worked new railways which were in their turn connected with those already in existence. Gradually the branches, which were made and worked by independent companies, were either leased by the original company, who then worked them in conjunction with their own line, or were simply *worked* by the company owning the main line.

Then, as the number of main lines increased, it became necessary to transfer traffic from one main line to another. In order to avoid inconvenience, this transfer was effected by the engine and carriages of one company passing over the railway of a second company, for the use of which toll was paid; either in virtue of the original theory of railways, or by virtue of special agreements.

Again, the proprietors of main lines of railway have extended their property, either by the purchase of railways made by others, or by the renting of them or parts of them. Where one railway is rented by another company, the rent agreed to be paid has been arranged upon a variety of bases.

In the progress of railway extension it has sometimes occurred that the proprietors of a railway have been unable to purchase the ground, or parts thereof, upon which the railway has been built, and have therefore been obliged to rent the same ; or they have rented a part of a railway, and made the extensions therefrom.

At this time railways will be found to exist under one or other of the following conditions :—

1st. An entire system of railway from beginning to end is owned and worked by its proprietors.

2nd. A system is but partly the property of the company who work it, and have the use of the remainder secured by some, or all, of the following means—

a. They may have rented a railway made entirely by another company, for which railway they pay a fixed rent for a term of years, or a rent dependent upon the net profits made.

b. They may have rented some portion of the site, and subsequently made the railway and such station accommodation as exists thereon.

c. They may simply have running powers over a portion, of which portion they have not the sole use. These running powers may have been secured by the payment of a lump sum down, or by a certain annual payment for a term of years, or by a payment, the amount of which is periodically revised, or by a payment of toll for each carriage or vehicle running.

d. They may undertake to work a portion of the railway for a certain fixed proportion of the gross receipts.

However a railway system is constituted, the entire system will always be found to extend through many parishes.

The question that now presents itself is, how to determine the rent of the whole system, and of any parochial portion of it under any or all of the above conditions.

It will first be evident, from what has already been said, that if a railway, under whichever of the above conditions it exists, were situate entirely in one parish, its rateable value is not, as a whole, in any way affected by the conditions under which its various portions are held; for the hereditament will, as a *whole*, command a certain rent, and the rent depends upon what, as a whole, the railway can produce. Neither will the magnitude of the occupation affect the principle upon which the rent must be determined.

What then is the produce of the land occupied as a railway, to enjoy which a tenant is willing to give a rent? Evidently an amount of money arising from the traffic that can be carried over that land.

The first question which has arisen from this subject is, as to what that amount is, having regard to two maxims which are indisputable?—first, that whatever is produced by the land is the foundation of the rent (*the return due to the* PROPERTY); and secondly, that profits in trade (*the reward of* LABOUR) are not liable to be rated.

It may be remarked, that railways are of that class of property which is almost invariably occupied by its owners, and that consequently the entire produce received by them represents not only the return due to the property, but also the reward due to labour.

Under the original constitution of railways the proprietors could perform two functions. First, they could receive the tolls allowed to be charged to any person wishing to run carriages upon the railway. Second, they could themselves run carriages, and so make a profit. And when it became necessary to rate the proprietors for their occupation of land used as a railway, they made the objection that, though their total receipts included receipts from both these sources, yet, as the receipts from running the carriages were entirely due to the trade of a carrier carried on by themselves upon their own railway, these receipts ought not to be taken into account, but that the receipts from *the toll* charged for vehicles running upon the railway (whether the vehicles belonged to themselves or to others) were alone the produce of the land, and consequently the sole basis of the rent that might be expected.

This question was brought before the Court of Queen's Bench in the case of *R. v. The South Western Railway Company* (1 A. & E., N. S. 558).

After a long argument, the Court took time to consider its judgment, which was given by Lord Denman, who, after reviewing the facts of the case, proceeded to discuss the proposition laid down by the company—viz., that to determine the rent, the property must be supposed to be let from year to year. The question would then be—

"What the tenant would take by the demise. The answer to which would be the railway itself and the perception of the tolls as before fixed by the company."

But it was pointed out by Lord Denman, that a lease of the railway would involve a demise of the stations, warehouses, and approaches.

" The supposition of a lease of a portion of a railway with no demise of the stations, warehouses, and approaches to it, or, at all events, some provision for the use of them, is merely absurd."

It was also pointed out, that though the railway itself was

" Thrown open to the public as a highway; no corresponding provision appears to have been made with regard to the warehouses, wharfs, stations, and landing-places."

And as these were necessary adjuncts to the railway, it would follow that a

" Free competition of carriers upon the same railway is practically little less than absurd."

" If all difficulties were removed as to the stations, warehouses, landing-places, and approaches, and all these were supposed as much laid open to the public as the railway itself, the very nature of the mode of conveyance forbids the free competition of rival carriers. But how can we suppose any competition possible with the company, now the carriers, or indeed any free use of the railway, even by a private carriage, the company retaining the independent occupation and control over all the existing approaches?'

Lord Denman next proceeded to inquire how the company would have been rated before the Parochial Assessment Act was passed; for the proviso therein declares that the principles of rating are not to be altered or affected by it.

" They would then have been found occupying buildings and lands on an entire line of railway, and carrying on a trade not merely *therein, and thereon, but thereby, a trade inseparably connected with such buildings and such lands,* and for the sake of which, in a great measure, the lands themselves are occupied in a particular manner. The profits of this trade would be included in the fares received for the conveyance of goods and passengers; and the question would be, whether these profits ought in any or what degree to affect the rateable value of the lands and buildings?'

Having referred to previously-decided cases, and compared them with the present, Lord Denman continued:

" Then do the *fares* increase the value of the buildings and land. No one can doubt; indeed, the case has answered that they do; that a higher *rent* for the buildings and land might be obtained in consequence of the facility afforded by the occupation of them to the carrying on a lucrative trade, and earning the profits on those fares."

Having thus shown that the rent is to include the fares, or receipts for the use of the carriages, and not *merely* the toll, the remainder of the judgment was devoted to a consideration of the question of the *local* value, which is at present immaterial. A second case, wherein the same question as to the *tolls only* being the basis of the rent, was shortly afterwards brought before the Court. This was the case of *R.* v. *The Grand Junction Railway Company*, 4 Q. B. 18.

This case differed from the last in this, that in it there only *existed a possibility* that other persons might run their own carriages upon the company's railway, while in the present other persons actually *did* do so.

The total receipts of the company were made up from four sources :—

First. Receipts accruing from the use of their own engines and carriages upon their own railways.

Second. Receipts, being toll paid by other persons who ran their own engines and carriages upon the appellants' railway, and who had, independently of the appellants, "coke and watering places, and all other things necessary and convenient for the conveyance of passengers and goods, and separate stations, with needful branches into or communication with the same."

Third. Receipts from persons who paid to the appellants sums of money for the use of the stations, and the hire of locomotive engines, and as toll for running over the appellants' line, but who themselves provided carriages.

Fourth. Receipts produced by the appellants' own carriages and engines running upon another company's line, for which they paid toll to the other company.

It was contended by the company that, in consequence of other persons actually running their carriages upon the appellants' railway, the *principle* laid down in the case of *R.* v. *South Western Railway* did not hold in their case.

Lord Denman in this case also delivered judgment. He began by contrasting the facts in the two cases, in order to ascertain whether the difference in the facts of the cases necessitated the application of a different principle of rating. He showed that in the South Western case,

Gross receipts to be the basis of the rate.

" The company was in the *sole and exclusive* occupation of the railway, warehouses, stations, and landing places ; and being so, were solely and exclusively carrying on a large business as carriers thereon,"

although in theory other persons might have carried on a business on the company's railway.

" To this state of facts we applied the established principles of rating—that the rate is to be on the occupier in respect of the beneficial nature of his occupation—in estimating which, as to amount, or, to put it in other words, in ascertaining how much net rent such and such an occupation may be expected to command, parish officers are to consider not drily and only what would legally pass by a demise of it. *but all the existing circumstances, whether permanent or temporary*, wherever situated, however arising or secured, which would reasonably influence the parties to a negotiation for a tenancy as to the amount of rent to be asked or given. We therefore thought it impossible in that case to separate . . . that whole line from the warehouses, stations, and landing places, or these again from the peculiar conveniences which a tenant would have for carrying on, as occupier, a lucrative business, if not the effective monopoly, which the provisions of the act appear to give to the occupier for carrying it on. What under the act was possible by law, what, in point of fact, might be in future, however near, we thought immaterial as to the principle, though very fit to be taken into account when making the calculation as to the quantum ; but in principle the parish officers were to look to the actual state and *value of the occupation*."

Here, however, the appellants were not in sole possession of the railway, nor the warehouses, nor stations ; for, as has been stated, other persons ran engines and carriages upon the railway, and others, again, hired from the appellants the use of their warehouses, stations, &c., and of locomotive engines, but supplied their own carriages.

With respect to this state of things, Lord Denman said : " It is unnecessary after this statement to point out the difference in fact between the two cases. But we cannot perceive how this *difference* bears upon the *principle* on which the present rate is to be examined, or which governed the Court in the former decision, for that proceeded not upon speculations as to what might be in future, but expressly on the then existing state of facts.

" Each of the two companies" (i.e., the South-Western and the Grand Junction) " must be rated in respect of the occupation of land ; one of them " (the South-Western) " derives no benefit from that occupation, except by carrying on upon the land the business of conveying goods and passengers, the division of that profit on tolls and fares being merely* nominal ; the other " (the Grand Junction), " in addition to this mode of profitably carrying, *also* derives a profit from allowing others to carry goods and passengers, and this latter profit is properly called tolls. Still in both the inquiry must be the same—*What is the value of the occupation from whatever source derived? In neither can the profits of trade as such be brought into the rate; but if the ability for carrying on a gainful trade upon the land adds to the value of the land, that value cannot be excluded because it is referable to the trade.*

" But it is said that in the cases supposed, all is referable to the occupation under the supposed lease; that conveys the exclusive dominion, thence flow entirely the means of making profits. We have in truth already given the answer to this ; but it will be plainer if it be observed that there is a fallacy in confounding that *which the lease conveys a legal title to* and, that *which it gives the lessee the means of doing or enjoying.* No two things can be more distinguishable, and it is the latter which regulates the rent a tenant can give, and not the former. . . . .   It is quite true that if the railway were let to a tenant, the lease would convey the land and railway only, and give a title to the *tolls* only : but the lessee would undoubtedly consider the facilities and advantages which the occupation as tenant would afford him of carrying on a locomotive trade as carrier, and in whatever proportion that consideration would increase the rents, in the same proportion, after due allowances, would his rate be raised also.

" Two propositions are equally true—that the rate is not to be imposed in respect of the profit of the trade, and that it is to be imposed in respect of the value of the occupation; and two propositions that are true and applicable to the same subject-matter cannot be inconsistent; we think that the respondents in the present case, by the scheme they propose, have shown that they are not so. The *gross yearly receipts* of the company as *occupiers of and carriers on* the railway, must at least *include* the proper subject-matter of the rate. They have, therefore, taken a sum agreed to represent them as the first point to start from. They then assume an amount of capital employed in the trade, and deduct from the former sum two percentages upon the latter for the interest of this capital, and the profits which ought to be made upon it, and a third for the depreciation of stock beyond usual repairs and expenses ; fourthly, they deduct from the gross receipts the annual cost of conducting the trade ; fifthly, they deduct the annual value of all the land occupied by stations, &c., and elsewhere rated; and, sixthly, a sum per mile for reproduction of rails, chairs, sleepers. These *deductions taken together* seem *to us to include whatever is properly referable to trade*, and distinguishable from the increased value which that trade gives to the land. We do not now speak of the amounts allowed under each item ; and we decline to give any opinion upon this point, which is properly for the sessions; but if these are the proper heads of deduction, *then the residue must represent the* VALUE OF THE OCCUPATION ; and if so, this alone is brought into rate, and the profits of the trade are excluded ; accordingly the sessions have found as an inference from the facts, that the residue is the sum which a tenant from year to year might reasonably be expected to give for the railway and corporeal hereditaments, now occupied by the company in connection with the railway, exclusive of the stations and other buildings rated separately, and such tenant being assumed to have the same and no other power of using the railway, the same and no other advantages and privileges as the company now possess. If the deductions exhaust that portion of receipts referable to trade, the inference of the sessions is fair. If the advantages and privileges which the company possess are attributable to their occupation, and would pass with it, their assumption is well-founded. We agree with them in both."

From these judgments it will be seen that the *gross receipts* of a railway company must be taken as the basis of the estimate of the rent the hereditament would command. Such gross receipts must, in all cases, be those arising from the *entire* hereditament *occupied*. No inquiries must, in the first instance, be made respecting the different tenures by which the various parts are held. But the gross receipts are the produce of the entire hereditament as a whole.

It may, and does happen, that the gross receipts of a railway company include certain sums, not the produce of the hereditament which the company occupies, but the produce of trade carried on upon another company's lines.

Of this nature was the fourth item of receipt in the above case of the Grand Junction Company.

And with reference to this, Lord Denman said :

"Again, it is contended that the existing facts of this case show the unreasonableness of the rate. The carrying trade of the company goes beyond their

own line upon the railways of the other set of proprietors; but the receipts
arising from this have been excluded from the rate. This, it is said, is inconsistent. How can the profits which the same engine earns by drawing goods
over one mile, be of a different character from those which it earns in the same
employ over the next mile? So far from there being any inconsistency in this
it is necessarily involved in the principle on which the rate rests. That the
distinction can be made, and has been made, is no slight proof of the sound-
ness of the principle. The moment that the engine leaves the railway of the
company, what it earns ceases to have any connection with their occupation of
the railway; it may, and of course does, increase the value of the occupation of
that other line on which it then works, and will, of course, in the shape of toll,
proportionably increase the rate which the occupier will pay; but if it were
allowed to swell the charge upon the company, it could only do so in respect
of the profits of trade, and these our principle excludes."

Let it be assumed that the whole gross receipts of a railway
company have been earned entirely upon a system of railway
occupied by the company.

The first step in deducing the rent from such gross receipts is,
to deduct therefrom the annual "costs of conduct-
ing the trade," which of necessity are borne by a
tenant from year to year. These expenses will
be:—

Tenant's working expenses.

1st. Locomotive power.

2nd. Carriage and waggon repairs.

3rd. Passenger traffic charges.

4th. Goods traffic charges.

5th. Mineral traffic charges.

6th. General charges.

7th. Miscellaneous charges.

8th. Legal expenses.

9th. Government duty.

The sum of these deducted from the *gross receipts* leaves the *net
receipts*, out of which the tenant must be compensated, and the
rent and taxes paid.

It is not pretended that the above are all the expenses which
are found in companies' accounts. But they are all the working

expenses *that would be incurred by a tenant from year to year.* Sometimes it happens that the companies' accounts contain charges for rent paid. Such will be the case when a portion of the entire system occupied is rented; or when rent is paid for land upon which the company may have made a portion of a railway; or when they have rented a station or part of a station from some other company.

But such an item cannot properly be deducted in ascertaining the rent which the whole would command; for it is the rent of a part, and must necessarily be included in the rent of the whole, and if deducted as one of the working expenses, would not be included in the whole.

Again, companies' accounts will sometimes contain large sums that have been actually expended in *parliamentary business,* but such sums are not expenses which *a tenant from year to year would have to incur,* for they are incurred in respect of new lines, and it is no business of the tenant from year to year to engage in such constructions. It must be borne in mind that a railway company, occupying its own property, fills the two functions of landlord and tenant, and care must be taken that the respective interests of the two functions must be clearly separated in deducing the rent which the railway company, as landlord, will expect to receive from itself in the capacity of tenant.

Again, the accounts frequently contain also a large item in respect of income tax. But when this is in respect of the total net receipts, a great portion ought not to be charged; for, as pointed out by the Court of Queen's Bench in the case of *R.* v. *Goodchild,* already noticed, the income tax upon the rent is a landlord's tax, not a tenant's.

Having found the net receipts, the first diminution thereof to be made is in respect of tenant's profits.

Upon this point the question has been raised, as to the basis on which these profits are to be computed; whether on that of the gross receipts, or on that of the capital employed. This question was raised in the case of the *Queen* v. *The Great Western Railway*

Company, 6 Q. B. 179, when it was contended by the company that the profit ought to be computed on the gross receipts. It was also raised in the Mile End Old Town case ; but then it was found by the arbitrator that "the tenant's profits bear no definite proportion to the gross receipts, and cannot be ascertained solely by reference to such receipts, but are governed by other extrinsic considerations."

In the Great Western case the Court refused to entertain the question, pointing out that "this was not a principle of law," but a matter entirely for the sessions ; and in the Mile End case no remark seems to have been made upon the subject. These profits are usually based upon the capital which a tenant would have to find.

Then comes the question, What capital will the tenant of a railway have to employ ?

The total capital of a railway company is expended for two purposes. One to create (if *it* does create) the entire

Tenant's capital. system of the railway, with all the requisite stations, warehouses, approaches, watering places complete, so that a tenant from year to year could, upon taking possession, *at once* begin business.

The other purpose for which the remainder of the capital is employed is to provide locomotive engines, carriages, and waggons, the requisite moveable furniture at the stations, and a certain quantity of stores and movable tools.

It will be seen that these two divisions of a company's capital correspond with the two functions of landlord and tenant which the company fills. The expenditure in the first division—a very large proportion of the whole capital, is in respect of the company's position of landlord, and the expenditure in the second division is in respect of the company's position of tenant. The latter sum, though in itself a large amount, is but small in proportion to the total capital. And it is this sum only which has to be dealt with in deducing the rent a tenant can give.

If the company only filled the position of landlord, it would only have to provide the amount required for the creation of the hereditament.

The tenant of the company would have to find the capital required for the purchase of locomotive engines, carriages and waggons, &c., &c., and upon this amount he would require his profit. Although these things are the only movable property connected with a railway, and consequently such only as a tenant from year to year would naturally be expected to find, yet it has frequently been claimed that, in addition, a tenant would himself have to provide certain other things.

Upon this point the decision of the Court has been taken. In the case of *R. v. The North Staffordshire Railway Company*, 30 L. J. (N. S.) M. C. 68, it was stated that—

" In addition to this (rolling) stock, the company has been obliged to provide, at a cost of £52,950, turn tables, cranes, weighing machines, stationary steam engines, lathes, electric telegraph and apparatus, office and station furniture and gas works used for supplying the stations with gas. The turn tables, and some of the weighing machines, are affixed to the freehold by means of an iron bolt, inserted in a large stone sunk in the land. The lathes and steam engines are connected with the buildings in which they are placed by means of iron bolts. The electric telegraph consists, first, of posts driven into the ground; secondly, of wires passed through sockets annexed to such posts, but which wires may be disconnected from the posts without injury or displacing them; thirdly, of the electrifying machines, which are in no way affixed to the freehold. The gas works consist partly of buildings and partly of gasometers, retorts, and the other usual plant for making gas, and of the pipes for conveying the same from the gas works to the railway station."

The questions for the opinion of this Court are—

" Secondly, whether the appellants are entitled to a deduction for interest on capital and tenant's profits upon the said sum of £52,950, the additional amount of capital invested in turn tables, cranes, weighing machines, stationary steam engines, lathes, electric telegraph and apparatus, office and station furniture, and gas works, or upon any and what portion of such items?"

To this question the Court replied:

" The second question is, whether the company are entitled to a deduction in respect of the various articles therein specified, being things necessary for

carrying on the business of the company? The articles to which such a
question may have reference may be divided into three classes—first, things
movable, such as office and station furniture; secondly, things so attached to
the freehold as to become part of it; and, thirdly, things which, though capable
of being removed, are yet so far attached as that it is intended that they shall
remain permanently connected with the railway or the premises used with it,
and remain permanent appendages to it as essential to its working. It is clear
that in respect of the first class of articles, a deduction should be allowed. It is
equally clear that no deduction should be allowed as to the second. As to the
third, the question is finally settled by the decision of this Court in the case of
the *Queen v. The Southampton Dock Company*, 11 Q. B. 587, 20 L. J. (N. S.)
M. C. 155."

In that case the facts found were:

"In addition to the deductions allowed by the Court, the appellants claimed
two further deductions; they contended that certain fixtures or fixed plant,
consisting of cranes, steam engines, shears, derricks, dolphins, and other like
ponderous machinery attached to the freehold and essential to the business of
the company, should be taken into account in estimating the rent, as fixtures
for which a tenant would require to pay on taking possession of the premises,
and ought to be treated as personal stock in the nature of stock in trade, and
part of the capital which a tenant would have to invest in the business; that
if so considered, such fixtures would diminish instead of increase the rateable
value of the property of the company. The fair value of the fixtures, if purchased by an incoming tenant, would be £6,550; and the sessions find as a
fact, that the fixtures in question were attached to the freehold, but are capable
of being detached from the freehold as easily and with as little injury to it as
other fixtures put up for the purpose of trade or business of the tenant, and
usually valued as between incoming and outgoing tenants. If those fixtures
ought to be regarded as stock in trade, or personal stock, then the appellants
are entitled to the same deduction in respect of interest and tenant's profit as
on the sum of £15,000 above mentioned."

Judgment was delivered by Lord Campbell, C.J., who said:

"The fourth question arose upon a deduction claimed by the appellants,
which was disallowed. They contended that their cranes, steam engines, and
other like ponderous machinery, although attached to the freehold, ought to be
treated as stock in trade, and part of the capital which a tenant would have
to invest in the business, so as to diminish, instead of increasing, the rateable
value of the property of the company. The sessions did find, as a fact,
that these fixtures, worth £6,550 to an incoming tenant, although attached to

the freehold, are capable of being detached from the freehold as easily, and with as little injury to it, as other fixtures put up for the purpose of the trade of the tenant, and usually valued as between incoming and outgoing tenants. But this is a rate upon buildings, to which machinery is attached for the purpose of trade, and it has been solemnly decided that such real property ought to be assessed according to its existing value, as combined with the machinery, without considering whether the machinery be real or personal property, or whether it be liable or not to distress or seizure under a *fieri facias*, or whether it would go to the heir or executor, or, at the expiration of a lease, to the landlord or tenant—*The King* v. *The Birmingham and Staffordshire Gas-Light Company.* In this last case, all the arguments pressed upon us to show that such fixtures are stock-in-trade, and not to be taken into account in a rate on the reality were urged, but urged in vain. It is of the greatest importance that a rule upon such a subject, which has been laid down and acted upon should be adhered to, and we see no reason why this rule should be now disturbed."

In determining the tenant's profits, the following considerations must be weighed.

In the first place, the tenant must be assured of such a sum as will induce him to invest his capital in any under-taking, rather than let it remain invested in other securities. But he must have something more than this, he must be repaid for his personal labour and responsibility. Yet, on the other hand, the value of this labour, and the amount of this responsibility must not be unduly exaggerated. The labour which it is necessary to bestow is not of that highly-skilled kind which commands for itself a high remuneration. The tenant himself is not assumed to undertake the technical business matters ; for this purpose he employs the requisite skilled labour in the secretary, engineer, traffic manager, general manager, &c., the remuneration for which is a charge, among the other expenses, upon the *gross* receipts. The labour which he himself expends is that of general supervision.

Tenant's profits.

Then as regards the responsibility. Its existence must not be denied, but be fairly measured and recompensed in all cases.

In addition to the allowances for tenant's interest and profits, other deductions are required. It will be clear that whatever

amount the tenant receives for his own remuneration, he will expect to receive that amount free from any deduction; hence the
taxes he must pay upon his profits will be one of the deductions
from the net receipts.   Of this nature is *tenant's* income tax, which
is payable in respect of his profits, and which must be distinguished from the income tax payable in respect of rent.

Again, the property in which the tenant's capital is invested is
liable to much wear and tear, and possibly to depreciation, by
which, if not counteracted, its value will, at the end of the tenancy,
be much diminished.   Against any loss from this diminution in
value the tenant will also expect to be secured; for it would be of
small benefit to him if he made a certain sum by his occupation,
and then found, when that terminated, that he retired with a
diminished capital.

With regard to the wear and tear of the tenant's stock, it will
usually be found that it is continually counteracted by constant
repairs, the expense of which is included under the heads of
locomotive power, and of carriage and waggon repairs.   In consequence of these repairs the rolling stock is kept in a constantly
efficient condition.   This system is to a greater or less extent
adopted on almost every railway; but the practice as to thorough-
ness of repairs varies.   Before, therefore, it can be determined
whether any allowance is to be made, it must be ascertained
whether the repairs executed are of a fair average amount.

But notwithstanding repairs, the engines and carriages will ultimately require renewing.   Even in this respect it
is usually found that the working expenses include
a charge not only for repairs, but also for renewals;
if in any particular case this is not found to be the fact, it is clear
that some allowance should be made under this head; if a charge
for renewals is contained in the accounts, then it only remains to
be seen whether such charge is a fair average amount.

Depreciation of
rolling-stock.

The question as to the principle on which the allowance for the
depreciation of rolling-stock is to be made, was raised in the *Haughley* case, 1 Law Reports, Q. B. 666.   The case stated that—

" (6*a*.) The arbitrator was also requested by the appellants to raise, as a question of law for the opinion of the Court, the proper mode of making the allowance for the depreciation of rolling stock.

" The arbitrator has, in the items for locomotive expenses, and carriage and waggon expenses, made a full allowance for the annual repairs of rolling stock taken upon an average of several years ; and as the stock would, after a certain number of years, be worn out, he has allowed the item of £76, in paragraph 4, as the proportional part of a fund for the renewal of the stock worn out. The appellants contended that the arbitrator ought, as a matter of law, to have allowed for the depreciation of stock by taking its value at the beginning of the year, and then ascertaining what a new tenant would give for it at the end of the year, and making the difference the amount to be distributed over the line for this deduction.

" The arbitrator understood the question to be brought before him as a question of fact, and as the mode of arriving at the supposed value, both at the beginning and the end of the year, is by estimate and valuation, and not satisfactory (the parish not having the means of testing it), he adopted the first-mentioned mode as more easily applied, as well as more correct in principle.

" If the Court should be of opinion that the arbitrator ought, as a matter of law, to have adopted the mode contended for by the appellants, then this item of deduction should be increased by the sum of £56, and the rateable value diminished by a corresponding amount."

On which Lord Chief-Justice Cockburn said :

" The other question is, whether in making the allowance in respect of the depreciation of railway stock which, of course, must be deducted before the profits can be got at, the learned arbitrator has been right in proceeding upon the assumption that the hypothetical tenant will make his estimate of what he can afford in the way of rent, upon the supposition that the stock is to be replaced and renewed at the termination of what may be called its natural life ; or whether the deduction is to be taken as the difference between the value of the stock at the beginning of the hypothetical year and termination of it . Mr. Coleridge urged upon us very strongly that we should be departing altogether from the statute, and, in point of fact, making law instead of expounding it. if we said the arbitrator was right in his view, namely that you are to make the deduction on an average, over the whole of what may be called the supposed natural life of the stock. I quite agree with Mr. Coleridge that, if we were to start upon any other assumption than that we are dealing with, a case of letting from year to year, we should be construing this statute in a manner in which we should not be warranted in doing.

Q

"But I think it is one thing to start with the assumption that you are dealing with a tenancy from year to year, and another thing to say that the hypothetical tenant, in calculating what he can reasonably pay as rent for the premises, is necessarily to assume that his tenancy is not to last beyond a year. I think the possibility of its longer duration is one of the surrounding circumstances which the tenant from year to year would take into account. It may be that the circumstances are such that it is worth his while to deal with the stock as though he were certain that his tenancy would not be put an end to at the expiration of the year. He is to calculate for himself how much his stock will be depreciated, and what it is worth his while to give, having taken that matter sufficiently into consideration. Now that seems to me to be a question of fact for the sessions; if there were five hundred such tenants, and it was found in all instances, except a very small minority, that tenants of that class did deal with their stock in a given manner, that would be a circumstance for the sessions; or, in the present case, for the arbitrator to take into account in ascertaining what a tenant from year to year would be reasonably expected to give as rent for the premises which are the subject-matter of the assessment. A tenant might make the deduction upon the one principle, or he might make it upon the other; that is a question of fact to be ascertained by those who are the judges of it. I do not think there is anything in the statute that makes it necessary or incumbent upon us to say that if the sessions or arbitrator have found that fact in a particular way, they must necessarily be wrong. The tenant must be taken as coming in as a tenant from year to year, and then the question remains, what may he be reasonably expected to give as the annual rent of such premises. Before that fact can be arrived at, a deduction must be made from his profits in respect of what he would allow for the depreciation in the stock used for the purposes for which he takes the premises, and how he would calculate this is a pure question of fact dependent on the surrounding circumstances. Being, then, a question of fact, we are not called upon to express an opinion; it is sufficient to say that the arbitrator has not deviated from the rule laid down in the statute in taking into account the surrounding circumstances."

Justices Mellor and Shee delivered judgments to the same effect.

But it may be objected that, granting the fact that the accounts contain charges both for renewals and repairs, yet, inasmuch as the conditions of the tenancy are to be from year to year, the tenant might be exposed to much loss in consequence of his receiving a smaller sum for his stock at the end of his tenancy than he gave for it, not because it was really less effective, but because the market price might then be lower, or simply because it is not actually new.

To this it may be answered, that although the tenancy is to be assumed to be from year to year, yet this assumption does not involve a *change of tenancy* yearly, but it simply allows the possibility of a yearly revision of the rent, and that, therefore, under this assumption, the time might never arrive when a change of tenancy takes place. Then, subject to this remark, it must be considered that such a depreciation does take place. It must be borne in mind that such depreciation is not cumulative, and that, therefore, the stock will simply cease to be worth the same amount it originally cost, and that the time will never arrive when it is worth nothing. Of course, it is assumed that the necessary depreciation, owing to *wear and tear*, is being counteracted by continual renewals. The liability of the stock to depreciate to some extent from its prime cost has caused the question to be raised as to the amount upon which the interest and tenant's capital is to be computed; whether upon the amount the stock originally cost, or upon its present value.

This question was determined by the Court of Queen's Bench, in the above mentioned case of *R. v. The North Staffordshire Railway Company.* Therein it was stated that the rolling stock of the company, the appellants, had cost £356,843, which, it was admitted, was a fair price at the time the stock was purchased.

Reduced value of stock.

Chief Justice Cockburn, in delivering judgment, said:

" Four questions are propounded in this case for the decision of the Court. The first is, whether the percentage amount to be allowed for interest on capital and tenant's profits is to be calculated upon the cost price of the rolling stock, or on the depreciated value which that stock may bear at the time the rate is actually made. We are of opinion that the allowance must be made with reference to the actual, and not to the original, value. The point has already been decided by this Court in the case of *The Queen v. The Great Western Railway Company,* 6 Q. B. 179, in which decision we entirely concur. In addition to the reasons given in the judgment of the Court in the case, it may be observed that, as under the Parochial Assessment Act, tenant's profits upon stock must necessarily be calculated with a view to their deduction from the gross earnings, in order to ascertain what a tenant would give for the entire property, nothing could be more inconvenient than that a different principle should prevail in calculating the profits in the two cases.

"Now, the question, when considered under the Parochial Assessment Act, must be looked at not with reference to the railway company, who may have expended on the purchase of the stock a much larger sum than such stock would now realise, but with reference to an incoming tenant, and the amount of capital which such tenant would have to lay out in the purchase of the rolling stock necessary to carry on the undertaking. It is obvious that what it would be worth the while of a person or company about to embark in a commercial undertaking to give as rent for the premises in which it was to be carried on, would depend on the amount to be deducted, in addition to repairs and other necessary outgoings, from the gross earnings, in respect of the profits due to the capital to be employed in the concern. But it is plain that a tenant would calculate such profits on the amount of capital actually required to be expended, not on what may have been the value of such stock at some other time, or in other hands. Now, it must be assumed, that the stock in its existing condition is sufficiently effective to produce the earnings, which, after the necessary deductions, constitute the improved value of the railway; and it cannot reasonably be supposed, that if the company were about to give up the undertaking, they would not be willing to part with their stock at its actual value, or that, if they refused to do so, the incoming tenant could not procure other stock of an equally efficient character at its real value to supply the deficiency. In estimating, therefore, under the 6 and 7 Will. IV., cap. 96, what a tenant would pay, the profits must be calculated on the *actual value of the stock*."

The amount of the tenant's interest and profits having been ascertained and deducted from the net receipts, the remainder is the amount which a tenant could afford to pay if he neither paid rates nor taxes nor did any repairs.

But as he is assumed to pay rates and taxes, the amount in respect of them must be deducted. The method of computing this has already been indicated under the head of the tithe rent charge. The rates and taxes having been deducted, the remainder is the rent which a tenant can give for the entire hereditament.

Rates and Taxes.

The rent having been ascertained, the next step is to deduce the

rateable value of the whole. It will be remembered that the Parochial Assessment Act assumes that the tenant does not execute
repairs, &c., but that the landlord does. This assumption may
very reasonably be made, and although, as a matter of fact, the
repairs are always done by the railway company, and form the first
charge against the gross receipts, yet this reparation must be taken
to be done by them in their character of landlords.

The *probable average annual* amount of the repairs of way and
works must be deducted, and the only question of
fact that can arise upon this point is whether the amount which appears in the company's accounts
is the *probable average* amount.

Deductions from the rent.

But the hereditament, like the rolling stock, is liable to an amount
of wear and tear greater than can be met by *mere repairs*. A time
ultimately arrives when a certain amount of reconstruction is
required to maintain the premises in a state to command the rent.
In the earlier cases the claim for an allowance to meet this renewal,
when it should occur, was disallowed by the Court of Queen's
Bench; but subsequently, in the case of *R.* v. *The London, Brighton,
and South Coast Railway Company*, 15 Q. B. 313, the question was
again raised, and the Court requested to review its former decision,
which it did, and as follows:—

"The second question submitted to us is on the right to a deduction from
the rateable value in order to counteract the depreciation which takes place in
the value of the permanent way, and to maintain it in a state to command the
supposed rent, which is the measure of the assessment. As a general principle
we do not understand the respondents to deny that a deduction for the purpose here stated, and as stated, is proper to be made. The objection which
they raise to the particular claim of the company is founded on two circumstances: first, that the proper provision is already made under a head called
working expenses, in which we do not agree; secondly, that if more may be at
any time necessary, the necessity has not yet arisen, because the company has
not yet incurred the expense, nor laid by from their receipts any sum to meet it
when it shall arise. This question, under nearly the same circumstances, came
before the Court in the case of *R.* v. *The Great Western Railway Company* (6
Q. B. 179, 203), and was decided against the company. But we are desired to
review that decision. We then said that we thought such an expense, as

distinct from mere annual repair, fell under the same principle, and was an unobjectionable head of deduction when it should either be actually incurred or provided for ; we thought that as no allowance would be made for annual repairs in any year in which no repairs took place, so none should be made for this annual depreciation in value, unless, at least, there were funds set aside to meet it when it should be thought expedient to do the work of renewal. In that case too there was a further circumstance which had some influence on our judgment, and which is not found here; that whatever expenses had been in fact incurred, the company had chosen, rightly or wrongly, at all events conclusively on themselves, to make a charge on their capital and not on their receipts, converting it, therefore, into landlord's improvements rather than tenant's repairs. The difficulty which we now feel arises from the same fact. that no charge has, in fact, either by way of outlay or setting apart, been made on the company's receipts. If the depreciation be, as probably it is, both certain and capable of an annual average, though not proper to be, in fact, repaired annually, we think it should be met by laying by a certain sum annually ; and that if the company, in order to swell their dividend, or for any other motive, neglect to do so, they act unlawfully in one of two ways: either they make a dividend which in substance impairs their capital, because they throw a burden on the latter which ought to be thrown upon the former, or they cast the whole burden of a heavy restoration of the permanent way on the dividend of some future year, to the manifest injury of the then proprietors, and for the unfair benefit of the present body. In such case, too, there may arise some difficulty in resisting the claim to be allowed—the whole deduction from the rate of the year in which the expense shall actually be incurred, although it would be manifestly unjust to allow it twice over, first in detail and then in lump. This difficulty was met in the argument by instancing the ordinary case of house property, as to which a larger difference is made between ' gross estimated rental ' and ' rateable value ' than in the case of land, on account of this very annual depreciation of the thing itself and the necessary prospective restoration ; and yet it was said you never inquired whether the owner did in fact lay by a portion of his annual rent to meet that distant expense.

 "We have considered this question with much attention, and, upon the whole, we think that the company are entitled to a deduction on this head. We cannot make a substantial distinction between this and house property, or any other of a perishable nature which must require renewal ; and although we think that the company ought to set apart the sum which they claim to deduct, we cannot compel them to do so in this indirect way. And we think that whenever the time shall come for actually making the restoration, they will be stopped from claiming more than that annual deduction which they now insist on. exactly as a landlord could not claim to deduct the expense of restoration made by him of a house."

At the present time the accounts of railway companies usually do contain charges in respect of renewal of way and works, although, it may be, that such charges are either above or below the average. But they sometimes contain sums, under this head, which are not a legitimate deduction from the rent. These charges are in respect of operations which are really landlord's improvements. An illustration will make this clear. In one case a railway had originally been built in a less durable manner than usual; there were many wooden bridges, and the permanent way was less substantial than was advisable. The consequence was that the expense of the repairs and renewals necessary to maintain the premises in a state to command the rent were large, and consequently the rateable value or net produce of the land less than it would have been had the original construction of the railway been better. Moreover, even the way and works had not been kept in such a perfect state of repair as sound economy would require. The result was that, latterly, for *a series* of years, the expense of maintenance and renewal of way was very high, and not only so, but, a better system of management having been adopted, the wooden bridges were gradually transformed into brick and iron ones, and an improved way substituted for the inferior. Part of the expense of these improvements was charged to revenue, and part to capital. But no part of this expenditure could be allowed as a deduction from the rent, for the expenditure was in respect of an improvement of the property, and not merely for the conservation thereof. Although by this improvement the entire hereditament would not command more *rent*, yet, inasmuch as the annual expense of maintenance and renewals of way and works would be less, there would be a less deduction from the rent, and, consequently, an increased rateable value—that is, an increased net produce of the land.

A case having reference to the deduction to be made under the head of *maintenance of the permanent way* was brought before the Court of Queen's Bench on the 20th of January last (1870).

The appellants were the *London and North Western Railway Company*, and the respondents were the *Assessment Committee of the King's Norton Union.*

The case stated for the opinion of the Court was that, the appellants are the owners and occupiers of the London and North Western Railway, a portion of which, called the Stour Valley line, runs through the parish of Harborne, in the King's Norton Union. The whole length of the Stour Valley line is fourteen and a half miles, of which a length of two miles thirty-eight chains is situate in Harborne parish. A poor rate for that parish was made on the 30th of November, 1867, in which the company were assessed at a rateable value of £5,538 for the portion of the railway and the stations in the parish. Against this rate the company appealed to the Quarter Sessions. The question which was raised being as to the amount of deductions to be made from the gross receipts in the parish in respect of the expense of maintaining and renewing the permanent way. It appeared that the London and North Western Railway is divided into several sections, and a separate account is kept of the cost of maintaining the permanent way upon each of those sections. It is possible, therefore, to ascertain exactly the amount so expended upon each section of the system. The Stour Valley line is the section of the system which lies between Birmingham and Wolverhampton. There are several coal mines near to some parts of the Stour Valley line, and, consequently, the cost of maintaining the permanent way upon that section is much greater than over the rest of the system. None of these mines, however, are in the parish of Harborne, and the maintenance of the permanent way in that parish is not affected by the existence of those mines. The bulk of the traffic passing over the Stour Valley line is local, but a portion of the passengers and goods traffic over the Stour Valley line, before arriving at and after leaving that line, passes over other parts of the London and North Western system.

The *appellants* contended that the amount of the expense of maintaining the permanent way to be deducted from the gross receipts earned on that portion of the Stour Valley line within the parish of Harborne, should be arrived at by ascertaining as nearly as practicable *the average actual expense per mile of maintaining the way on the whole of that section of the line.* The *respondents* contended that the amount of the expense of maintaining the permanent way to be deducted from the gross receipts earned in the parish, should be arrived at in one of the three following ways—that is to say, either by taking the average actual expenses per mile of maintaining the permanent way over the whole system, or that the extraordinary expense of maintaining the permanent way on the Stour Valley line should be distributed amongst all the parishes through which the traffic carried over this section of the railway also passed, in proportion to the amount of such traffic passing through each parish, or that, *the appellant should be entitled to deduct only the expense of maintaining the permanent way within the parish.*

The Court of Quarter Session, subject to the opinion of this Court, affirmed the principle contended for by the appellants.

A. S. Hill, Q.C., appeared for the appellants; and *Gray*, Q.C., and *Bosanquet*, for the respondents.

Per Curiam :

Each parish is entitled to the benefit of the value which the land within it has acquired for the purposes of rating. The proper mode of making the deduction in respect of the maintenance of the railway from the gross annual value is not by following the mileage principle, *but simply by taking the actual outlay in the parish ;* and this item is not to be varied by expenses under this head in *other parishes* along the same railway. The judgment must therefore be for the *respondents*.

It will now be well to speak of certain claims which have been made, but disallowed by the Court. These claims must be considered here, because they can be arranged under no other head than as a deduction from the rent.

As to claims for rent paid, and on other points.

They cannot be made a deduction from the gross receipts, for they are not tenant's working expenses, nor, some of them, even expenses at all ; neither can they be deducted from the net receipts, for they in no way concern the tenant. Neither can they be deducted from the rateable value, for the rateable value is that which remains after all deductions have been made.

The first of these is for an allowance for goodwill. In making this claim the allegation is practically, that the amount paid by the tenant, and which has hitherto been called the rent, is not so, in fact; but that it includes, not merely the rateable value and the amount for repairs, but also an amount in respect of the lessor's goodwill, which amount is not the produce of the hereditament, but of a something which is not liable to be rated. This claim was made in the case of *R.* v. *The Grand Junction Railway*, 4 Q. B. 18, and also in the case of *R.* v. *The East London Water Company*. With respect to the claim for an allowance in respect of goodwill, made by the Grand Junction Railway Company, Lord Denman, in his judgment, said:

"The appellants, however, contend that, even if the *principle* of the rate be fair, some reasonable deductions are omitted. We have used the sufficiency of the deductions made as a mode of trying the principle; but the objection of the appellants, now to be considered, is one of detail. The only instance which they specify and rely on, is, that an allowance ought to be made, and is not for goodwill. We presume by this is meant that a person bargaining with the company to become their yearly tenant of the railway in expectation of succeeding to their trade, as a probable consequence of succeeding to their occupation, would probably be called upon to pay them something for the goodwill of that trade: and this would be, in the nature of an outgoing, a deduction from profits. This objection appears capable of two answers: the first and a decisive one, is, that the purchase of a goodwill implies that a *trade* is sold: that the company are bound to surrender their trade to the lessee, and to be no longer carriers on that line. But the calculation of the sessions proceeds on no such supposition. All those *special advantages*, indeed, for carrying it on, which the occupation gives them, whatever they may be, they must necessarily surrender; but the moment they had leased the railway, they would become a part of the public, and have the right to carry on their trade, retaining all the goodwill, with all those advantages which the statutes have carefully reserved for the public. Secondly, though the supposition of a tenancy is to be made, yet what the incidents of a tenancy must be, as to actual terms and allowances, must be determined for the purpose of fixing the amount of rate by the actual state of things; for this supposition of a tenancy is only the mode of ascertaining the existing value of the occupation to the existing occupier. Now, here there is no tenancy in fact; no goodwill is in fact paid for, and therefore no deduction ought, in fact, to be made on account of its price."

The next claim to be noticed was that made by the *Great Western Railway Company*, 6 Q. B. 184, for an allowance of 5 per cent. interest on £420,000, being the outlay for promoting the Great Western Railway Company, obtaining the act of incorporation, and the like. It is evident that such a deduction as this cannot be one which concerns a tenant from year to year, for it is no part of his business to incur *any* expenses, even in *creating* the hereditament, much less in *preparing* to create it, and the deduction must therefore, if made at all, be made from the rent.

Respecting this claim, Lord Denman, in his judgment, said:

"One of the claims made by the appellants, and rejected by the respondents, was for a sum of £21,000 yearly, interest on the sum expended in raising the capital of the company, getting the Act of Parliament, purchasing land, and other similar expenses. The Court was of opinion that there was not the slightest foundation for this claim. These expenses were not in any way connected with a rateable value of the railway. As well might the purchaser of an estate, who had borrowed money to complete his purchase, claim, after the termination of expensive litigation, deductions from the poor rate in respect of the money he had thereby been compelled to spend."

Another claim made in the same case must also be treated of before proceeding to discuss the question of the apportionment of the entire rateable value, inasmuch as, if allowed, the deduction would have had the effect of reducing the rateable value.

This was in respect of a deduction of £10,500, the annual loss upon two branch lines *rented* by the company.

Here the entire hereditament occupied was, as a whole, created by the Great Western Railway Company, they having made some and rented other parts thereof, and by that means secured the occupation of the whole. They, if the entire hereditament had been let, would have secured to themselves a greater annual rent than if the part only which they themselves had made had been let. But the rent which they had agreed to pay for the branch lines was

greater than the rent which the net produce of the branch lines
would have yielded.   But in consequence of the occupation of
these, the extra net produce on the main line was much greater
than it would have been without them, and moreover was so much
greater that, after bearing the loss occasioned by those branches
which the company rented, the rent remaining in the hands of the
company, in respect of that part which they had themselves made,
was greater than would have been the case had the company not
rented those branches.   The Court disallowed this claim also,
saying :

"Then came the claim for deduction in respect of the losses on the two
branch lines. This claim would be well enough if the rate was laid on the
land which formed part of those lines; but though those lines were themselves
worked at a loss, they must, so long as they were worked, be considered, in the
ordinary sense of the term, a means of profit, and the loss would not be
deducted from the profits on the main line, but must be treated as money
laid out in the improvement of that line."

This renting of the branch lines to secure a profit on the main
lines is analogous to the case of the owner of a house securing a
piece of ground as a garden, at a rent much higher than the garden
itself is worth ; but the effect is to make the house and garden
command a rent so much higher, that out of the increased rent of
the whole, the owner can well afford to bear the loss on the
garden.

This matter may be put in another way, thus—That it is no
concern of the tenant of the whole how the whole was created : he
can give for the whole a certain rent, and the rent of any part
thereof is no concern of his, and consequently he would not deduct
it before arriving at the rent of the whole ; neither can it be
deducted from the rent of the whole in deducing the rateable value,
for it is not a deduction necessary to maintain the premises in a
state to command such rent : hence it cannot be deducted at all.

Rateable value of   The next question is, how the rateable value of
stations.   the stations and warehouses must be arrived at ?

If the whole hereditament were situate in one parish, no such question as this would arise, but the inquiry would be complete.

It will be convenient to assume that the entire hereditament, which, as already has been seen, consists of the line of railway itself, and "warehouses, wharfs, stations, or landing places," necessary to the occupation of the railway, is situate in but two parishes; and that the line of railway is situate in one parish, and the warehouses and stations in the other.

It will at once be evident that it would not be just to assign the whole rateable value to the parish in which the railway is situate, neither would it be just to assign the whole to the parish in which are the stations. But the whole rateable value which has been earned by the joint co-operation of each part must be divided between the two parishes. And in doing this, regard must be had to the *value of the occupation in each.*

In the earlier cases which came before the Court, this question seems somewhat obscure.

In the first case, that of *R.* v. *The Great Western Railway Company,* no dispute respecting the stations arose. In the next case, that of *R.* v. *Grand Junction Railway Company,* a rateable value of the entire line was found in the case, *exclusive* of the rateable value of the stations, which were separately rated in the parishes where they were situate, at an aggregate sum of £9,150. In this case no question was raised either as to the correctness of the amount at which they were rated, or as to the principles on which the amount should be determined. But in the case of *R.* v. *The Great Western Railway Company,* 15 L. J., M. C. 80, wherein the parish of Tilehurst was the respondent, in which there was no station, the case stated that the entire rateable value of the stations, "rated separately from the railway," was, on the main line, £35,000 a year, and on the branch, £10,000; and the appellants claimed that a proportion of this total amount should be deducted from the rateable value of the line in Tilehurst.

The judgment of the Court upon this point was not clear.

"Another objection related to the mode of calculating the outgoings that were allowed. The respondents treated the deductions as if they ought to be made in respect of outgoings upon the whole line, assuming it to be indifferent in point of principle whether the stations were in one parish or in another; and the Court agreed with them."

In the case of *R.* v. *The North Staffordshire Railway Company,* 50 L. J. (N. S.) M. C. 68, a question relating to the stations was again raised. It was

" Whether the deduction to be allowed in respect of the stations, buildings, and sidings, along the line of railway, ought to be ascertained by taking the rateable value at which the same are assessed to the relief of the poor, or by allowing 6 per cent. upon the original cost of construction, as contended for by the appellants; or how, otherwise, a deduction should be made in respect of the said station, buildings, and sidings."

It was agreed that £360,000 was the amount of the original cost of construction.

To this the answer of the Court was:

" As regards the fourth question, we are of opinion that the deduction to be allowed in respect of stations, buildings, and sidings, must be calculated on the actual value at which they ought to be assessed, and not on the original cost of construction."

This judgment was rather of a negative than a positive character, inasmuch as it did not point out the principle upon which the "actual value" ought to be ascertained.

The case of *The Eastern Counties Railway Company* v. *The Overseers of Great Amwell,* 32 L. J. (N. S.) M. C. 174, progressed another step in determining this principle, by further showing how the rateable value must *not* be ascertained.

The point in this case was, that the rateable value should be based upon the capacity which the stations have, to earn certain monies which, it was said, were received in respect solely of the use of the stations.

Continuing the assumption that has already been made, that the business of a railway company is carried on entirely upon a railway occupied by themselves, it is apparent that, in order to earn the fare which is paid by a passenger for conveyance from one place to another, certain accommodation must be provided in addition to a service rendered. The accommodation is the use of the stations at each end of his journey. The service rendered is the transport of the passenger from one station to another. It is perfectly possible to divide the total amount of the fare into two parts; one part may be assigned as the recompense for the use of the station, and the other part as the recompense for the service rendered in transit. When the carriages of a railway company pass on to the railway of another company, the total fare paid is actually thus divided into parts. This division is made by mutual agreement between the various companies concerned, and is affected through the medium of the clearing house.

Of the various parts into which the whole fare is in such a case divided, one part is assigned for the use of the station, and for the services of the staff at the station from whence the passenger departs; another part for the like use of the station, and the staff of the station at which he arrives; another part for the payment of the expenses of transit; another part for the use of the engine; another for the use of the carriages; and the other parts for the use of the railways over which the traveller passes. The same system is adopted for goods. The amounts allotted for the use of the stations at either end are called " terminals."

Where, however, a company only uses its own stations and railway, no such division of the fare is made.

In the above case of *The Great Eastern Railway Company* v. *The Overseers of Great Amwell*, the company claimed to deduct from the gross receipts the amount that would have been received for the use of their stations, had they been used to the extent they were by the passengers and goods of other companies, instead of by their own passengers and goods.

" The questions for this Court are—1. Whether, in ascertaining the general earnings of the said portion of the said line, the appellants are entitled to deduct the said sum of £2,829, the amount that would have been received for the terminals under the above hypothesis. 2. Whether the capacity to earn the said sum is to be considered in determining the rateable value of the station.

" *May* 23.—The judgment of the Court was now delivered by Mr. Justice

Blackburn : In this case it appears that if the station and line in Amwell belonged to different companies, and if the clearing house system were in force, certain allowances would be made to the company owning the stations by way of remuneration for the accommodation afforded in receiving and unloading, despatching and delivering goods, either taken in or given out at the station. The appellants contend that these allowances, which are called "terminals," are not part of the earnings of the line, but are to be considered as earnings of the stations. We are, however, of opinion that we must, in conformity with the established practice, treat the station as *only indirectly contributing* to the profits of the line, and, consequently, as being to be rated as land and buildings whose value is to some extent enhanced by their capacity of being employed in connexion with the line. We think the amount of those terminals, and the amount of the expenses in earning them, are parts of the general earnings and general expenses of the line, and are to be treated in the same way as any other part of the gross receipts and outgoings."

The Court having by this judgment laid down the principle that the stations are only "*indirectly contributing to the profits of the line*," and having also laid down in the *West Middlesex Water* case, 28 L. J. (N. S.) M. C. 135, the principles upon which those parts indirectly contributing to the profit are to be rated, the proper principle of deducing the rateable value of the stations, &c., may from this time be taken to have been judicially determined.

This has been confirmed by the judgment recently given in the case of *The Company of Proprietors of the Birmingham Canal Navigation* v. *The Overseers of the Parish of Birmingham*, 19 Law Times Reports (N. S.), 311. The company were owners and occupiers of a portion of a canal, and of wharves and reservoirs ancillary thereto, situate in the parish of Birmingham. Some of the reservoirs being "summit" reservoirs, it was necessary to provide an engine for the purpose of pumping water into them. It was only necessary to work this engine for a *few days during the year*, but it was necessary to keep it always ready for work. The quantity of work it did depended on the rainfall during the year.

The company were authorised by their act to levy tolls on goods carried on their canal, and other tolls on the goods landed at their wharves, and further tolls if the goods landed remained on the wharves more than forty-eight hours. The company were authorised to demise certain of their wharves if they should so think fit. They do not, however, either collect any demurrage tolls, nor demise any of their wharves, but they allow certain of their customers, wood merchants and coal merchants, to store wood and coal on their wharves. They require certain paths and spaces on their wharves to be kept always clear so as to allow free passage to the canal.

Under these circumstances the parish officers of Birmingham rated the wharves and reservoirs as

" Land and fixed capital vested therein, and deriving some additional value from its capacity of being applied to such purposes as that of a canal company."

And they rated the canal by ascertaining the gross receipts from tolls, making the necessary deductions and allowances.

The company objected to the amount at which they were rated for their wharves and reservoirs, and contended that they ought to have been rated either at the net value of the tolls they charged for the use of their wharf, or at the net value of those tolls *plus* the value of the demurrage tolls had they charged them, or at the rent they could have got had they let their wharves. The assessment arrived at by the respondents was higher than any of these modes would have given. They moreover contended that even were the respondents right in their method of arriving at the rateable value, they ought not to have included in their calculation the land which was used solely as pathways ; also " that the reservoirs have no *rateable value beyond* what is dealt with in rating the other parts of the undertaking ;" and also that in rating the engine power, the respondents ought to have rated it only to the extent to which it was actually used during the year, and for that portion of the year during which it was unused ; that it ought to have been rated on the principle laid down in the case of *Staley* v. *Castleton*, 33 L. J., M. C. 178 (in which it was decided that a building in which a large quantity of machinery was erected, but which machinery was standing idle in consequence of a failure of trade, was rateable as a warehouse used for the purpose of storing

R

machinery ; the position taken up by the appellants being, that so long as the machinery was standing idle the building was not rateable).

Cockburn, C. J. :

"I must say I think Mr. Keane is right. You cannot give the whole canal or those who travel the whole length of the canal, a benefit at the expense of the parish. The parish is entitled to a rate upon the property of the canal for what occurs in Birmingham, and for the profits which might be made in Birmingham—that is to say, not only in respect of the profits which the company do make, but in respect of the profits which the company might make, *but which they are pleased to forego, from no doubt a very wise policy*—namely, that by foregoing those profits in Birmingham *they make a greater profit upon the whole area of the canal.* Therefore Mr. Keane's contention is right, that whatever might be the value of this property in Birmingham, the company which is to make the value that they might extract from it with respect to that, to that extent would be rated. I have expressed my opinion before, that as to the reservoir the rate is right. With regard to the engine house. it has a certain value by reason of the land or the building erected upon it. and of the machinery attached to that building, all of which is necessary for the purpose of the canal. It is situated in Birmingham ; it is only made available, and put to a particular use *on certain occasions*, or if you like, in *certain contingencies ;* nevertheless *it must always be there ;* it has a certain value with respect to the land, and the buildings upon it, and the machinery permanently affixed to it; and in that respect I think it ought to be rated *whether it is used all the year or not.*

"Lush, J., concurred. Judgment for the respondents."

The rateable value of the stations having been determined and deducted from the rateable value of the whole, the residue is the rateable value of the line of railway.

But before proceeding to consider the principle upon which that rateable value must be apportioned amongst those parishes in which the railway is situate, it will be desirable to notice a case which has been decided in the Court of Queen's Bench affecting the rateable value of a station in some particular cases.

Special local values.

It has already been seen that a railway company may pay toll to another company for the use of that company's railway. They may also pay a rent for the use of a station or stations; for the mere payment of toll does not, as it has been pointed out in the case of *R. v. South Western Railway*, give a right to the use of a station. In like manner they may also *receive* tolls from other companies, which tolls would constitute part of the gross receipts. Also they may receive a remuneration for the *use* of a particular station. The amount of such remuneration would be included in their gross receipts, and, consequently, in the rateable value of the whole hereditament. But in apportioning—since the receipt of this rent for the use of any station makes the value of the occupation in the parish where such station is situate greater than it would be if such station were used by the company only—the rateable value of such station must include the entire annual value of the occupation, even when it has been decided, the remuneration received by the company is greater than the accommodation afforded is worth.

In the case of *The Great Eastern Railway Company v. The Overseers of Fletton*, 30 L. J. M. C. 89, the Great Eastern Company had granted the use of the Peterboro' Station to the London and North Western Railway Company, at a fixed amount, for 999 years. Subsequently, in consequence of a change of circumstances, the value of the occupation to the London and North Western was much below the amount they paid for such accommodation.

The Great Eastern Company raised the question

"Whether they were to be deemed the occupiers, and were liable to be rated in respect of this amount paid to them, as well as in respect of the value of their own occupation of the station?"

Judgment was delivered by Lord Chief-Justice Cockburn, who held that the Eastern Counties Company were still the occupiers, subject to the easement granted to the London and North Western.

"It was true the value of the easement to the London and North Western Railway had greatly decreased, but the Eastern Counties Company were the occupiers, and they were liable to be assessed in the full value which they derived in respect of their occupation of the station, both by their own use of it and what they received from the London and North Western Company."

The whole force of this judgment depends upon the fact that the Great Eastern Company had not ceased to be the *occupiers* of the

Peterboro' Station ; and the payment of a certain sum for a long and definite period having been *guaranteed*, a property would thereby be created, for which a tenant from year to year would give a rent.

In a subsequent case, *R.* v. *Lord Sherrard*, the extent to which the Eastern Counties Company, and that to which the London and North Western, respectively were to be considered as occupiers, was determined ; this was merely a local question, and involved only the amount at which the Great Eastern Company should be rated in respect of the rent paid by the London and North Western.

Apportionment of the entire rateable value. The next question that arises is the manner in which the rateable value of the whole *line of railway*, exclusive of the stations, must be apportioned amongst the various parishes in which the railway is situate.

The assumption that has been made that the railway lies wholly in one parish, and the stations in another, must no longer be regarded. The *principle* upon which the rateable value of the stations must be determined having been ascertained, it is immaterial in how many parishes the stations are situate.

In the earlier cases which were submitted to the Court for decision, the rateable value of the *railway, per se,* it was *agreed* should be apportioned to each parish by a mileage division.

It was thereby practically allowed that the value of the occupation was in proportion to the length of the railway. But it very soon became evident that this proposition was not true ; but that, on the contrary, the value of the occupation of a mile of railway near to a large town was much greater than that of a mile further off; the mile nearer to the town *producing* much more than one remoter.

Such being the case, it was contended, by those interested, that the *parochial earnings* in each parish must be ascertained, and the rate for that parish based upon them.

This important question was raised in the cases of *R.* v. *The London and Brighton Railway Company*, 15 Q. B. 313, already referred to, *R.* v. *The South Eastern Railway*, 15 Q. B. R. 314, *R.* v. *The Midland Railway*, 15 Q. B. R. 353.

In the Brighton case the question was raised by the parish officers, the respondents, who

"claimed a right to rate the company on the principle of *parochial earnings*—that is to say, at such a sum as a solvent tenant should pay as annual rent for the stations and portions of railway within the parish, regard being had to the net revenue earned within the parish."

In the South Eastern case the company raised the question :

"The appellants contended that the rate ought to have been based on the principle of *parochial earnings*, that is to say, that they ought to have been rated at such a sum as a tenant might be expected to give as annual rent for that portion of the branch railway situate within *Westbere*, regard being had to the net revenue earned by the portion of the branch railway situate within that parish, such rent being ascertained by taking the gross annual receipts of the company, arising from that portion of the *Ashford, Ramsgate,* and *Margate* branch of railway, situate in *Westbere* parish (such gross receipts being ascertained by taking a proportion of the fare paid by every passenger who has, during the course of the year, been carried by the company over any part of the railway in *Westbere*, such proportion bearing the same ratio to the whole sum paid by such passenger for his fare for the whole distance travelled by him over the company's main line and branches, as the distance travelled by him in *Westbere* bears to the whole distance travelled by him on the company's main line and branches), and also by taking a proportion of the gross receipts for goods traffic in *Westbere*, calculated on a similar principle ; then by taking from such gross receipts for passengers and goods traffic in *Westbere* the deductions prescribed and directed by the Parochial Assessment Act, 6 and 7 Will. IV. c. 96, according to the mileage principle, applied to such Ashford, Margate, and Ramsgate line only ; the result showing the rent which a tenant might reasonably be expected to give for the portion of the railway situate within *Westbere*; which mileage principle the appellants contend gives the nearest approximation to the actual expenses and usual allowances in respect of the respondent parish which can with any certainty be arrived at."

In the Midland case the question was raised by the company, the appellants, who contended that the rateable value ought to be estimated "with reference solely to the *net profits* earned by the railway within that parish."

In the above proposition of the South Eastern Company, three propositions are made.

1st. That the rate ought to have been based on the principle of the parochial earnings.

2ndly. That the rent of the parish is represented by the difference between the gross receipts in the parish, and the expenses necessary to earn those receipts.

3rdly. That the expenses are to be ascertained by a mileage apportionment.

Of these propositions it is the first only which is now immediately under consideration. Of the second no further remark need be made, the proposition having almost become an axiom.

Judgment in all the cases was given as a whole by Mr. Justice Coleridge, February 22, 1851, who in a very detailed ruling, decided that the company must be rated upon the principle of *parochial earnings*, regard being had to the *net revenue* earned within the parish.

It will have been seen from the quotation from the South Eastern case, that the foundation of the *net revenue* is allowed to be the *gross receipts*. But questions have been raised by the London and Brighton, and by the Great Eastern Counties Railway companies as to what are to be *deemed the gross receipts in the parish*.

In the case of this Brighton Company, 15 Q. B. 313, the circumstances were somewhat peculiar. The company not only used the railway themselves, but they allowed the South Eastern Company also to use it. For this use they did not charge the South Eastern Company toll, because they themselves used a portion of the South Eastern Company's lines without paying tolls.

Under these circumstances, the company contended that if they were to be assessed upon the net revenue, such assessment should be upon the *actual* net revenue, and not upon what the *net revenue* would have been had they received toll from the South Eastern Company. But the Court disallowed this claim, considering that this exchange toll, represented "rent in kind," and as such would add to the "annual value" of the occupation.

" It seems to us exactly the same in substance as if so many tickets were daily issued without money paid for them to the South Eastern Railway Company, in return for so many received from them. The tickets mutually transferred would on either side represent so much money earned. But then we think these earnings must be subject to exactly the same deduction as if they were received in money."

Again, in the case of *The Eastern Counties Railway Company* v. *The Overseers of Amwell*, 32 L. J. (N. S.) M. C. 174, wherein the company claimed to base their rateable value of the stations upon their capacity for earning certain terminals, and to deduct the amount of these terminals from the gross receipts earned in the parish; but the Court disallowed the claim, ruling that the amount of those terminals were parts of the general earnings of the line, and the expenses of earning those terminals part of the gross expenses.

Notwithstanding this judgment, railway companies even now often make a deduction from the gross receipts, the right to make which must some day come before the Court. The nature of the claim may be thus explained :

Let A and B be two terminal stations. Let station A belong to the X railway company, and station B to the Z railway company. Assume a gross amount earned for the carriage of goods between A and B. Assume (to make the case clear) that the engines and carriages of the X company do all the transport work, and in doing it use the station A of the X company, the railway X of the X company, the railway Y of the Y company, the railway Z of the Z company, and the station B of that company.

Now, it is a fact, in many systems of railway, that goods are carried between A and B at two rates, called by the clearing house "cartage rates," and "non-cartage rates." When goods are carried at "cartage rates," the X company would collect, or cause to be collected, into their station A the goods to be carried to B. Arrived at B, the Z company would distribute the goods. When goods are carried at "non-cartage rates," the senders of the goods take them to the one station (A), and the consignees of the goods fetch them from the other station (B).

The gross amount above assumed to have been earned would be distributed between the companies X, Y, Z by the clearing house. First, the X company is remunerated for the cost of transport, and for the use of its engines and carriages. Next (in the case of goods carried at cartage rates), a deduction for the expenses of cartage at each end of the journey is made. Then a deduction is made for the use of the stations, *i.e.*, for terminals, and the residue, which is for the use of the railway between the two stations, is divided between the X, the Y, and the Z companies, in proportion to the length of railway belonging to each.

Now, when one railway company occupies both the terminal stations and the railway between them, the aid of the clearing house is not required to distribute the amount earned. In arriving at the gross receipts per mile in any parish, the proper mode is to divide the total amount so earned by the distance between the two stations.

In the Amwell case, the company had not done this, but had deducted from the total earnings the amount the clearing house would have assigned to the stations, and then divided the residue only. This the Court declared was wrong, and ruled that the "*terminals*" ought not to have been divided.

Notwithstanding this, some companies, in arriving at the gross receipts, deduct not the amount which the *cartage* has cost them, but the amount the clearing house would allow for *cartage* (such amount being more than the cartage would cost the company), and so make the gross receipts less than they would be if the actual payment for cartage only were deducted.

From these judgments it may be gathered that the proper gross receipts, from which to deduce the net profits, are the total gross receipts which *ought* to be received in any parish. The gross receipts *in any parish* being settled, the next question is, in what manner is the *net revenue* in that parish to be deduced.

It has already been shown what items must be deducted from the total *gross receipts of the entire hereditament* in order to arrive at the *rateable value* of the *whole railway, exclusive of the stations*, and the question now becomes, in what manner is a due proportion of these items, to be charged in any parish *against the gross receipts therein*, to be ascertained,

Deductions
from local re-
ceipts.

Before proceeding to consider this question, it will be as well to notice a distinction which it has been sought to make between the parishes upon a branch railway and the parishes upon a main line.

This occurred in the second *Great Western Railway* case, 21 Law Journal, M. C. 84. The Great Western Company possessed and occupied a branch railway twenty-five miles long. It was *managed* in common, with the remainder of the whole Great Western system. No separate accounts were kept of the receipts and expenses on the branch, but the amounts were merged in the general accounts of the Great Western Company. But a certain number of engines and carriages were specially devoted to working that particular branch, and a certain number of officers and men specially employed thereon. Under these circumstances the appellants claimed to be rated at the sum of £30 per mile, being an amount arrived at by considering the railway in the parish as a portion of the branch railway, and which was considered as being an independent line. Whereas, the respondents claimed to rate the company at the sum of £254 per mile, which amount was arrived at on the consideration that the branch railway was a portion of the entire system of the Great Western Railway.

Upon this point the Court said:

"But the separation of the branch from the trunk is in its effect the substantial ground of dispute between the two parties, producing, it may be said, nearly the whole difference between £254 and £30 per mile; and, unless they are justified in this, it is impossible that their mode of ascertaining the rateable value can prevail, and we think they are not. We wish it to be distinctly understood that we came to this conclusion solely on the facts of the case. We are far from saying that there may not be cases in which the two lines, connected for many purposes, and worked by the same company, may yet have been kept so distinct by the statute or agreement which creates the connexion, or by the circumstances under which they are worked, that for the purpose of rating they would have to be separately considered as two distinct subject-matters. When such cases arise they must be dealt with according to their respective circumstances ; but in the present case the fusion of the two lines is complete."

After examining the circumstances of the case, the Court continued :

" We conclude, therefore, that a rateable value, ascertained by considering twenty-five miles as a distinct whole, cannot be correct."

Reverting to the consideration of the question—

"In what manner is the due proportion of expenses and allowances, to be charged in any parish against the gross receipts therein, to be ascertained ?"

Let it be assumed, in virtue of the above judgment, that the railway in any parish is a portion of a whole system.

In the case of *R*. v. *The South Eastern Railway*, already alluded to, 15 Q. B. R. 344, it was seen that the company claimed to charge the expenses and allowances against the receipts according to a mileage division.

In the above case of *R*. v. *The Great Western Railway Company*, the *appellants* had apportioned the expenses as follows :—

" They took the gross receipts per mile per annum in the respondent parish exactly as the respondents had done, and they deducted from these the actual expenses of each mile ascertained or estimated. In order to do so, they ascertained the actual expenses incurred on the branch alone; and where those expenses were common to the entire branch, they divided such expenses by the number of miles in the branch ; and they consider the result to be the expense of each mile in the branch. A small portion of the general expenses of the entire railway, being those of central superintendence, printing, and advertising, were apportioned on the branch in the ratio of the business or traffic upon it ; and such portion was then subdivided as before on the mileage principle."

In the same case the *respondents* had apportioned the rateable value of the whole railway, "*qua*" railway, in the ratio of the gross receipts :—

" And they assessed the appellants, in respect of the said two miles and a half of railway in their parish, in the ratio which such annual receipts bore to the gross annual receipts of the company in respect of the entire Great Western Railway, trunk and branches ; the rateable value of a mile of railway in the respondent parish being calculated in the same proportion to the rateable value of the whole line of railway, exclusive of the stations, as the gross annual receipts in respect of such mile bore to the total of such actual annual receipts of the company."

By this mode they practically apportioned the expenses and allowances in proportion to the gross receipts.

The case, however, found that

" The actual expenses of the company are not in the proportion of the actual gross receipts on the branch or through the entire railway ; nor are either such gross receipts or such expenses at one uniform rate per mile throughout the entire railway."

Upon this point the Court said :

" The remaining question is, what is the net rateable value of the two miles and a half. Now as the net rateable value is that which remains of the gross receipts after all just deductions are made, it might seem at first sight that we might confine our inquiry to the two miles and a half, and that we only encumber the investigation uselessly by introducing into it any consideration of the gross and rateable value of the whole line. But the circumstances of a railway make this absolutely necessary. The inquiry may become, and undoubtedly does become, more complicated and difficult thereby, but it would be wholly incomplete and illusory, even in its result, unless we did so. Of the outgoings of a railway, some are general, having no more connexion with or influence on one part of the whole line than on any other incurred for the sake of the whole line, and contributing to the profits everywhere. Of course these must be distributed, and to every mile must be apportioned some share, on whatever principle the apportionment is to be settled. Some, again, seem purely local—a tunnel here, an inclined plane there (we purposely mention striking and definite peculiarities) : yet even *these are contributing to the earnings everywhere :* without these, the traffic upon either side could have no existence. It would be wrong to set these wholly and exclusively against the receipts earned in the same part of the line. We need not dwell on this, because in principle some distribution is on all hands agreed to be necessary, the only difficulty is in determining what is to be adopted for making it justly —a difficulty we believe actually insurmountable in fact, if strict mathematical accuracy were insisted on.

"It is our business, however, only to lay down the general rule, and applying it must be left. not only to the experience and acuteness, but also to the good sense. and good faith, and candour of the parties concerned, whose interest will be found in the end to be best consulted by this mode of dealing. How, then. are the deductions from the total gross revenue, which constitute the difference between it and the total net rateable value, to be apportioned, so as to arrive at the actual sum which constitutes the rateable value of the two miles and a half. There is no difficulty in giving the first answer; indeed principle and authority leave us no option; it must be done by acting upon what is called the parochial principle. We are dealing with a parochial question, with one in which the interests of the several parishes on a line of railway are quite distinct. We are to ascertain what expenses are incurred in earning the gross receipts on the two miles and a half; what charges, parochial or otherwise, they are liable to: and what is fairly to be deducted for tenant's profits, and so on. The same process in kind is to be gone through with regard to the two miles and a half as would be with regard to the whole line if that were all in one parish. We need not now repeat the reasoning which appears in our judgment before referred to, *R. v. The London and Brighton Railway.* But, as we then said, and have now repeated, this principle does not preclude a consideration of charges and expenses wherever arising locally, which are necessary for keeping the subject of assessment at the value which is made the measure of that assessment.

"And further we must add, that wherever it is found that such charges and expenses do in fact apply equally to every mile of railway, it is a convenient and allowable mode to arrive by a mileage division at the proportionate part to be assigned to the miles in any particular parish. This is no departure from the parochial principle, if it be assumed as to particular charges (central superintendence, for instance), that a separate investigation of them, as they actually arise in. or are referable to a particular parish, would lead us to the same result as a mileage distribution of the whole. It becomes by the hypothesis but another mode of arriving at it; in many cases it will be the more convenient and just. in some perhaps it may be the only practical mode."

The Court having thus laid down the *principle*, proceeded to review the method of apportionment employed by the appellants. Having done this, the Court continued :

"This explanation shows that the appellants have, in fact, separated the branch from the trunk. except as to what they call a small portion of the general expenses of the entire railway, and then divided the expenses of the branch thus separated on the *mileage principle.* We do not think them *necessarily wrong* in this last particular; it may have been no practical departure from the true principle, but only an allowable instance of what we have above stated to be a convenient practice where the actual expenses were the same on every mile; and as no objection is made by the respondents, we must assume that it was so."

The case, however, had found—

"Nor are either such gross receipts, or such expenses at one uniform rate per mile throughout the entire railway."

The Court then proceeded to consider the mode of rating adopted by the respondents.

"It appears by the statement in the case that the respondents have taken the deductions at the same rate for every mile of railway, for, they say, as the gross receipts of one mile to the gross receipts of the whole, so the rateable value of one mile to the rateable value of the whole. This is in effect to strike off from the gross receipts of a mile an aliquot part of the sum which is struck off from the gross receipts of the whole, and assumes at least that the expenses are at one uniform rate throughout the whole line. If the case were silent on this subject, we might have presumed that the respondents had ascertained this to be fact, and then there would have been no objection to a mileage division; but the case, reasonably understood, excludes this, for it finds that the actual expenses of the company are not in the proportion of the actual gross receipts, either on the branch, or throughout the entire railway; nor are either such gross receipts or such expenses at one uniform rate per mile throughout the entire railway. The counsel for the respondents laboured in vain to explain away the clear meaning of this passage, and, failing in that, they equally laboured in vain to show that all the expenses on a railway were necessarily to be distributed in calculation equally over the whole line. In the result we cannot adopt either of the modes suggested to us, or confirm the rate at either of the sums stated; the consequence must be, which we very much regret, that the award must be referred back to the learned arbitrators, to whom the parties, and we ourselves, are so much indebted for the labour and ability which they have bestowed on the case. We trust that the principles we have laid down will enable them to agree on a satisfactory rate, and there may be no more litigation on the subject."

The whole of a tenant's working expenses of a railway, the tenant's allowances, and the landlord's deductions, may be divided into two classes.

1st. Those which depend on the amount of business done—that is, on the receipts.

2ndly. Those which depend on the work done, *i.e*, the number of trains run.

Of the first-class is the item "passenger traffic charges." Under this head are placed such items of expense as the following :— Salaries of superintendents, clerks, wages of guards, ticket porters, collectors, police, clothing, &c. It will be evident that such items will vary more or less according to the receipts. On those parts of the railway where there are many passengers, there will be required many booking clerks, porters, &c., while on those parts of the line where there are not many passengers, but few of these officers and servants will be needful. It would, therefore, be incorrect to divide such an expense as passenger traffic charges by a general mileage division.

Again, such an expense as locomotive power does not depend so *much* on the number of passengers, as it does on the number of miles travelled and the weights moved. The dead weight of an empty train is great. To move this dead weight a given distance a certain expense must be incurred. If the train be full of people, its weight is of course somewhat increased, but the increase in weight does not involve a proportionate increase of expense. For of the various items which make up the whole cost of moving a train, say one mile, some will remain constant, whether the train is full or empty ; such an item is "wages to drivers and stokers." The passage of a train over any parish does not necessarily involve the production of gross receipts to that parish, for the train may be almost empty, and consequently the receipts in respect of that train due to the parish will be but small. The same train, before passing through another parish much further "up" the line, may have been filled, when the gross receipts due to that parish in respect of the same train will be great, but the expense of haulage will not have been proportionally increased. Hence it would not be just to divide the expense of haulage in proportion to the gross receipts. Again, over some parishes many more trains pass in the course of the year than over others. In such a case it would not be

right to divide the total expense of locomotive power by a general
mileage.

Then, to comply with the principle laid down, that parochial
expenses must be deducted from parochial receipts, it is usual to
apportion such expenses as locomotive power, &c., in the ratio of
the train miles run in a parish to the total train miles run, and
other expenses in proportion to the gross receipts. Other expenses
again, having merely a local existence, having been incurred *to
secure a local benefit only*, must be charged locally, just as local
receipts, such as the rent paid to the Great Eastern Company for
the use of Peterbro' Station must be locally assigned.

The result of this apportioning is to assign to parishes in which
the gross receipts are great, great working expenses; and to
parishes in which the gross receipts are small, less working expenses; but in *neither case do the expenses vary in proportion to the
receipts*.

This mode of apportionment is unquestionably not mathemati-
cally correct. But it is much more correct than either of the
others suggested.

In whichever of the above methods the expenses are apportioned, it continually happens that in some parishes
situate far from large towns no *net revenue*, and
consequently no rateable value, remains. This
effect was foreseen by the Court in giving judgment
in the Brighton case, wherein the Court said :

Parishes in which
there appears to be
no rateable value
of a railway.

"And this suggests the answer to a difficulty raised in the argument in this
case. If you give Croydon the full benefit of all the earnings made by the
railway in the parish, what is to be done in the case of a parish on some
branch line, and which the company may work at a loss? The answer is,
that that case must be decided when it arises between the company and
that parish on the same principle as the present, without reference to Croydon."

Such a case did very soon arise. It continually happened that
in certain parishes the working expenses and *allowances* absorbed
the whole gross receipts in that parish. And this anomaly existed,

that while a station, which only *indirectly* contributed to the profits of the line, was rateable (inasmuch as the rateable value of the indirectly contributing portion is the first charge upon the rateable value of the whole property), and the *line of railway*, as a whole, had a large rateable value, yet a portion of the same line appeared to have no rateable value at all. Although this state of things appeared to exist, it was found, nevertheless, that companies continued to work lines which appeared to produce nothing; and further, for lines which were not the property of the occupying company, such company was frequently paying a large rent.

The first case that occurred affecting the question of the rateable value of a railway in a parish in which there *appeared* to be no rateable value was that of *R. v. Newmarket Railway Company*, 23 Law Journal, M. C. 76.

In this case the Newmarket Railway Company had made a railway from the Eastern Counties Railway to Newmarket.

The Eastern Counties Railway Company,

"In consideration of the benefit likely to accrue to them from the construction of the branch and the working of the railway,"

guaranteed that if the profits of the Newmarket Company were not sufficient to pay £3 per cent. on the Newmarket Company's capital, they would make up the dividend to that amount. The gross receipts of the Newmarket Railway in the respondent parish were insufficient to provide for all the working expenses and allowances, and on the entire railway, insufficient to pay the £3 per cent. to the shareholders. Consequently the Eastern Counties Company had, during the year in question, paid £3,700 to the Newmarket Company to make up the dividend.

Under these circumstances, the question was raised, whether the overseers were entitled to rate upon a proportion of this £3,700? The Court, however, ruled that they were not, inasmuch as this sum did not arise out of the occupation, and would not of necessity pass to a tenant of the Newmarket Company's Railway.

The Court, however, were not unanimous, Lord Campbell dissenting from Mr. Justice Coleridge and Mr. Justice Erle.

The next case that came before the Court on this point was that of *R.* v. *The South Eastern Railway Company,* 24 Law Journal, M. C. 84.

In that case the South Eastern Company had leased for a thousand years, the railway from Reading to Reigate, at a rent of £33,000 per annum, and also undertook to pay £8,000 per annum, the interest on a debt incurred in making the line. Subsequently the Reading Company was dissolved, and its powers transferred to the South Eastern Railway Company, and a perpetual annuity of £41,000, payable to the shareholders of the dissolved company, was charged on the revenue of the South Eastern Railway Company. Two rates were made on the South Eastern Company. The first before the dissolution of the Reading Company as *occupiers* of the branch railway, and the second, after the dissolution of the Reading Company, when the South Eastern were both *owners* and *occupiers* of the branch. In the first rate, the rent, £41,000—viz., £33,000 and £8,000, *paid*, was made the basis of the rate, and the case found that, if the rent paid under lease was the proper criterion of the rateable value, then the rate appealed against was correct. The case further found, that the gross earnings of the South Eastern Railway on the Reading railway, less the proper deductions did not amount to £41,000, less the statutory deductions. It was also found that the Reading line brought a great deal of additional traffic to the main line of the South Eastern Railway, and that the latter company thus derived benefit from the Reading line as a feeder of the main line in respect of the traffic conveyed upon that line. It was also found, that the Reading line, if in the market, might be an object of competition between the South Eastern and other companies. The questions for the Court were—

" First, whether the appellants were properly assessed in the two rates appealed against in certain specified amounts, the assessments being founded on the said rent as to the first, and the said annuity as to the second rate, which assessments were taken as the proper criterion of annual value in each case?

" Secondly, whether they were liable to be assessed in respect only of the net profit derived from the traffic passing through Dorking, irrespective of any rent paid by the company, and the value of the Reading, Guildford, and Reigate line as increasing the traffic on the main line?

"Thirdly, whether the respondents were entitled to take into consideration, in their assessment, the value of the line to the appellants as an integral part of the South Eastern Railway, *in addition* to the net profit as derived from the traffic passing through the parish of Dorking?"

Upon the first question the judges were unanimously of opinion

Rent actually paid not sole criterion of the rateable value. that the rent or the annuity paid under the lease or agreement *could not be taken to be the sole criterion of the annual value.*

But upon the second and third questions the Court were divided; Lord Campbell, Mr. Justice Crompton, and Mr. Justice Coleridge being of opinion that the appellants were liable to be assessed for the *total profit* arising from the occupation of the land in Dorking parish.

Lord Campbell said :

"I am of opinion that the liability of the appellants cannot be *confined to the net profit derived by the appellants from the traffic passing through the parish of Dorking*. They are only to be assessed in that parish in respect of property occupied by them in that parish; but *its value in the parish* may be *enhanced by circumstances existing out of the parish.*

"The appellants say truly that *they are not to be rated in this parish for profits made elsewhere*. I wish implicitly to abide by what is called the 'parochial principle' of rating. But upon that principle we must see of what value the property rated in that parish is to the occupiers, and this is not *necessarily determined by the pecuniary receipts for the use of it within the parish.* The rent that was paid by the appellants is strong evidence that it was of greater value to them than the mere net profit from the traffic upon it.

"We have an express admission that the Reading line brings a great deal of additional traffic to the main line, and that they derive benefit from the Reading line as a feeder to the main line in respect of traffic conveyed upon that line, and that the Reading line, if in the market, might be an object of competition between the South Eastern Company and other railway companies, the traffic on the main lines of which would be increased by the possession and control of the Reading line. Therefore, *plus* the net profits derived from the traffic passing through the parish of Dorking, the appellants do derive a profit from the occupation of the portion of the line in that parish. But it is said that in respect of this last profit they ought only to be assessed in the parishes through which the main line passes. I am of a contrary opinion. This profit, although not *received* for the traffic upon the line in the parish of Dorking, originates from the occupation by the appellants of land in the parish of Dorking; and if they are assessed in that parish in respect of this profit, in estimating their profits in the parishes through which the main line passes, there ought to be a deduction in respect of what is paid for the line which is worked as a feeder to the main line. This calculation, though difficult, may be made upon data which are accessible, and is not more difficult than calculations which must be made in railway rating, where stations and inclined planes affect the traffic in another parish. Adhering to the parochial principle, I inquire of what value the land rated is to the occupier. Of this value the rent which he is willing to pay affords evidence, and from any profit which he indirectly makes from it out of the parish, part of the rent which he pays for it in the parish is to be regarded as a deduction. At the bar it was hardly denied that this would be the result if the two railways belonged to two companies, and if the company whose railway is fed were to pay a regular fixed annual sum to the company whose railway is the feeder. But I do not see how it would make any difference to the parish of Dorking that both lines are occupied by one company, and are worked as one concern. The advantage derived from the occupation of the portion of the line in the parish is still the same, although the process by which the amount of that advantage is to be calculated has changed. I adhere to the rule of rating which is laid down in *R.* v. *The Newmarket Railway Company*, which I there attempted to support and illustrate. This, I think, is in entire harmony with our decision in *R.* v. *The Great Western Railway Company*, 15 Q. B. 379. In many cases the supposed advantage derived by a railway company from a portion of a railway in a particular parish, bringing passengers and goods to another portion out of the parish, may be almost inappreciable, and I would earnestly dissuade parishes from ever making any claim under this head, unless upon clear evidence that the claim can in point of fact be established."

Mr. Justice Coleridge said: "I understand the second and third questions to be intended to raise three points. First, must the assessment be made only on the net profits earned by the passage of goods over the land occupied in Dorking, and must any additional value, which the occupation in truth may have, as increasing the traffic on the main line, be excluded? Secondly, *may any additional value*, which the occupation of the land in Dorking may have, by reason of the amalgamation of the two lines, *be included in the assessment*? These two questions, I presume, were framed with a view to the different circumstances under which the two rates were made in respect of the amalgamation. My answer to these questions will be this—nothing is to be excluded which—I do not say has a tendency to add to (for of this no notice

can be taken—but which actually adds to the value of the occupation ; for the
rate is to be regulated in amount by that value, and it is a principle which I
believe to be established by numerous 'decisions, that the inquiry is not so
much where the profits are produced, as whether any alleged profits are so
directly referable to it as properly to be considered profits of the occupation,
so that, to adopt the words of Mr. Crisp, in his sensible essay on the subject,
' the rateable value within the parish may depend on matter without the
parish.'"

Mr. Justice Crompton said : " Secondly, I think that in strictness the value
of the branch as a feeder is to be taken into account in ascertaining the
rateable value. It is a profit derived from the occupation of land, and it
seems to me impossible to say that the value to the person willing to take the
lines, or the rent likely to be got from them, would not be increased by the
advantage of this line to, and from its being a feeder of, the large railway.
The value of the land in the parish is increased and enhanced by its being
useful as increasing the profit that may be made in another place, and I
think that the rateable value within the parish may clearly be enhanced by
matter in another parish."

Mr. Justice Erle dissented. In his judgment he reviewed the various cases
that had been decided, and showed that, in the Great Western case (15 Q. B.
1085), the Court sanctioned a rateable value founded upon the *net earnings* in
each parish, and that, in the cases of *R.* v. *London and Brighton*, *R.* v
South Eastern, *R.* v. *Midland*, this principle was, after much consideration,
confirmed.   Mr. Justice Erle thus concluded : " Also it is clear that no
tendency to create profit is rateable ; no tenant would pay rent for a tendency
to profit unless it resulted in profit ; and certainly no tenant of part of the line
in Dorking would pay rent to increase the profit of some other tenant of some
other part of the line, as was mentioned in the case of *R.* v. *The Newmarket
Railway* in this term.   I have disposed of all that was material in the questions submitted : but as the judges differ on the question whether a railway
can be rated for more than it produces in the parish, on account of its
tendency to make profit elsewhere, which is expressed by a metaphor from
feeling ; and, on the question whether, in a case for apportionment, one parish,
in making its rate, can disregard the positions of other parishes within the
apportionment, and as a generality cannot be tested without a specific application, I suggest, if a case is again brought up relating to these points, it
should state specifically what is the railway profit arising out of the parish
which is liable to be rated within it."

In a subsequent case, that of *The London and North Western
Railway* v. *The Parish Officers of Cannock, Staffordshire*, reported

in the *Times* of November 12, 1863, and in 9 *Law Times*, N. S.
325, the parish officers had rated the London and North Western
Railway at the sum of £325 in respect of their occupation of two
and a half miles of the Cannock Mineral Railway, situate in the
parish of Cannock, wherein the gross receipts were £358 for the
two and a half miles, and the *working expenses* alone £807 for the
same distance. The London and North Western Company had
leased this line, the total length of which is seven and a half miles,
paying £5,500 per annum. In the course of the argument it was
admitted that the line, though worked at a loss, was necessary to
the earning of profit on the rest of the London and North
Western Railway.

After much discussion judgment was given in favour of the
parish, although no formal judgment is reported.

The principle that the rateable value within any parish is to be
measured by the *entire* profit derived from the occupation of land
therein, and not merely by the profit which actually arises in the
parish, being by these judgments laid down and confirmed, the
question presents itself, as to how that entire profit is to be ascertained?

To determine this, it will be first desirable to analyse the entire
gross receipts in some one parish, which, it shall be assumed, is
near a large town. The manner in which such gross receipts
will have been calculated has already been described in the
extract from the case *R. v. South Eastern Railway*. From that
description it will be seen that the gross receipts in such parish
are produced by the conveyance, during the year, of passengers
and goods from various stations to various other stations situate at
distances above and below the parish in question. From any one
station, a certain number of passengers and quantity of goods have
been conveyed, during the year, to each of the other stations on the
railway. The gross receipts arising from the conveyance of passengers and goods will be made up of as many parts as there are
different stations. Any one of those parts will be the result of
the traffic between any one station, and one of the other stations,

on the railway. The amount of one of these parts has been earned by the railway lying between the two stations. And, moreover, each mile of railway lying between these two stations has *equally* earned the amount; for, without the joint co-operation of each portion of the railway, this amount could not have been earned. Hence, then, the receipts, divided by the distance between these two places, will give the gross receipt per mile in respect of this particular traffic. The total amount of receipts between any two places shall be termed a "*stream of traffic.*" From each station there will emanate many streams of traffic. Now, over the parish of which we are at present speaking many such streams of traffic may pass, each stream travelling over a *different total length*. Then the entire gross receipts in such parish will be made up of the aggregate of the share of the parish of *each stream* of traffic. Consider one stream of traffic only, which shall have passed between two places, say one hundred miles apart; each mile of railway between these places would be entitled to one hundredth part of the whole stream. Now, take a parish through which only this single stream of traffic passes. The gross receipts of that parish per mile would then be one hundredth part only of this stream. Again, take another parish through which this stream, as well as many others, passed; the gross receipts in such parish would be the aggregate of its shares in each stream.

Next, with regard to the *net profit*. It has already been seen that the expenses do not vary in proportion to the receipts. It is therefore evident that, an increase in a receipt for traffic does not involve a corresponding and proportionate increase in the expenses. Hence, if the gross receipts can be increased in some parish, wherein there are already many streams of traffic, the *profits* in that parish will be increased to a greater ratio than the gross receipts.

"Gross receipts" in a parish may be increased in two ways. First, by increasing the total annual amount of a *stream of traffic*. This is the result of increase of population or of business in any two places between which the stream of traffic passes. Secondly, by increasing the *number of streams*. This is effected when the *number of places between* which traffic is carried on is increased.

Now, since " gross receipts " may be increased without increasing the expenses in the same proportion, it follows that an increase of " gross receipts " may produce a greater proportionate increase of net profits.

It will now be clear how a railway company may secure to itself a benefit by securing to itself the occupation of branch lines. For, by so doing, it increases the number of places to which it carries. By securing the occupation of branch lines, in consideration of a rent, the company avoids increasing its capital account by the construction of the railway. And the rent which the company can afford to pay is measured, not by the net profit it makes upon the branch, which may be nothing at all, but by the net profit it makes *altogether* out of the extra streams of traffic which it secures by the occupation of a branch.

Reverting to the consideration of the particular stream of traffic referred to above, it will readily be seen that in a parish through which the single stream only of traffic passed, no rateable value in respect of the railway might exist, because it is possible that no net profit may exist there; inasmuch as the expenses and allowances apportioned to that parish by being all charged against that one stream of traffic, might considerably exceed the gross receipts. Follow that stream until it reaches a parish through which many other streams also flow. The expenses apportioned to such parish will be chargeable against the *sum* of all the streams. Now, as the expenses are not in proportion to the receipts, there will exist in this latter parish a large net receipt in respect of the total gross receipts. Consequently there will exist a net receipt in respect of each stream which makes up the total gross receipts, and consequently, of the particular stream in question.

As the stream may be assumed to pass through many parishes, in some of which there may be no net receipts, but in others, a considerable amount of profit, the *entire profit of the stream* will consist of the sum of the profits in each parish in which profits do arise, less the losses in those parishes in which the losses arise.

This is the condition of things as they actually exist, and up to this point no argument can arise. But it does become a matter of argument as to which parishes are to have a share of this net profit.

From each stream of traffic there will accrue a certain amount of *net receipt*. And this net receipt, in respect of any stream, being really equally earned by each portion of the railway over which the stream has passed, ought to be equally divided between the various miles over which it has passed.

The result would be, that every portion of the railway on account of the holding of which any profit has *anywhere* been made, would have, as rateable value, *its share of that profit which it had helped to make*. But of those profits, in making which it had had no share, no part would be due, nor could be assigned to it. That parish through which one stream of traffic passed would have its share of the net profit of that stream *wherever made*. That parish through which twenty or thirty streams of traffic passed would have its share of each of those streams. The whole rateable value of the railway would thus be apportioned to all the parishes through which the railways passed, and the sum of the rateable value in each parish would together equal, and not exceed, the rateable value of the entire railway.

Neither could it be said that the profit due to the main line was rated on the branch. For, of the entire net profit of any stream only such proportion would be assigned to the branch as the length thereof bore to the whole length of the stream.

It may be objected that this profit derived from the occupation of a branch does not exist, because so many railways have been injured by renting branches. But the answer is, that it is not by *renting branches* that railways have been injured, but by *renting branches at a greater rent* than the branches are worth.

Whenever it happens that railway companies give as rent an amount greater than the *net profits* of the extra streams of traffic which they thereby secure, then such renting becomes a source of loss. If the company give as rent the entire net profit of the streams, then they, as landlords, secure no benefit and as tenants only secure the profit upon the extra stock required. But if the company secures the use of a branch at a rent less than the amount of net profit of the streams thereby added, then the branch becomes a source of benefit to the company as landlords, and so, because thereby the whole system of the railway, main line and branches, is made to command a higher rent than the main line *alone* would do ; and of the higher *rent* thus commanded the company has only to pay a part for the use of the branches.

The last case before the Court on this question of "contributive value," was that of *The Great Eastern Railway Company* v. *The Overseers of Haughley*, 1 Law Reports, Q. B. 666, in which the arbitrator adopted the suggestion of Mr. Justice Erle in the Dorking case, and stated in the case that, in addition to the rateable value in the parish, arrived at in the usual way, there was (under a certain hypothesis) a further amount of rateable value of £75, in respect of the *contributive value* of the land in Haughley parish. The hypothesis being, that a certain proposition made by the respondents should be pronounced by the Court to be correct.

The proposition was—

"That in respect of the traffic which passed over Haughley as well as other parts of the line, each mile of the railway over which that traffic passed must be regarded as contributing equally to the earning of the profits derived from that traffic ; in other words, that if the same traffic is carried at a much greater profit over one part of the line than over the other, still each part of the line must be considered as equally earning the profit."

The Court decided that this proposition was not true.

Cockburn, C. J. :

"Two questions have been presented to us in this case. The first is whether in assessing the railway in the parish of Haughley, the traffic beyond Haughley is to be taken into account, with a view to reduce the expenditure of the line in the parish of Haughley ; for of course the lower the expenditure can be reduced, the larger will be the amount of profit in Haughley, and therefore the greater the rateable value of the railway in that parish. After hearing the argument, it seems to me that the decision of the learned arbitrator is right. Let us take the case presented, of a through passenger from Norwich to London. It is correctly stated by Mr. Field, that beyond Haughley on the route to London, a great accession of traffic takes place, and then that the carriages which start from Norwich with a limited number of passengers, are, before they arrive at London, filled with a large accession. Mr. Field says, that the effect of this additional traffic is to reduce the expense with reference to each individual traveller, and that therefore, taking the case of those individuals who have started from Norwich, it is not the expense of carrying those passengers through the parish of Haughley for which the estimated expenditure is to be made, but all the other passengers that join the railway, and occupy carriages after the train has proceeded on, must be also taken into account. It is a very ingenious mode of putting the argument, but I think there is a plain and palpable fallacy in it. It is not with respect to each individual passenger that the expense is to be ascertained, according to my view. You must ascertain the expense of the whole traffic between Norwich and London.

"Upon parts of the line the expense of conveying that traffic would be less, and the profits would be greater than upon others, but the expenses upon an average are uniform throughout. I will illustrate what I mean by the case of the old stage-coaches. Take the coach from Norwich to London; the expense of running it from Norwich to London was so much per mile, with little or no variation throughout the journey; so it is upon an average the same with a railway. Sometimes the coach carries five passengers, and sometimes fifteen. If it carried five, it probably worked at a loss, and if it carried fifteen, it worked at a profit. When they are working from Norwich to Haughley they are probably working at a loss. When they are working beyond Haughley towards London, they take the traffic at Ipswich and other places of consequence that lie on the line, and then the traffic becomes remunerative; but the expense of working the train from one end to the other is uniformly the same. It seems to me, therefore, that there is a fallacy in the way Mr. Field puts his argument, and that we are not to take the additional traffic beyond Haughley into account as a matter of expense, but to take it into account as a matter of profit. Then if it is dealt with as a matter of profit, inasmuch as it occurs beyond the parish of Haughley, it is an accident with which the parish of Haughley has no concern, but which affects the rateability of the property where the profit accrues, and not elsewhere. Therefore, treated in that short and simple way, the hypothesis, or rather the assumption upon which Mr. Field's argument is based—namely, that you are to look at the expense of conveying each individual passenger, and not at the expense of conveying the whole traffic as one, is not true; and considering that as a fallacious assumption, the only way of looking at the case is that which I have suggested: consequently the arbitrator was right in the conclusion at which he arrived.

Mellor, J.: "I am of the same opinion. The question to be answered, according to the authorities, is, what is the rateable value in each parish throughout the line of railway which passes over a great number of parishes? That appears to me to be made up of these two elements, the actual earnings in the parish attributed to the parish, and the actual expenses attributed to the parish; and I think that it would be introducing a new difficulty into the determination of this question if we were to adopt Mr. Field's argument. Ingenious as it is, I cannot help thinking that there is a fallacy in it. It is this: the fare of the through passenger is necessarily received at one or the other end of the journey—Norwich or London: therefore, says Mr. Field, the fare must be divided equally throughout the journey, in order to ascertain the earnings in each parish on the journey; but he also says, with reference to the expenses, you must not deal with them in the same way, because the expense of carrying a passenger is diminished in certain parishes, and is greater in certain other parishes, and so the expense of conveying the passenger is not equal from one end of the journey to the other. That is true in a sense; but it is owing to the circumstance that in some parishes a large accession of traffic takes place, and the expense of carrying each passenger over those parishes would be diminished if those parishes could be isolated for the purpose: but I think that it is an accident to be assigned to the benefit of those parishes in which the accession of traffic takes place, and not to a parish which has nothing to do with it. It seems to me, on the simple ground that the actual profit earned is much greater in some parishes than it is in others, that the rateable value in those parishes is greater than it is in others; therefore, with regard to the first point, I think the arbitrator was right.

Shee, J.: "I am of the same opinion." After describing the manner in which the arbitrator arrived at the rateable value, Mr. Justice Shee continued: "The respondents attack this mode of ascertaining the rateable value by excepting to the first item of the calculation the item of gross receipts: not that they say it is a sum improperly arrived at, if no item which ought to have been admitted has been excluded by the arbitrator, but they say that it is a sum which is not properly taken as the datum of his calculation, because he has omitted from his estimate what is called contributive value—that is, a value additional to the value to be ascertained by the actual receipts in the parish of Haughley, arising, as they allege, from the circumstances that the occupation of the railway company in the parish of Haughley is more valuable on account of their occupation on other parts of their line, and

particularly between Ipswich and London. The respondents say that this
contributive value ought to be added to the actual value found by the
arbitrator upon the calculation which he sets out in the case. It appears to
me that that cannot be done without adopting the mileage principle instead of
the parochial principle, the mileage principle never having in any of the
decided cases been adopted, and the parochial principle having been always
adopted in estimating the value of property in a parish for the purposes of a
poor rate. It appears from all the cases that a railway is rateable in the
parish where the particular profits are earned ; it matters not where they are
received. It is so laid down in several cases, and particularly in the case of
R. v. Kinswinford, 7 B. and C. 236, and *R. v. London and South Western
Railway Company*, 1 Q. B. 558. So again in *R. v. Lower Hutton*, 9 B. and
C. 818, it is laid down that if a portion of a canal in one parish is more
productive than portions in other parishes, either because there is more traffic,
or because the yearly outgoings and expenses there are less, it ought to be
assessed at a higher proportionate value ; and it is decided in *R. v. The
London, Brighton, and South Coast Railway*, 20 L. J. M. C. 124, 144, that
' the value which the land occupied in each parish produces after the due
allowances, is that upon which the occupier is to be rated in each.' No
doubt it is very difficult in the case of railway companies, and in the case
of a part only in one parish of a long line of railway, to apply the principle of
the Parochial Assessment Act, that principle being that the rate on the property
in a parish (and on a railway like all other property, for there is no distinction)
is to be made ' upon an estimate of the net annual value of the several hereditaments rated thereunto—that is to say, of the rent at which the same might
reasonably be expected to let from year to year.' "

Lord Chief Justice Cockburn, Mr. Justice Mellor, and Mr.
Justice Shee arrived at the same conclusion—viz., that the
arbitrator was right ; but they arrived at this conclusion by two
different roads.

The Lord Chief Justice and Mr. Justice Mellor laid down the
proposition that the accession of traffic below Ipswich was an
accident, and therefore the value of the railway in Haughley
ought not to benefit by that accident.

Let it be granted that the accession of traffic is an accident.
Then assume that such accident does not happen, but that the
traffic which has passed through Haughley continues unincreased
as far as London. Its passage through Haughley produces a certain
rateable value in that parish. Now assume that just before it

reaches London it must pass up a steep incline. This incline
necessarily involves much increased expense in working the traffic.
But it was ruled in the Great Western case, 21 L. J. M. C. 81,
that this expense must not be a *local* charge. "Yet, even these
(the tunnel or inclined plane) are contributing to the earnings
everywhere."

Therefore, in such a case, since the expenses of the incline must
be shared by all those parishes whose traffic uses the incline, the
rateable value in Haughley would be affected by it ; that is, the
rateable value in the parish is to be *lessened* by an accident (for the
existence of the incline is essentially an accident in the sense in
which the term has been used in the argument) occurring out of
the parish. Yet by the decision in the Haughley case the rateable
value in the parish is not to be *increased* by some accident which
exists out of the parish. But is this accession of traffic an accident?
Is it not in the very nature of things? Is it not a necessary consequence when traffic approaches a large town? What would be
the state of things if there were no railway between Norwich and
Ipswich? Why, the expense per mile of working between Ipswich
and London would continue nearly the same, but the gross receipts
per mile would be very much lessened, and therefore the profits
per mile would be lessened. That is, the possession of land in
the parish of Haughley (and in the other parishes between
Norwich and Ipswich) does, as a fact, enable the company to
make greater profits than they otherwise would, between Ipswich
and London.

Mr. Justice Shee said that the contributive value could not be
taken into account without adopting the mileage principle and
abandoning the parochial. But giving each parish a mileage proportion of all the profit *it had helped to earn* (for that was in effect
the contention of the respondents), is a very different thing from
giving each parish a mileage proportion of *all* the profits *made*,
whether that parish had contributed to earn them or not. In the
one case, if a parish had helped to earn profit from many streams of
traffic, it would claim its share of the many, and so have a high

rateable value. If it had helped to earn profit from *one* stream only, it would claim a share in *one* stream only.

Mr. Justice Shee says that :

" It appears from all the cases that a railway is rateable in the parish where the particular profits are earned."

But Mr. Justice Coleridge, in the Dorking case, 23 L. J. M. C. 84, said that :

" It is a principle which I believe to be established by numerous decisions, that the inquiry is not so much where the profits of the occupation are produced, as whether any alleged profits are so directly referable to it as properly to be considered parts of the occupation."

In the Haughley case it was not deemed that profits were made elsewhere.

There are many miles of railway in England and Wales which have no rateable value, because the expenses alone exhaust all the receipts; and yet we find railway companies giving high rents for such lines. And why? Because these lines are the means of enabling the renting companies to make greater profits on their own main lines. Surely if such lines, when rented, have a value *somewhere*, they have equally a value if the renting companies *purchase* them.

If this decision of the **Court** *be not reviewed, this anomaly will exist, viz., that miles and miles of railway, forming parts of a valuable whole, will themselves have no rateable value ; yet if they were cut off from the whole, the value of the whole would be seriously diminished.*

On the 24th of April, 1869, the following case was brought before the Court of Queen's Bench with the evident intention of inducing the judges to review their decision in the Haughley case:—*Reg. v. Llantrissant.*

This was a case stated by the Quarter Sessions of Glamorganshire, upon an appeal by the Great Western Railway Company against an assessment of the company to a poor rate of the parish of Llantrissant, in the Pontypridd Union, in respect of the Ely Valley Railway.

The Ely Valley Railway is leased to the Great Western Railway

Company for 999 years, they undertaking to pay a fixed rent of £4,000 a year. The entire length of the railway is about ten miles, of which about seven are in the parish of Llantrissant. The traffic is chiefly minerals; and the greatest portion of that traffic is brought by the Ely Valley Railway to the South Wales Railway, which it joins a short distance beyond the boundary of the parish, and is conveyed for some distance over that line and over other portions of the Great Western lines. The South Wales line is the property of the Great Western Company, and the Ely Valley Railway acts as a feeder to that line.

In assessing the Ely Valley Railway within the parish, the value of the traffic contributed by that line as bringing traffic to the South Wales line was taken into consideration; and it was agreed that, if this contributive value was to be excluded in the computation, the rate was to be reduced from £400 to £270.

Mr. Field, Q.C., contended that the case was concluded by the decision in *The Great Eastern Railway Company* v. *The Overseers of Haughley*, 35 L. J., 229, M. C., where it was held that the rateable value of a portion of a railway, consisting of the net annual profits from the traffic upon the portion rated, cannot be increased by any part of the profits caused by the same traffic upon the other portions of the line.

Mr. Michael, *contra*, relied on the decision in the case of *The London and North Western Railway Company* v. *The Overseers of Cannock*, 9 L. T. Rep., N. S. 325, where it was held that the rateable value of land in a parish may be increased by its producing a return to the occupiers out of the parish, as when a branch railway, occupied by a company owning the main line into which it runs, produces a profit by virtue of the traffic which it carries over such main line. *The Newmarket Railway Company* v. *St. Andrew's-the-Less*, 23 L. J., 76, M. C., was also cited.

Mr. Justice Mellor (Lord Chief Justice Cockburn being absent):

"It appears to me that it is immaterial whether the line be a branch line or a portion of the main line; the question is—what is the value of the line to the parish? It is, what would be the amount that the hypothetical tenant would give? The question asked is whether the respondents are entitled to take into consideration in their assessment the value of the line to the appellants, as bringing traffic to the Great Western Railway Company's South Wales line, in addition to the net profit derived from the traffic passing through the parish of Llantrissant? I think the case is governed by the Haughley case, and that the Lord Chief Justice did not intend to abide in that case by what he said in the Cannock case. I think there should be no addition to the rating in Llantrissant because the traffic of Llantrissant comes on to the Great Western Railway's line."

Mr. Justice Hayes:

"The Haughley case settles the question, and reduced to the ordinary rule certain aberrations which had crept into the subject."

Judgment accordingly.

It only now remains to speak of cases in which the entire re-

Tolls.

ceipts of a railway company are earned, partly on the system occupied by the company, and partly on some other system occupied by another company.

It will be seen, from the case of *R. v. The Grand Junction Railway Company,* that so much of the receipts as have been earned on foreign lines, and so much of the expenses attending such earnings, must be deducted from the gross receipts before proceeding to deduce the rent of that portion of the system which the company do so occupy, for the rent is to be founded upon a consideration of what is produced. And it cannot be said that that which is produced on another company's line is any part of the produce of the hereditament occupied by the company, the value of whose occupation is the subject of inquiry.

With regard to the expenses attending the receipts earned over foreign lines, it may be remarked that the expenses may be arranged in two classes. In the first class will be placed those expenses and allowances which are necessary to the carrying on of the trade. In the second class will be placed those expenses which, if the company were the occupiers, instead of the users merely, would represent the rent and taxes.

To the question, how these receipts are to be ascertained, it may be replied that the receipts between any two places will be equally earned by each portion of the railway lying between those places, whether some of it is owned and occupied by one company, and some owned and occupied by another company; or whether it is all occupied by one company. So that, whatever proportion of the distance between those places is *used* only by one railway company, that proportion of the traffic between those places can be justly deemed to be the gross receipts earned otherwhere than on the hereditament occupied by that company.

The difference between the gross receipts and the carrying expenses and allowances will be the toll the company can afford to pay for the use of the other company's railway.

But it does not always happen that the use of a railway is secured by the payment of the amount of toll which a company can afford to pay. Sometimes it happens that such user is secured in one or other of the following ways:—

Firstly. The use may have been secured for ever by a lump sum paid down.

Secondly. The use may have been secured by an annual rent paid for a term of years, under agreement.

Thirdly. The use may have been secured by a payment, depending upon the use made of the railway.

Fourthly. The use may be derived from the exercise of the right given to the public to use a railway upon payment to the occupiers of such toll as the special Act of Parliament authorises them to demand.

In each case the amount of payment for such user may be either less than, equal to, or greater than the difference between the receipts earned, and the expenses and allowances incurred.

In the event of the amount of toll payable being greater than the difference between the receipts and expenses, the important question arises whether the *extra amount* is to be paid to the detriment of the rateable value of the hereditament which the company does occupy, or whether such extra amount must be deemed

T

a landlord's improvement, just as the extra rent paid for a branch railway was deemed to be of that nature.

An attempt was made to raise this question in the case of the *North London Railway Company, appellants,* v. *The Churchwardens of St. Pancras parish, respondents,* 32 L. J. M. C. 145.

The North London Railway Company occupied their own railway of a length of about seven miles, situate between Hampstead Road and Bow. At Bow it joined the Blackwall Railway. The North London Company carried passengers from Hampstead to Fenchurch Street and all intermediate stations; their engines and carriages ran over their own line as far as Bow, and then, for about two and three-quarter miles, over the railway of the Blackwall Company, which they *used.* For the use of this railway the North London Company paid to the Blackwall Company the sum of 1d. for each single passenger, and 1½d. for each return passenger. The amount of the payment to the Blackwall Company. was, for the year in question, £10,900. The Blackwall Company, previous to the opening of the North London Railway, had a station at Bow, to and from which they used to carry passengers. When the North London Railway was opened, the North London Railway Company then carried in their carriages that Bow Station traffic which had previously been carried by the Blackwall Company. And in addition to the above sum of £10,900, they handed over to the Blackwall Company the entire receipts for the Bow traffic, subject only to a very small payment (about 11 per cent.) for working expenses.

It was contended, in deducing the rateable value of the North London Railway, that the toll *actually paid* to the Blackwall was not, *as a matter of course,* to be deducted, but that the inquiry was first to be made whether the toll so agreed upon to be paid was a fair amount, and such as, had the railway been *occupied* by the North London Company, would represent the rent a tenant could reasonably give for that portion of the line. Upon investigation it was found that the toll actually paid to the Blackwall Company was greater than the *net receipts* earned over the Blackwall Railway, and not only so, but that it was greater also than the net profit arising from the whole of those receipts which were earned in consequence of their connection with the Blackwall Railway. But it appeared in evidence that the amounts actually paid to the Blackwall Company were less than the company could, under their Act of Parliament, have charged if no special agreement had been made by them.

Under these circumstances *it was found, as a fact,* that the amount paid to the Blackwall Company was a reasonable sum.

"The questions for the opinion of the court are—first, whether in ascertaining the rateable value of the subject matter of the rate, any sum should be deducted in respect of the said payments by the appellants to the Blackwall Company? Second, whether, if any sum ought to be deducted, as the first question mentioned, the sums mentioned in the said agreement payable by the appellants to the Blackwall Company for passenger tolls are the sums which ought to be deducted? If the court should answer both questions in the affirmative, the order of sessions and amendment to be confirmed.

Lord Chief Justice Cockburn gave judgment :

" This case is very clear, and I think the sessions came to a right decision upon it. Complaints have often been made of the inapplicability of the landlord and tenant principle mentioned in the Parochial Assessment Act to railways. But in this instance, that principle may be advantageously applied, because in considering the yearly tenantable value of the land in the possession of the North London Railway in the parish of St. Pancras, it would be proper to exclude the amount paid over to the London and Blackwall Railway Company.

" It appears that the entire line is made up of two parts. That in the possession of the North London Railway extends to Bow Junction, and there they would have to put their passengers out, if it were not for the agreement they have entered into with the Blackwall Company to pay to the latter one penny or three-halfpence, as the case may be, for each passenger carried on to Fenchurch Street. But not a farthing of this last mentioned sum goes into the pockets of the North London Railway Company ; it is taken wholly on behalf of the Blackwall Railway Company ; and therefore it could not be included in any rent which a tenant would give to the North London Railway, in respect of land in the parish of St. Pancras. Again, the Blackwall Railway Company are assessable in their own parish for all their receipts, and the money paid them by the North London is a part of those receipts. If, therefore, St. Pancras parish

T 2

were to receive a rate in respect of this sum, and the Blackwall Railway Company were also to pay a rate in respect of the same, the result would be that a rate would be raised in two different parishes upon the same subject matter. I think, therefore, that the amount in question was rightly allowed to be deducted."

Crompton, Blackburn, and Mellor, J.J., concurred.

This judgment was a necessary consequence of the sessions having found "*that the payments made by the appellants to the Blackwall Company were reasonable.*" It leaves undecided the question whether, if the toll or rent, or other compensation which has been agreed upon to be paid by one company to another for the use of that other company's railway, or railway and station, be found to be greater than the net receipts arising from such user, the actual amount so agreed upon to be paid, *whatever it may be*, is to be deducted in determining the rent of those premises which the one company do so occupy, or whether such amount only as is represented by the difference between the gross receipts earned over the other company's property, and the carrier's expenses and allowances incurred in earning such gross receipts, is to be deducted.

The latest decisions on this question of toll are those in the two cases of *The Midland Railway Company* v. *The Overseers of the Parish of Badgworth*, 34 L. J. M. C. 25, and *The Great Western Railway Company* v. *The Overseers of the Parish of Badgworth*, 2 Law Reports, Q. B. 251.

In this instance, the railway between Cheltenham and Gloucester was made under the authority of 6 Will. IV. c. 77. It was to be made by the joint payments of two companies, one of which ultimately became united with the Midland Railway Company, the other with the Great Western Railway Company. The railway was actually made by the Midland Company, and the Great Western Company subsequently paid to the Midland one half the cost of construction. The Midland Company repaired and maintained the half nearest to Gloucester, the Great Western the half nearest to Cheltenham. The line was used by the trains of both companies, and was laid with three rails to accommodate both broad and narrow guage traffic. The traffic of the Midland Company far exceeded the traffic of the Great Western Company. The parish of Badgworth was situate on the half of the railway nearest to Cheltenham. The Great Western Company, seeing that their traffic over the Midland Company's half was less than the Midland Company's over their half, had brought an action against the Midland to recover tolls from that company ; but it was ultimately decided by the House of Lords that the Midland, under the peculiar circumstances of the case (the railway having been authorised to be made by the two companies jointly), were not liable to pay toll to the Great Western Railway. Under these circumstances, the Midland Company contended that they were not rateable in Badgworth, as they had merely an user of the railway there situate.

The Court decided in their favour.

After this decision the parish officers of Badgworth rated the Great Western at an amount made up of the value of the Great Western's own occupation, *plus* the value of the toll that would have been paid by the Midland had they had to pay such.

The Great Western Company raised the question whether they were properly rated.

The Court decided that the company was rateable for the value of its own occupation in the parish, *plus*, not the value of the Midland toll, but the value of the Great Western Company's easement over the Midland Company's half.

This decision, as it depends entirely on the peculiar circumstances of a particular case, cannot influence the general principle of rating.

During argument, the Lord Chief Justice said :

"No doubt, if there were no mutual running powers, but the case were simply that the Midland Company had the right, either by Parliamentary enactment, or by agreement, of running over the appellants' half of the line on payment of tolls, and the appellants had a corresponding right of running over the Midland's half of the line, then the amount of tolls received by the appellants would enhance the rateable value of their line, and they would be rateable accordingly ; but, when the appellants receive no tolls, the only way in which the value of their property is enhanced is by their having an easement over the Midland half of the line."

Mellor, J. :

" The value to the appellants, who are the occupiers, is not the value of the actual amount of use made by the Midland Company over the appellant's half of the line, but the value to them of the arrangement by which they run free over the Midland half."

The judgment was to the same effect. Thus was the principle laid down by Mr. Justice Coleridge when he said :

" It is a principle which I believe to be established by numerous decisions, that the inquiry is not so much WHERE the profits of the occupation are produced, as whether any alleged profits are so directly referable to it as properly to be considered parts of the occupation."

Again judicially asserted.

APPENDIX.

Some remarks upon the present system of railway rating, together with a suggestion as to the best mode for the prevention of railway companies escaping the payment of their due share of the parochial rates.

The following important article on railway rating appeared in the *Journal of the Chamber of Agriculture*, on the 25th of April last, and, as I believe the subject discussed to be of considerable interest to ratepayers generally throughout the kingdom, and particularly to those who hold large tracts of land in agricultural districts, through which lines of railway pass, I here insert it, *in extenso*, and am of opinion that, in addition to its being of general interest, it may also be the means of more fully demonstrating the present unsatisfactory system of rating such properties.

"Producing a veritable egg out of a palpably empty bag is a conjuror's feat not to be paralleled by any Chancellor of the Exchequer two years in succession; but Mr. Goschen has an excellent chance of rivalling Mr. Lowe's financial magic of last year if he will but bring in a supplementary Budget for dealing with the minor taxation called 'rates.' The black stick might work wonders in many different directions: meanwhile we can astonish some of our readers by declaring it both possible and easy to relieve the ratepayers of England and Wales *to the extent of three-pence in the pound, or,* in other words, *to pay one-half of the county rate, hundred rate, borough rate, and police rate, without diminishing the present scale of expenditure, without advancing a sixpence out of the imperial revenue, without introducing an additional tax of any kind, without equalising the rates between one union and another, without disturbing the system of assessment now existing, and without rating any description of property that does not already contribute to the poor rate.* To lower the average ratal burden of England and Wales by threepence in the pound, thereby saving the present ratepayers ONE MILLION AND A QUARTER STERLING PER ANNUM, we have only to insist upon an adequate valuation of the property in the hands of railway companies. What is the true 'rateable value' of that property. In compliance with the terms of the Parochial Assessment Act of 1836 this value must be the estimated rental, free of all tenants' rates, taxes, and tithe rentcharge, if any, which a supposed tenant might reasonably be expected to give for the occupation from year to year of all the railway property in England and Wales, deducting therefrom the probable average annual cost of repairs, insurance, and other expenses, if any, necessary to maintain the property in a state to command such rent. And the figures and data by which the estimate may be framed are given in the returns made to the Board of Trade by the several railway companies—the latest published being for the year 1867. If we subtract the total working expenses from the total receipts from all sources of traffic, we shall have the net receipts which are to be divided between the landlord and the hypothetical tenant. What were these working expenses in 1867? They consisted of maintenance of way and works, £3,036,862; locomotive power, £4,620,641; repairs and renewals of carriages and waggons, £1,392,644; traffic charges, £4,818,903; Government duty, £411,755; compensation for injury, &c., £322,985; compensation for loss, &c., £140,400; legal and parliamentary expenses, £310,724; and miscellaneous expenses, £956,066; making a total of £16,040,980. The item

of rates and taxes is omitted, as it will be deducted later in the calculation. The total receipts from all sources of traffic amounted
to £33,398,222; and the difference between this sum and the
working expenses, £16,040,980, is £17,357,242. This has to be
divided between the landlord and the supposed tenant, the tenant's
share being arrived at first; and the calculation proceeds in the
following manner:—The prime cost of the rolling stock, furniture,
stores, &c., which a tenant would have to take to on entry, is
known to be about equal to the gross receipts—namely,
£33,398,223; but, according to the decision of the Court of
Queen's Bench in the case of *R.* v. *North Staffordshire
Railway Company* (30 L. J. M.C., 68), the tenant's profit is not
to be calculated upon the "prime cost," but upon the "present
value" of the stock. Hence an allowance must be made for
depreciation. The correct deduction under this head might be
stated at 30 per cent; but as railway companies do sometimes admit
as much as 25 per cent., we will take this rate, making the depreciation of stock £8,349,555, and the present value of stock, therefore,
£25,048,667. This represents the amount of capital which
a tenant would require to take to the stock upon entry at a
valuation, and upon this capital he must be allowed a fair
remuneration. But, in ascertaining what this remuneration
should be, it is to be borne in mind that no *skill* or *labour* is
required of the tenant in the management: this is already provided for in the working expenses, which include *directors' fees*,
salaries to *managers, secretaries*, &c.; and, in fact, every outgoing,
both actual and contingent. And further, *if the accounts have been
properly and honestly audited, no depreciation, either in the stock or
in the way, or works, can have taken place during the year in question.*
Under such conditions as these 10 per cent. should be an ample
allowance; but as Courts of Quarter Sessions, not going very
deeply into the subject, have allowed more, we may, perhaps,
venture to take the liberal rate of 15 per cent. as the profit upon
tenant's capital, amounting to £3,757,300. This being the
supposed tenant's share of the net receipts, which we have shown

to be £17,357,242, the remainder of the net receipts, or a sum of £13,599,942, represents the landlord's share, or net rental, together with the rates which we have not yet deducted. The next step in our calculation is to find this net rental or rateable value by separating from the sum of £13,599,942 the proper amount of local rates. We cannot take this item as it appears in the returns, because it is wholly inadequate, the sum actually paid for rates being far below the just and rightful amount. According to the twenty-first Report of the Poor Law Board and the Local Taxation Returns (497), the total rateable value of property in England and Wales in the year 1867 was £100,612,734; and the total amount of local taxation raised by rates on that property in the same year was £16,727,174, the average rate in the pound being thus 3s. 3·9d. But as railway companies are exempt from the full payment of certain of the rates—paying on only one-fourth of the 'net annual value' rates which are levied under the Local Board of Health Act, the proportionate average rate payable by railway companies is reduced to as nearly as possible 3s. in the pound. So that we have now merely to work out this simple equation:—As 20s. + 3s. : 3s. : : £13,599,942 : x,—where £13,599,942 is the sum to be divided into net rental and the amount for rates, and x represents this amount for rates. Multiplying the second and third terms and dividing by the first, in the usual way, we find that x=£1,773,905; and this is the amount of local rates which ought to be paid by the railway companies, if they contributed their proportionate share in common with owners and occupiers of other rateable property. Lastly, deducting this proper amount of rates, namely, £1,773,905, from the sum of £13,599,942, we have £11,826,037 as the net rental or rateable value of the railway property in England and Wales for the year 1867. That this cannot be very far from the *minimum* of rateable value may be verified in the following manner. According to the returns, the total amount of capital expended in the construction and planting of railways (including rolling stock, &c.) to the end of December, 1867, was

£327,250,569 : and subtracting from this total the prime cost of tenant's working plant, namely, £33,398,222, there remains the sum of £293,852,347 as landlord's capital expenditure. The net rental, £11,826,037, as calculated above, amounts to only 4 per cent. upon this capital ; and is the least that can be allowed to the supposed landlord or owner of the *corpus* for his investment. The result has been arrived at by allowing the supposed tenant a liberal profit of 15 per cent. net upon his capital. But, as already remarked, 10 per cent. should be considered enough ; and we will, therefore, see what would be the rateable value under that more moderate allowance to the tenant. Ten per cent. upon the tenant's capital amounts to £2,504,866, which, deducted from the net receipts, leaves £14,852,376 for the landlord's rental and the rates. By the same equation as before, the calculated amount of rates which ought to be paid is £1,937,266; and this being subtracted from the £14,852,376, makes the net rental or rateable value £12,915,110. This rental is 4·39 per cent. upon the landlord's capital. Having now shown that the true rateable value of railway property in England and Wales for the year 1867 was at least £11,826,037, and might very well be stated at £12,915,110, and having shown that the amount of local rates which ought to have been paid in that year was from £1,773,905 to £1,937,266, we are able to say that the railway companies escaped the payment of a very large proportion of those rates. Under the head of 'rates and taxes,' the total given in the returns is £723,540. But it is known to include payments for law in settling appeals, salaries to surveyors, to rating officers, and various other expenses, amounting in the aggregate to £50,000, if not more. It further includes a very large amount for income tax, which item is in many cases included under this head in the accounts of railway companies. Not knowing what portion of the income tax from railways is charged under this head of 'rates and taxes,' we must make a guess and put the total sum actually paid for local rates in 1867 at, say, £650,000. Then it appears that, if the normal amount of rates due for that year was £1,773,905, *the railway companies* escaped the payment of £1,123,905 ; and if the normal amount of rates was £1,937,266, they escaped the payment of no less than £1,287,266. We have no hesitation, therefore, in asserting that, if the matter were thoroughly sifted, it would be found that rail-way companies in England and Wales are escaping the payment of local rates justly due from them to the extent of *one and a quarter million pounds annually*. While the average rate in the pound upon the rateable property of England and Wales in 1867 was 39.9d. upon rateable railway property, it was practically 12d. or 13.18d. in the pound. The deficiency of payment, amounting to £1,123,905, or to £1,287,266, is equivalent to a rate of 2·68d. or 3d. in the pound upon the whole rateable property of England and Wales, and would defray, as we said at starting, half the county rate, half the hundred rate, half the borough rate, and half the police rate. What would be the effect of fairly assessing the rail-way property? If we suppose the £650,000 of local rates to have been paid by the railways at the general average for 1867 of 39.9d. in the pound, this will represent a rateable value of £3,909,774, paying its fair proportion of rates. Deduct this from the total rateable value of the railway property—namely, either £11,826,037 or £12,915,110, and we see that £7,916,263 or £9,005,336 worth of railway property remains to be brought under assessment. Or, in other words, instead of the total rateable property of England and Wales for 1867 having been £100,612,734, it would have been, by a proper valuation of railways, £108,528,997, or £109,618,070 ; and the total of local rates—namely, £16,727,174 —would have averaged not 39·9d. in the pound, but only 36·62d. or 36·98d. in the pound, being a reduction of 2·92d. or 3·28d. in the pound. That railway companies are heavily burdened with *imperial taxes* we are quite aware; and if the Chancellor of the Exchequer bleeds them too much, let them be relieved at the cost of the whole community of taxpayers. But we will not admit that inequality of imperial taxation is to excuse them from paying their rightful quota to the local rates, or that the faults of any number of Budgets are to be made good by those unlucky scapegoats, the ratepayers."

If the above figures be correct, of which there can be little doubt, it must be evident that railway companies *do* escape the payment of local rates to the extent mentioned—viz., *one and a quarter million of pounds annually*, and that other ratepayers are paying on the average *about 3d. in the pound more than they ought.* Railway directors, as a body, are too honourable to wish those burdens to be thrown upon others which ought to be borne by their companies. I therefore attribute the inequality which now exists to the present unsound system of rating railways. Before suggesting any remedy for this state of things, I will briefly review the changes which have been made by the legislature, in the law of rating, during recent years.

Until the passing of the Union Assessment Committee Act of 1862, the assessment of property was entirely in the hands of overseers, the majority of whom were wholly unacquainted with the value of property, and with the principle upon which it ought to be assessed.

In the greater number of cases the only document they had for their guidance was the *old rate book* transmitted to them by their predecessors, and this rate book had probably remained for years and years unaltered except by the insertion of new property.

The cause of this was to be attributed to the fact that although the Parochial Assessment Act of 1836 clearly defined the principle of assessing all rateable property, it provided no machinery by which such principle could be carried into effect, beyond the appointment of overseers, who were to receive no remuneration, and consequently incurred all the responsibility and expense of establishing a proper basis of assessment.

One result was that if an overseer on coming into office attempted to increase any of the old assessments he incurred much local hostility, and if he happened to be in a business ran great risk of losing his customers. Hence, it usually happened that overseers contented themselves with levying rates upon the old assessment.

Occasionally, however, in parishes where the property of railway companies happened to be situate, the overseers, not fearing the hostility of such neighbours, would raise the assessment of their property. The result of so doing, might be an appeal to Quarter Sessions, or it might not. When the company *did* threaten the overseers with an appeal to Quarter Sessions, and at the same time questioned the correctness of the assessment of other property in the parish, they, seeing the justice of the objection, would often again reduce the amount.

Further, even assuming that such objections were, in a particular case, groundless, an appeal to Quarter Sessions is a very expensive contingency. A solicitor must be employed to conduct the case, briefs prepared, professional witnesses engaged, and counsel retained. The risk of incurring the expense of all this to a single parish is a serious matter, and was of itself sufficient to deter the parish officers from contesting the point. It has, however, happened that Overseers, having persuaded themselves of the importance of such property being fairly assessed, have defended their rate before the Quarter Sessions.

When the case came on for hearing, important points as to facts would at times arise, the settlement of which would have kept the Court sitting for many days and even weeks, and to avoid such lengthened occupation of the time of the Court the case was usually referred to arbitration.

The arbitrator chosen was generally a Queen's Counsel in large practice.

It might then happen that either his engagements, or those of other persons engaged in the case, would necessitate the postponement of a sitting from day to day, and in some cases the arbitration was thus protracted for months and even years.

And during the whole of this time the appellants might either be paying no rates at all, or else merely paying on the original low assessment.

Is it, therefore, a matter of surprise that, with such difficulties to contend with, parish officers generally should have been chary of disturbing the original assessment of railway property?

The Union Assessment Act changed this state of things, and caused Assessment Committees to be established in every Union throughout England and Wales, and conferred upon them, at the same time, powers very extensive.

The overseers of the various parishes in the Unions were compelled to prepare and return to the respective committees, annual valuation lists, showing the gross rental and rateable value of each of the hereditaments in their respective parishes.

These valuation lists the committee were empowered to alter and amend as they thought proper; and they were further empowered, if they deemed it necessary, to employ professional valuers to re-value the whole or any portion of the Union under their jurisdiction.

In some cases the committees have themselves entirely revised the valuation lists, in others they have had the whole Union re-valued by professional valuers; and in others, again, they have only had the special properties, such as railways, gas and water works, manufactories, brick fields, coal mines, chalk and clay pits, &c., re-valued. These lists, then, having been settled one way or another, were handed over by the committee to the overseers of the various parishes, who were compelled to make their rates upon the amounts contained in such lists. But here the power of the committee ended.

The responsibility of defending the rate *still* remained with the overseers, and the entire expense so incurred had still to be borne by their parish alone.

If, therefore, the assessment of the property of wealthy rate-payers (and the railway companies were the wealthiest) was increased and an appeal to the Quarter Sessions ensued, the overseers were at times unprepared with the necessary evidence to support their rate, and, their witnesses understanding very little of the

subject, were unable successfully to coup with those whom the
railway companies were able to call.

The Court of Quarter Sessions, having to decide according to
the evidence before it, would reduce the rate; and thus it happened that property which ought to have been assessed at a high
amount was really assessed at a mere fraction of its true value.

And thus it was that the assessment committees, although invested with important functions, still lacked the power requisite
to enable them to establish the proper assessment of such property
as that held by wealthy and influential companies. It is evident
that the Legislature quite understood the bearing of the case when
it passed the Union Assessment Act of 1864, by which assessment committees are empowered to become co-respondents with
the parish overseers in the event of appeal, and to charge the
expenses so incurred in supporting the rate to the common fund of
the Union, thereby relieving, to a wonderful extent, an individual
parish of the very serious burden to which it had hitherto been
subject.

The Poor Law Amendment Act of 1868 still advanced another
step in the same direction as that of 1864, inasmuch as it empowered the guardians of *adjoining Unions* to *combine* in defending
a rate appealed against in which a question of principle was involved.

But, although assessment committees have these powers, it is
only a very few that have so far availed themselves of them; and
to this general unwillingness to exercise such power is, in my
opinion, to be attributed the fact that at the present time we
find the railway companies in England and Wales escaping the
payment of parochial rates to the extent of something like ONE
AND A QUARTER MILLION STERLING annually. And what is true
of railway companies is equally true, I believe, of gas and water
companies also, though perhaps, it may be, not to quite the same
extent, yet still in a very considerable degree.

Having thus briefly investigated the origin of the shortcomings
of the system, and at the same time endeavoured to demonstrate

its unsoundness, I next propose to show how, in my opinion, these defects should be remedied.

In the first place, speaking from my own practical knowledge as a railway valuer, I may say that to ascertain the rateable value of the *whole* of the property of *one* railway company is not a very difficult matter, and as long as railway companies are assessed at no more in the aggregate than this total amount, they should have little cause to complain.

In the second place the question arises as to how this total rateable value should be apportioned among the parishes in which the particular company possesses property. I would suggest that it should be done in this way : Having ascertained the rateable value of the whole, divide it into two portions, viz., rateable value of line proper and rateable value of station buildings, &c. I would then apportion the rateable value of the line *in proportion to its gross parochial earnings*, that is to say, if the rateable value of the whole line proved to be 25 per cent. of the gross earnings over the whole system, and, supposing the earnings in a particular parish were £10,000, I should say that the rateable value of the line in that parish was £2,500, and to this amount I would add the rateable value of the station buildings, &c. (if any), in that parish. This mode of apportionment, I admit, would not be *strictly* accurate, but still it would be far more accurate than the mileage system which has for many years been adopted in Scotland, and I feel convinced that a more accurate and practical mode could not be adopted without leading to many complications.

If such a system were adopted, the railway companies would be required, say every five years, to extract from their traffic ledgers for the previous year the gross earnings between the various stations on their system, and to submit them to the officers specially appointed by Government to make the necessary apportionment. Upon this the rates should be made for the ensuing five years, when a revision would again take place. Assuming such a plan as the above to be adopted, what would be its effect ? It would

U

effectually put a stop to all litigation between railway companies and parishes on questions of rating.

And such a result would unquestionably be to the interest of both parties, and would therefore be mutually beneficial. It would certainly—and this I do not wish to deny—impose upon railway companies the necessity of paying more rates than they do at *present*; but, on the other hand, the companies would have the satisfaction of knowing that they were only paying their fair and just proportion of the burdens borne by their neighbours. Further, it would satisfactorily settle the vexatious question as to the assessment of branch lines of railway, the receipts on which are, in most cases, entirely swallowed up by the expenses incurred in working them in such a manner as to be of profit in the capacity of feeders to the traffic of the main line.

To do this many trains are run, *which would not be run* if the branch line was a distinct occupation. For such lines companies are willing to pay heavy rents, for by securing them they are enabled to work their main line traffic to much greater advantage. Assuming one or two of these branch lines not to be in the occupation of the company to whom the main line belonged, what would be the result? Why, the occupiers of those branch lines instead of running perhaps eight trains each way daily *half full*, would run only four each way *full*. If only four trains ran there might not be quite so much traffic I admit, but it would not make *much* difference. Upon the arrival of these well filled trains at the junction, the main line company would have to put on trains specially to convey the traffic to its destination. This system of working the traffic would be most inconvenient to the main line company; therefore, rather than do it, they find it pays them better to rent the branch lines at such a sum as their owners could make out of them, or perhaps a little more, and then work them as I said before, to act as feeders to the trains running upon their main line. The law as it is at present defined by the judges of the Court of Queen's Bench declares such branch lines to have no value, because the receipts are absorbed by the expenses, and transfers the whole value to the main line, which, it is easily seen, would, without the branch lines or feeders, be of considerably less value.

It seems to me that the judges cannot have had the matter clearly placed before them. In the Haughley case C. J. Cockburn said—

"Two questions have been presented to us in this case. The first is whether in assessing the railway in the parish of Haughley, the traffic beyond Haughley is to be taken into account with a view to reduce the expenditure of the line in the parish of Haughley; for of course the lower the expenditure can be reduced, the larger will be the amount of profit in Haughley, and therefore the greater the rateable value of the railway in that parish."

The learned judge, after giving as an illustration the earnings of a stage coach running between London and Norwich, went on to say—

"So it is with a railway. When they are working from Norwich to Haughley they are probably working at a loss. When they are working beyond Haughley towards London they take the traffic at Ipswich and other places of consequence that lie on the line, and then the traffic becomes remunerative."

Now I will put the question: Assuming the line from Norwich to Haughley belonged to a distinct company, would they work it at a loss?—that is to say, would they require so much stock, or run so many trains daily as to cause the whole of the earnings to be swallowed up by the expenses which the Great Eastern Railway Company may find it necessary to do in order to make a greater profit elsewhere? Certainly not. I will put another question. In estimating the rent such a branch line was worth from year to year, would the Great Eastern Railway Company take into consideration the local expenses they might *themselves* incur in working it, or would they not rather consider the expense it might be worked at by an independent company, which had its own interests alone to study, and not those of the Great Eastern Railway Company?

I say most decidedly the latter, and this, in my opinion, is the clear solution of railway companies paying heavy rents for branch lines, which appear to be worked at a loss, but are not so actually.

The result of all this is, that parishes having *main lines* of railway passing through them are to benefit at the expense of parishes having *only branch lines* passing through them.

The system, however, which I propose would be the means of apportioning to every parish having railway property in it, its fair share of the rateable value of the whole, which I again say ought to depend upon the *gross parochial earnings* and *not* upon the local net earnings, which entirely depend upon the number of trains run by the company to the junction station, to suit the convenience of their main line traffic, and not the number of trains which *would* be run if the branch was a distinct occupation.

I trust, therefore, that in order to establish a more equitable mode of rating, this subject may be considered worthy of the attention of the committee of the House of Commons appointed to inquire into the *incidents* of local taxation.

W. MARSHALL.

COPPER, TIN, AND LEAD MINES.

As it seems to be the intention of the Legislature to make the occupiers of the above, and all other mines hitherto held to be exempt
from rating, now conform to the intention of the Act of Elizabeth—
viz., "that every man should assist in supporting the poor according to his ability"—a few practical remarks on the principle of
ascertaining the rent a tenant may reasonably be expected to give
for such hereditaments, may shortly be found to be of some assistance.

The inquiry to be made will be the same as in the case of coal
mines. What are the receipts and what are the working expenses?
Take one from the other and a sum is left representing two things
—profit and rent. Then, how much profit and how much rent?

As an example may be useful, I will take the revenue accounts
for twelve months of one of the large Cornish copper mines, and
then proceed to ascertain its rateable value approximately. I say
approximately, since the amount of tenant's capital required is a
matter of uncertainty which could only be correctly ascertained by
an actual inspection.

RECEIPTS.

By sale of 18,500 tons of copper ore	£143,040		
Do.	tin . .	2,533	
Do.	arsenic. .	144	
			£145,717

EXPENSES.

Agents' salaries.		£3,344
Tutwork bargains.		26,177
Bargains on surface, wages, &c. .		2,539
Carried forward . . .		32,060

Brought forward £32,060

Carpenters, masons, smiths, engineers, &c.	3,099	
Carriage and horse work	922	
Materials	15,008	
Engine or water cost.	15,415	
Expenses on ores	7,803	
Tribute, subsist, and balances . . .	25,031	
Sundry payments	1,872	
Doctor and club	795	
		102,005

Net receipts £43,712

TENANT'S WORKING CAPITAL.

Cash required for wages, timber,
candles, iron, safety fuse, oil,
gunpowder, repairing and renewing tools, &c. — say 4½
months' expenses—viz . . .   £38,250

Cash required to provide picks,
wedges, shovels, mallets, borers,
scrapers, tamping bars, &c., say   550

Sundries, say   1,000
                                 ———————
                                 £39,800

Capital required by a tenant from
year to year, say £40,000

Tenant's profits, including an amount
for risks and casualties, say
25 per cent. on £40,000 . . .   10,000
                                      ———————
Carried forward . . .   £33,712

THE PRINCIPLE OF RATING. 295

Carried forward	£33,712
Less for renewal of buildings and machinery (ordinary repairs, insurance, &c., have already been deducted), say 2 per cent. on £80,000	£1,600
Rateable value and rates . . .	£32,112
Less rates at 3s. in the pound .	4,188
Rateable value . . .	£27,924

Now, if this mine happened to be entirely in one parish, the above sum of £27,924 would be about the amount upon which the parochial rates ought to be levied. But in this particular case (and I might say in nearly every case), the workings extend through many parishes. The pit's mouth is in one parish, but the ore is obtained from several. It, therefore, becomes necessary to deduct from the rateable value of the whole, the rateable value of the indirectly productive portion of the hereditament, viz., the buildings, machinery, &c., which should be assessed in the particular parish in which it is situate. What then remains will be the value which should be apportioned to the various parishes out of which the ore has been taken, in proportion to the quantity extracted from each.

The royalty, or lord's dues, paid for the ore raised during the years in question amounted to £6,071. It will therefore be seen that the rent paid for the privilege of exhausting the earth, is no measure of the value the hereditament may reasonably be expected to let for from year to year, enhanced as it had been in value by the expenditure of capital to the extent of nearly £100,000 in buildings, machinery, &c.

In making estimates of the rateable value of tin, copper, and lead mines, it must be borne in mind that, like the mining of precious metals, the work is very precarious.

Veins which are very promising when first opened, may suddenly

---

fall off and occasion immense loss, or they may be worked with little or no profit.

On the other hand, veins which at first promise little, may in time yield large profits.

Therefore, before arriving at the rent which a prudent tenant might reasonably be expected to give, a very liberal allowance ought to be made him to provide against such risks, but the amount of this allowance ought to entirely depend upon the character of the mine. Some mines produce a steady profit for a series of years, while others fluctuate very much from year to year.

To give a specimen of this fluctuation, I insert the following, which were the profits made out of a large Cornish copper mine in ten successive years:—

£10,336
16,800
28,520
38,880
60,480
47,040
29,760
48,000
32,640
31,680

Parochial authorities, in estimating the rent of such hereditaments, would also do well to remember the words pronounced by Lord Denman in his judgment in the case of *Queen* v. *Everest*, 10 Q. B. 178—

" Parish officers having to make a *prospective rate* may well look to see what it is probable the land will be made to produce in the *current year*."

In the case of a mine certainly no better criterion of the produce of the current year can be found, assuming the same state of things still to exist, than what it produced during the past.

In the Succession Duty Act, 16 and 17 Vict., cap. 51, section 26, it is enacted that—

"The *yearly value* of any *manor, opened mine,* or *other real property of a fluctuating yearly income* shall either be calculated upon the *average profits* or *income derived therefrom, after deducting all necessary outgoings* during such a number of preceding years as shall be agreed upon for this purpose between the commissioners and the successor, before the first payment of duty on the succession shall have become due ; or. if no such period shall be agreed upon, then the *principal value* of such property shall be ascertained, and the *annual value* thereof shall be considered to be equal to interest calculated at the rate of *three pounds per centum per annum* on the amount of such *principal value.*"

It may be mentioned that the value of the minerals annually raised in England and Wales, and which are at present not rateable, amounts to about £5,600,000. Assuming, then, that the proportion of rateable to gross value which we have just deduced in the foregoing example holds generally — viz., in the proportion of £145,717 to £27,924 we shall have upon the law being extended, the present aggregate amount upon which rates are now being levied in England and Wales increased by about £1,100,000.

W. M.

ON CERTAIN INEQUALITIES IN THE RATING OF RAILWAYS.

Inequalities in the rating of railways, as between company and company, with some remarks attached, to show the unsoundness of certain claims made by the witnesses of railway companies, in order to reduce the rateable value.

The following extract from an article on the subject of railway rating which appeared in *The Chamber of Agriculture Journal* on the 12th of last September may be found interesting, as it points out the great inequality the present unsatisfactory system of rating this class of property causes to exist, as between company and company :—

" We have shown that the railways, as a whole, escape the payment of about 3d. in the pound upon the rateable property of England and Wales. Is it easy to bring home the charge to particular companies ? In the first place, it is very evident, from the Board of Trade Returns of 1867, that great inequality exists in respect of rates and taxes between the *twelve companies* which have termini in the metropolis. Of the *net receipts*, the percentage paid for rates and taxes is by the London, Brighton and South Coast, *17.07 per cent.;* by the London, Chatham and Dover, *12.24 per cent.;* by the South Eastern, *9 per cent.;* by the London, Tilbury and Southend, *6.5 per cent.,;* by the London and South Western, *5.8 per cent.;* by the North London, *5.18 per cent.;* by the Great Eastern, *5 per cent.;* by the Metropolitan, *4.71 per cent.;* by the Great Northern, *4 per cent.;* by the Great Western, *3.92 per cent.;* by the Midland, *3.27 per cent.;* and by the London and North Western, *2.85 per cent.* The London, Brighton and South Coast, and the London, Chatham and Dover Railways are paying considerably more than their fair share of local rates ; which arises, we believe, from their occupying a large proportion of unprofitable line of railway; in fact, lines through the working of which they are annually losing large sums of money. Their Acts of Parlia-

ment, however, compel them to pay local rates, no matter whether
the portion of line assessed be profitable or unprofitable. If unprofitable, the company has to pay simply upon the *agricultural value*
of the land which it has abstracted from the parish ; but parish
officers being seldom satisfied with this, and insisting on something
more than *mere* agricultural value, the company commonly gives
way in order to avoid litigation upon what may be, in any one case,
a comparatively small amount.   The South Eastern Railway pays
somewhat less than the sum which ought to be levied upon it for
local rates ; and all the other railways having termini in London
pay *very much less than their fair share*, averaging, indeed, less than
half the sum due upon their proper rateable value. Let us take
the case of the London and North Western Railway.   The rateable
value is *the estimated rental, free of all tenants' rates and taxes, and
tithe rentcharge, which a supposed tenant might reasonably be expected
to give for the occupation of the property, from year to year, deducting from that rental the probable average annual cost of repairs,
insurance, and other expenses, if any, necessary to maintain the property in a state to command such rent.* If we subtract the total
working expenses from the total receipts from all sources of traffic,
we shall have the *net receipts* which are to be divided between *the
landlord* and the *hypothetical tenant.*   According to the Board of
Trade Returns, the gross receipts for the year 1867 were
£6,752,567 ; the working expenses, *including renewals*, but excluding *rates* and *taxes*, which will appear later in the calculation, were
£3,008,244 ; and deducting one amount from the other, we have
£3,744,323 to be divided between the supposed landlord and
tenant. The tenant's portion is a *fair* remunerative profit upon
the capital which he would require in order to take to the stock
upon entry *at a valuation*, every outgoing for management, and for
all expenses, both actual and contingent, having been allowed for
in the working expenses. The tenant's capital is represented by the
present value of the stock. The *prime cost* of the stock is usually
taken as equal to the gross annual receipts, being, in this case,
£6,752,567. Deducting 25 per cent. for *depreciation*, or £1,688,142,

we have £5,064,425 as the present value of the stock or *amount of tenant's capital*. A profit of *15 per cent.* upon this comes to £759,664 ; and this, deducted from the £3,744,323, which we had to divide between tenant and landlord, leaves £2,984,659 as the proprietor's share or net rental, together with the rates which we have not yet deducted. To ascertain what was the proper amount for rates that should have been paid by the London and North Western Railway Company in 1867, we ought to reckon the rate in the pound at the average rate of the poor law unions which are traversed by the main and branch lines of the company; but it will be sufficiently near the truth if we take the average rate *of the several counties* through which these lines pass. This will certainly be *favourable* to the company ; for as the railway cuts through the most populous districts, the rates payable will, in reality, be *more* than the general county averages. We have taken the trouble to calculate from the items of total rateable value and rate in the pound, deducting such portions of rate as are not payable by railways (Local Board of Health rates, for instance, which railways pay upon only one-fourth of the net annual value), as given in the Local Taxation Returns (497), the average rates in the pound payable by railways in the counties of Middlesex, Herts, Bucks, Northampton, Warwick, Leicester, Stafford, Salop, Cheshire and Lancashire. The average rates for these counties, through which the London and North Western Railway passes, range from 1s. 11½d. up to 3s. 2d.; the general average (not the mean) for the ten counties being 2s. 9½d. in the pound *properly payable by railways.* To separate the proper amount of rates from the sum of £2,984,659, which was for the landlord and the rates together, we must work the following simple equation :—As 20s. + 2s. 9½d. : 2s. 9½d. : : £2,984,659 : *x*. We find that *x* equals £365,580, *which is the amount of rates that the company ought to have paid in the year 1867;* and deducting this from the £2,984,659, the landlord's net rental, or the *true rateable value* of the *whole* of the London and North Western Railways and stations, is seen to be

£2,619.079. A rate of 2s. 9½d. upon this value comes to £365,580; *but the amount actually paid in the year 1867, as stated by the company itself, in the Board of Trade Returns, was only £103,884, showing that the company escaped the payment of no less than £261,696 in the year 1867,* in consequence of the property being assessed very far under its real value. Upon the net receipts, namely, £3,640,439, the amount of rates which ought to have been paid, namely, £365,580, are 10.04 per cent. The sum actually paid, namely, £103,884, was only 2.85 per cent."

In dividing the net receipts of the London and North Western Railway Company, in the above calculation between the *landlord* and the *hypothetical tenant*, I observe that the latter has been allowed a profit of 15 per cent. on the capital he would require to work the line. Now, I should like to know where any person, or body of persons, could invest a capital of *five million pounds sterling* and obtain a return of 15 per cent. profit, without incurring any of the ordinary risks; without requiring to give any portion of their time in conducting the undertaking, for this is all done for them by *paid* directors, managers, &c. ; and without any depreciation taking place in the value of their stock, which is prevented by repairs and extensive annual renewals charged to the revenue.

I know from experience that the rating officers of railway companies, in order to reduce the rent, are in the habit of claiming absurdly extravagant allowances for the assumed tenant. The following is a specimen of what they sometimes claim :—

Interest	5 per cent.
Profit.	10 ,,
Risks and casualties . . .	5 ,,
Depreciation of stock . .	5 ,,
Total	25 ,,

With regard to the first two claims—viz., *interest* and *profit,* observe what T. F. Ellis, Esq., recorder of Leeds, said in his judgment in the case of *The Midland Railway Company* v. *The Overseers of Armley.**

---

* "Railway Rating," by Hodgson, page 91.

" The next item I will consider together with the item which is next but one to it in the estimate of the appellants. They say that the value of the money which a supposed tenant of the line would have to invest in locomotive stock is £49,119 ; and such a tenant, they think, would, in estimating the rent which he is to pay, expect to be allowed—First, 5 per cent. interest on this sum, and then 15 per cent. for tenants' or trade profits. Secondly, they say that, if 5 per cent. is allowed for interest, no more than 10 per cent. ought in addition to be allowed for profits. *As to this, I cannot doubt that the allowance which they propose is extremely liberal.* A very short consideration of the principles upon which such deductions are allowed will, I think, show this.

" The subject of the rate is the value of the occupation. When we ask, what is the rateable value of any subject of occupation, we ask, in effect, what is it worth while to give for the permission to occupy ? This is what the legislature meant in proposing as a test of rateable value, what a tenant would pay as rack-rent. The tenant pays for the permission to apply his capital and labour to the subject of occupation and take the resulting profits. But, in applying this test, we must exclude any consideration of the greater or less ease in obtaining the capital required. The question is not, whether a tenant can easily be found? The tenant is introduced merely as a hypothetical test of the value of the right to occupy. *We must, therefore, take it as if we had tenants ready with unlimited capital, or (which, in practice, is the same thing) as if there were a large joint stock company intending to invest their money in the speculation.*

" Now, the considerations which determine (independently of local and accidental disturbing causes, which of course are not now to be taken into account) the rent which a tenant would pay for the right to occupy are—*Can he employ his money at better interest ? Can he employ his labour at better profit ?* In other words, can he, by employing the same money and labour, and at the same risk, get more return than, by giving the rent which is asked for, he will get here ? *The answer will be determined by the average value of capital and labour in the country, including the consideration for risk.*

" It does not much signify, therefore, whether we first allow interest for the money and then allow for the value of the labour and risk, or put the two together, and call them trade or tenant's profits. But it is clear that what the appellants in effect assert is, that money applied to the hire of this railway ought to produce 20 per cent. profit ; and that the respondents are content to allow 15 per cent.

" It is to be observed here, that *the risk is very little.* There is no specific charge made for insurance ; but the insurance of the buildings must have been taken into account in the estimate of the rateable value of the buildings ; and the risk upon the rest must, from the nature of the property, be very slight ;

less certainly, very much, than in the case of standing crops, ships, cotton goods, &c.

" Then, as to the labour, that has already been allowed for. The previous items include what, in the case of a farm, would correspond to the farmer's personal exertions in the tillage ; in the case of a ship, to the superintending the details connected with the navigation ; in the case of a shop, to the trouble of providing the goods, regulating the business, superintending the clerks, and so on. That which in agriculture or trade takes up most of a man's time, is here done for the supposed tenant. In the consols, the interest now attainable is between 3½ and 4 per cent. *How much more labour and risk would a party incur by embarking his money in the hire of this railroad, all expenses being paid! The trouble of taking the money* from the clerks would be somewhat more ; the risk of destruction is rather greater ; and something must be allowed for the less facility of shifting capital, once so embarked, to any new investment. But when all these allowances are made, the 15 per cent. which the respondents propose to allow, seems to me *far to exceed what would be suggested by comparison with other investments. The 5 per cent. interest must therefore be struck off.*"

As to the third claim—viz., 5 per cent. for *risks* and *casualties.*

It may be said that the amount *actually* spent under the head of *compensation for injuries and losses,* is already allowed in the working expenses.

With regard to any possible or imaginary risks beyond this amount, it may again be said that no person can get more than 3½ or 4 per cent. for their money without incurring *some* risk, and even then, they incur a *slight* risk.

Lastly—as to the claim of 5 per cent. for *depreciation of stock.*

When a line of railway is first opened, it is usually worked by *new* stock, but as years roll on, this stock annually decreases in value until about the tenth or fifteenth year, when it becomes depreciated in value about 25 or 30 per cent. of its original cost ; beyond this, it *cannot* depreciate, that is, if the accounts of the company are *honestly* audited, and the certificates attached to them and signed both by the auditors and engineers are to be relied upon ; for out of the yearly revenue, the whole of the working stock is not only obliged to be kept in repair, but the old worn out stock replaced by new stock being brought upon the line ; so that, the stock having once deteriorated to a certain extent in value, *cannot* deteriorate beyond. The 30th section of the Railway Companies' Act of 1867 has put a stop to the old system of robbing the line and stock for the benefit of present shareholders at the expense of future ones; and the 5th section of the Act of 31 and 32 Vict. c. 119 renders persons found guilty of signing false accounts liable, on conviction, to fine and imprisonment, or a penalty not exceeding fifty pounds.

To substantiate therefore such a claim as the above, even partially, companies would have to admit that the amounts spent annually out of the revenue, were insufficient to prevent deterioration going on, and that a time *would* come when a thorough renewal of stock would be required, but to provide against which, *no annual sinking fund had been laid by out of the revenue.* In plain words, that the accounts had been cooked in order to pay a larger dividend to the present shareholders, and that the certificates at the end of them, signed by the auditors and engineer, were mere fabrications to suit the convenience of *existing* circumstances.

The foregoing remarks will equally apply to a claim the witnesses of railway companies are in the habit of making for the ultimate *renewal* of the permanent way, &c.

When the Local Taxation Committee of the House of Commons deals with this important subject, it is to be hoped that it will not allow itself to be influenced by the opinions of the Chairmen of Railway Companies, as the Lords' Committee seems to have been in the year 1850; but will rely more upon the evidence of Accountants who are in the habit of auditing the accounts, not only of public companies, but those also of large mercantile firms.

The evidence of such gentlemen on the all important subject of *tenants' profits* would be invaluable. With regard to claims for imaginary risks, depreciation of stock, &c., the common sense of the Committee, without evidence, would be sufficient to determine such points.

W. M.

www.ingramcontent.com/pod-product-compliance
Lightning Source LLC
Chambersburg PA
CBHW021213270326
41929CB00010B/1117